Psychoanalytic and Historical Perspectives on the Leadership of Donald Trump

What is Donald Trump's personality? Is he mentally ill? What in American culture and history enabled him to become president? How does his personality shape his policies and leadership?

In this fascinating and highly relevant new book, these questions are answered by a selection of expert contributors, including psychoanalysts, historians, and a sociologist. Narcissism is defined and applied to Donald Trump, his personal history and style of leadership, and the relationship between Trump and his base is explored as a symptom of his needs and the needs of his followers. U.S. culture and U.S. politics are put under the lens, as chapters draw on contemporary academic and journalistic analysis, continuing discussions around gaslighting, demagoguery, and fascism in terms of their validity in application to Trump.

Psychoanalytic and Historical Perspectives on the Leadership of Donald Trump refutes many of the mental health experts who label Trump as suffering from a narcissistic personality disorder and makes the case that Trump's personality combines a marketing and narcissistic orientation that determines his behavior and policies. The authors also assert that to understand Trump's rise and his followers, it is valuable to combine psychoanalytic, historical, and sociological perspectives. This book will therefore be of great interest to academics in those fields and all those with an interest in contemporary American politics.

Michael Maccoby, PhD, is a psychoanalyst and anthropologist, who is a globally recognized expert on leadership. He has taught or consulted to leaders in 36 countries and has taught leadership at Oxford's Saïd Business School and Sciences Po, Paris. He is the author of *The Gamesman, Narcissistic Leaders, The Leaders We Need: And What Makes Us Follow*, and *Strategic Intelligence*.

Ken Fuchsman, EdD, has been President of the International Psychohistorical Association since 2016. He is Emeritus faculty from the University of Connecticut, where he taught American history and interdisciplinary studies. He has written on Presidents Kennedy, Nixon, Obama, and Trump.

Psychoanalytic and Historical Perspectives on the Leadership of Donald Trump

Narcissism and Marketing in an Age of Anxiety and Distrust

Edited by
Michael Maccoby and Ken Fuchsman

LONDON AND NEW YORK

First published 2020
by Routledge
2 Park Square, Milton Park, Abingdon, Oxon OX14 4RN

and by Routledge
52 Vanderbilt Avenue, New York, NY 10017

Routledge is an imprint of the Taylor & Francis Group, an informa business

© 2020 selection and editorial matter, Michael Maccoby and Ken Fuchsman; individual chapters, the contributors

The right of Michael Maccoby and Ken Fuchsman to be identified as the authors of the editorial material, and of the authors for their individual chapters, has been asserted in accordance with sections 77 and 78 of the Copyright, Designs and Patents Act 1988.

All rights reserved. No part of this book may be reprinted or reproduced or utilised in any form or by any electronic, mechanical, or other means, now known or hereafter invented, including photocopying and recording, or in any information storage or retrieval system, without permission in writing from the publishers.

Trademark notice: Product or corporate names may be trademarks or registered trademarks, and are used only for identification and explanation without intent to infringe.

British Library Cataloguing-in-Publication Data
A catalogue record for this book is available from the British Library

Library of Congress Cataloging-in-Publication Data
A catalog record has been requested for this book

ISBN: 978-0-367-89712-3 (hbk)
ISBN: 978-0-367-42648-4 (pbk)
ISBN: 978-1-003-02068-4 (ebk)

Typeset in Times New Roman
by Taylor & Francis Books

Contents

List of contributors	vii
Acknowledgments	x

Introduction 1

MICHAEL MACCOBY AND KEN FUCHSMAN

PART I
Who is Donald Trump and why do people follow him? 9

1 Trump's marketing narcissistic leadership in an age of anxiety 11

MICHAEL MACCOBY

2 The anatomy of narcissistic leadership: Interview with Otto
Kernberg 24

KEN FUCHSMAN AND MOLLY CASTELLOE

3 The allure of Trump's narcissism 34

ELIZABETH LUNBECK

PART II
How Trump leads 41

4 Probing Trump's disruptive narcissistic personality 43

PAUL H. ELOVITZ

5 Is Donald Trump competent and fit to be president? 58

KEN FUCHSMAN

vi Contents

6 Gaslighting and beyond 71
ROBIN STERN AND JUDITH LOGUE

7 Trump the demagogue 88
MICHAEL SIGNER

8 Is Trump a fascist? 92
PAUL GOTTFRIED

PART III
Social and historical factors in the rise of Trump 103

9 American Exceptionalism on steroids 105
DAVID LOTTO

10 What in our politics, history, economy, and culture enabled
Trump's rise? 114
KEN FUCHSMAN

11 A sociologist's view of the Trump phenomenon 125
CHARLES HECKSCHER

PART IV
Presidential personality and performance 145

12 How Trump's personality influences his policies 147
MICHAEL MACCOBY

13 The president we need 153
MICHAEL MACCOBY

14 Conclusion 161
KEN FUCHSMAN

Index 169

Contributors

Molly Castelloe, PhD, teaches at Metropolitan College of Manhattan. She earned her doctorate in Performance Studies at New York University. She writes a column at psychologytoday.com on group psychology and applied psychoanalysis. Her documentary film, *Vamik's Room* received the Gradiva Award of the National Association for the Advancement of Psychoanalysis.

Paul H. Elovitz, PhD, is a research psychoanalyst, presidential psychobiographer, historian, editor-in-chief of *Clio's Psyche* (1994–), professor (1963–), and founder/Director of the Psychohistory Forum (1982–). After teaching at Fairleigh Dickinson, Rutgers, and Temple universities, he became a founding faculty member of Ramapo College. His most recent book among his 360 publications is *The Making of Psychohistory: Origins, Controversies, and Pioneering Contributors*. Currently he is editing *The Many Roads to Insight of the Builders of Psychohistory*.

Ken Fuchsman, EdD, has been President of the International Psychohistorical Association since 2016. He is Emeritus faculty from the University of Connecticut, where he taught American history and interdisciplinary studies. He has written about Presidents Kennedy, Nixon, Obama, and Trump. In January 2016, he appeared on the Reelz cable network where he spoke about John Kennedy in World War II.

Paul Gottfried, PhD, is Raffensperger Professor of Humanities Emeritus at Elizabethtown College. He is President of the H. L. Mencken Club. He is the author of *After Liberalism: Mass Democracy in the Managerial State, Conservatism in America: Making Sense of the American Right, Fascism: The Career of a Concept, Leo Strauss and the Conservative Movement in America* and more than one hundred scholarly articles. He received a Guggenheim Fellowship in 1983.

Charles Heckscher, PhD, is a Distinguished Professor in the School of Management and Labor Relations at Rutgers University and co-Director of the Center for the Study of Collaboration. His research interests include societal trust, the design of collaborative organization, and the changing nature of employee representation. He has also worked as a practitioner and consultant on viii Contributors

processes of organizational development, primarily in telecommunications and currently in K-12 education. His most recent book is *Trust in a Complex World: Enriching Community.*

Otto F. Kernberg, MD, FAPA, is Director of the Personality Disorders Institute at The New York Presbyterian Hospital, Westchester Division, and Professor of Psychiatry at the Weill Cornell Medical College. He is Past President of the International Psychoanalytic Association. He is also Training and Supervising Analyst of the Columbia University Center for Psychoanalytic Training and Research. Dr. Kernberg is the author of 12 books and co-author of 11 others. These include *Borderline Conditions and Pathological Narcissism, Severe Personality Disorders: Psychotherapeutic Strategies*, and *Object Relations Theory and Clinical Psychoanalysis.*

Judith Logue, PhD, has been a practicing psychotherapist, and faculty, training and supervising psychoanalyst for 50 years. She co-founded the Institute for Psychoanalysis and Psychotherapy of NJ. She is a Former Board Member, APA, Division 39 (Psychoanalysis); Sections I, III and VIII, and Past President, Section III. She is an Executive Councilor, American Psychoanalytic Association. She is also a Captain, Civil Air Patrol, and teacher, Palm Beach County CAP Squadron.

David Lotto, PhD, is a psychoanalyst in practice in Pittsfield, Massachusetts. He is the editor of the *Journal of Psychoanalysis.* He has written on recent or current American political events, including the Gulf War, the origins of terrorism, the psychology of fundamentalism, the resurgence of fascism, American Exceptionalism, Obama's fatal flaw, the perils of patriotism, and the racist roots of the Tea Party.

Elizabeth Lunbeck, PhD, is Professor of the History of Science and Director of Graduate Studies in Harvard University's Department of the History of Science. She is the author of *The Americanization of Narcissism, The Psychiatric Persuasion: Knowledge, Gender, and Power in Modern America*, and with Bennett Simon, *Family Romance, Family Secrets: Case Notes from an American Psychoanalysis, 1912.*

Michael Maccoby, PhD, is a psychoanalyst and anthropologist, who is a globally recognized expert on leadership. He has taught or consulted to leaders in 36 countries and has taught leadership at Oxford's Saïd Business School and Sciences Po, Paris. He directed the Kennedy School's Program on Technology, Public Policy and Human Development from 1978 to 1990. He is the author or co-author of 15 books, including *Social Character in a Mexican Village* (with Erich Fromm), *The Gamesman, The New Corporate Leaders, Narcissistic Leaders, Who Succeeds and Who Fails, The Leaders We Need, and What Makes Us Follow*, and *Strategic Intelligence: Conceptual Tools for Leading Change.* In 2008, he received the Swedish honor of being made

Commander of the Royal Order of the Polar Star and in 2016 he received a lifetime achievement award from the Washington School of Psychiatry.

Michael Signer, an attorney and a lecturer in the Department of Politics at the University of Virginia, was Mayor of Charlottesville, VA, from 2016 to 2018 and currently sits on the City Council. He is founder and chair of Communities Overcoming Extremism: The After Charlottesville Project, and is the author of *Demagogue: The Fight to Save Democracy from Its Worst Enemies* and *Becoming Madison: The Extraordinary Origins of the Least Likely Founding Father.*

Robin Stern, PhD, is the Associate Director for the Yale Center for Emotional Intelligence and an Associate Research Scientist at the Child Study Center at Yale. She is a licensed psychoanalyst with 30 years of experience treating individuals, couples, and families. She co-developed RULER, the Yale Center's approach to bringing emotional intelligence to school communities and to the workplace; and is a lead trainer for the Center's Institutes. She is also on the faculty of Teachers College, Columbia University, and the author of two books, *The Gaslight Effect* and *Project Rebirth.*

Acknowledgments

During the 2017 International Psychohistorical Association Conference at New York University, there were a number of featured papers on Donald Trump. Dr. Molly Castelloe suggested to Ken Fuchsman that there could well be a book on Trump's leadership from these presentations. Without her suggestion, this book would not have come into being. Fuchsman later invited Michael Maccoby to contribute a chapter and to be lead editor of the book. The book benefited not only from those who contributed chapters, but also from experts who shared their understanding of the impact of Trump's behavior and policies. Dan Morgan described Trump's appeal to farmers. Dan was also a valuable editorial consultant offering advice on framing the ideas presented in the book, emphasizing what is original and suggesting that certain concepts needed clarification. Robert Shapiro, economist and former government official, contributed an analysis of the economic impact of Trump's policies. Todd Hathaway, nuclear engineer and retired army major, contributed an analysis of Trump's energy policies; John Rother, President of the National Coalition on Health Care, contributed an analysis of the impact of Trump's policies on health care and Steve Redburn, professor at George Washington University, described the impact of Trump's policies on the management of the federal government.

The book was accepted for publication by Russell George who made valuable editorial suggestions and suggested the title. Elliott Morsia and Alec Selwyn provided advice on preparing the book for production, Naomi Hill was a helpful production manager, and Susan Dunsmore did the copy-editing. Maria Stroffolino deserves the gratitude of the editors for her exceptional work in preparing the manuscript for publication.

Michael Maccoby and Ken Fuchsman
February 25, 2020

Introduction

Michael Maccoby and Ken Fuchsman

Who is Donald Trump? What is his personality? Is he mentally ill? Why is he followed by millions of Americans? How does his personality shape his policies and leadership style? What in the history and culture of the U.S. can help us explain the election of Donald Trump, the first president without previous experience in government?

These are the questions that the contributors to this book—psychoanalysts, historians, and a sociologist—try to answer. Trump has been labeled by many mental health professionals as suffering from pathological narcissism. The chapters by psychoanalysts Michael Maccoby, a globally recognized expert on leadership, and Otto Kernberg, known for his clinical studies of narcissism, reject that Trump's behavior can be understood in terms of a psychiatric diagnosis such as a narcissistic personality disorder.

Maccoby has studied the biographies of historic narcissistic leaders and coached or psychoanalyzed over 30 narcissistic leaders in business and government. Some have been effective leaders and some have been failures (Maccoby, 2007). None can be understood in terms of their narcissism alone. They, like all of us, are a mix of personality traits. It is also necessary to understand a leader's philosophy, competence, relations to associates, and the social and historical context that favor the rise of these invariably disruptive leaders. Trump's narcissism is combined with a marketing orientation; he is a marketing narcissist. He lacks any conviction other than his need to be a winner. He shapes his behavior and policies according to what pleases his base of supporters and maintains Republican support. He says whatever he thinks makes him sound good and look good.

Trump's success in gaining fervent followers can be understood only in a historical and cultural context of an anxious and distrustful electorate. In times of great change people fall for narcissistic leaders who give them hope. In less disruptive times, people tend to follow more traditional leaders. Trump has been a disruptive president in disruptive times. In Chapter 3, historian Elizabeth Lunbeck makes the case that Trump's narcissism is a resource, not an impediment to his electoral and political success. In an age of anxiety caused by social, economic, and technological change, some people have prospered and others have been left behind. Trump has persuaded many of the losers that he will recreate their idealized past by bringing back jobs from abroad and keeping out immigrants who have supposedly taken their jobs and brought alien cultures to America. Trump's marketing narcissistic personality explains some of his ability to distort reality and make convincing promises that he is unable to fulfill. Rather than alleviating anxiety, he uses it to promote himself as the only one who can make things better. Rather than building trust in national leadership and government, he tells his base of followers that he is the only one they should trust. In Chapter 2, Kernberg describes how a narcissistic leader like Trump can control followers so that they become a regressed social group that surrenders their moral reasoning to the leader.

A large part of Trump's appeal to his most fervent supporters has been his skill in branding, denigrating, stereotyping, and scapegoating. And his own unfiltered resentment and anger strike a chord with those who enthusiastically welcome his giving voice to their alienation and victimization.

Trump's labeling others is often the pot calling the kettle black. He said Ted Cruz was a liar, accused Hillary Clinton of being crooked, and called immigrants from Mexico rapists. Yet Trump has faced charges of making falsehoods, committing crimes, and allegations of sexual misconduct during the campaign and throughout his presidency.

These ironies, his falsehoods, incompetency, and frequent reversals of position do not appear to bother a good number of Trump's admirers. Some even make him over in their own image. Neo-Nazis, for instance, proclaimed "Hail Trump" at a 2017 pre-inauguration gathering, or another Nazi sympathizer while trolling Jews, happily declared "You are in Trump's America now." Trump is a brilliant entertainer whose outlandish and aggressive Tweets capture the attention of the press and the American people and take attention away from his reactionary and short-sighted policies. He is like a conjurer who tricks the audience to look in the wrong direction while he pulls off one of his tricks. What led to his ascendancy and the enduring Trump phenomenon is as much about many of us as it is about him. This volume addresses who he is and what we have become. The chapters present psychoanalytic, historical, and sociological perspectives on Trump in present-day American culture. After considering these analyses, Maccoby describes the kind of president America needs to put the country back on a progressive humanistic path.

Structure of the book

Part I Who is Donald Trump and why do people follow him?

Chapter 1 Trump's marketing narcissistic leadership in an age of anxiety, by Michael Maccoby

We are living in an age of anxiety with fears that are political, social, and individual, caused by threats to life and by economic and cultural changes. In times of great change and uncertainty, people become vulnerable to narcissistic leaders who promise to alleviate their fears. Donald Trump is such a leader. But Trump has not dealt with the real causes of anxiety. He has increased uncertainty and anxiety in America. Many mental health professionals have diagnosed Trump as suffering from a narcissistic personality disorder, but Trump is neither suffering nor sick. Many narcissists have become effective leaders, but some of them have had a purpose of working for the common good. Trump's only purpose is to be admired as a winner. His marketing attitude treats himself and others as commodities. Only successful and powerful people are valuable, weak and vulnerable people are not. In contrast to Trump, we need leaders who deal with the real causes of anxiety and work for the common good on five levels: global, national, community, organizational, and individual.

Chapter 2 The anatomy of narcissistic leadership, by Ken Fuchsman and Molly Castelloe

In Chapter 2, Otto F. Kernberg differentiates narcissistic personality disorders from malignant narcissism and the narcissistic personality. Narcissistic personalities lack internal representatives of people important to them. They are lonely and need continual admiration. They also need continual excitement. They have infantile value systems and want to be admired for their possessions, not for their character. They are excessively competitive and envious. Those with a personality disorder have serious problems in work and social relations. Malignant narcissists are extremely aggressive and want power and control. They have deteriorated ethics.

Narcissistic leaders create regressed groups with a common ideology who identify with each other and who let the leader determine their moral responsibility.

Kernberg doesn't believe in diagnosing living politicians he has not seen personally, in contrast to historical leaders like Hitler and Stalin, whom he terms malignant narcissists. Donald Trump should not be diagnosed, but he should be judged on his political behavior. Trump does employ techniques used by Hitler such as repeating basic phrases such as "crooked Hillary," "lock her up," "clean the swamp," "build the wall." The U.S. is basically an open culture. Trump has caused regressive anti-immigrant attitudes.

Chapter 3 The allure of Trump's narcissism, by Elizabeth Lunbeck

In Chapter 3, Lunbeck describes how Trump mobilizes his narcissism to connect with his followers. He holds out a fantasy of greatness that offers the mutual construction of a reality, one that gives reassurance and bolsters self-esteem. Narcissism's seductive qualities are a key to understanding what the figure of Trump means for his followers, and, more generally, for the emotional tenor of our country at this historical moment.

4 Michael Maccoby and Ken Fuchsman

Chapter 4 Probing Trump's disruptive narcissistic personality, by Paul H. Elovitz

President Trump has disrupted the American political system, the western world's alliances, international trade, domestic politics, and even his own administration, which has an incredibly high turnover rate. He narcissistically fails to distinguish between his own personal needs and those of the country and the office of the presidency. Trump's combativeness is an integral part of his interpersonal relationships, typically making him the center of the news. Disruption is an early and basic part of Trump's personality which is traced to a developmental crisis occurring when he was 2 years old. His mother almost died after the birth of her fifth child, leading to a series of operations and subsequent ill health that led her to not being emotionally available to Donald, her fourth child. Trump's father was a workaholic who paid little attention to his sons until they were old enough to follow him around his housing projects. Young Trump lived in the largest house in the neighborhood, walled off from others, with walls becoming a crucial issue in his life, mind, and politics. Trump craves constant adoration but will settle for any attention whatsoever, which is the primary root of his disruptive tweets.

Part II How Trump leads

Chapter 5 Is Donald Trump competent and fit to be president?, by Ken Fuchsman

Donald Trump is the first elected United States President with no prior government service. During the 2016 campaign he was more interested in branding his opponents than being informed on the issues. He would make policy statements then reverse his pronouncements. His few attempts at detailed policy proposals often resulted in dramatic revisions. The false and misleading statements he made during the campaign were rigorously tracked by news outlets. Trump seemed ignorant of what was written in the U.S. Constitution. Many former Republican foreign policy officials have questioned his capacity to competently conduct foreign affairs. It was both his incompetency and his character that led many observers to question his candidacy. Yet, 46 percent of those who voted for President did so for Trump, and he won the Electoral College. His campaign showed that being informed and interested in the details of government were not what drew much of the electorate to support a presidential candidate.

Chapter 6 Gaslighting and beyond, by Robin Stern and Judith Logue

Gaslighting is a term originating in a play and film. It refers to a person who persuades another that their perceptions are mistaken, and gets them to doubt themselves and believe the deceiver. Robin Stern reports how many of her patients in therapy have let themselves be taken in by gaslighting. She shows how HBO comedian John Oliver was gaslighted by candidate Trump. Judith Logue traces a number of instances in the campaign where Trump made misleading statements designed to undermine people's perceptions and thus gain followers and support for his candidacy. Logue also finds this gaslighting in popular entertainment and media advertising campaigns, and she shows how gaslighting can influence people who have been susceptible to prior deceptions.

Chapter 7 Trump the demagogue, by Michael Signer

Donald Trump is the first demagogue to be elected President of the United States. To be so labeled a demagogue, a politician has to meet four criteria. First, he identifies as a man of the masses, usually by attacking elites. Second, he creates great waves of passion. Third, he uses that passion for political benefit. Fourth, he tests or breaks established rules of governance. Taken together, this approach enables the demagogue to create a state within a state—a massive cult—that follows him alone. As President, Trump's vulgarity appeals to his base. His inflammatory rhetoric stirs their passions. In these regards he resembles other prominent American demagogues, such as Huey Long, Louisiana Governor and U.S. Senator in the 1930s. Trump also uses many of the appeals that made former Alabama Governor George Wallace a rousing candidate for President in 1968. Donald Trump has just risen to a higher status than his two predecessors did.

Chapter 8 Is Trump a fascist?, by Paul Gottfried

In Chapter 8, Paul Gottfried examines why Donald Trump's enemies routinely refer to him as a fascist or even a Nazi. He distinguishes mere partisan attacks from those charges made by intellectually more serious critics who seem convinced that Trump is what they say he is. Gottfried argues that what leads these critics to their ominous conclusion is their view of Trump as someone who through his election and presidency ended a process of cultural and social change that his opponents support. Although Trump has done little to undo what his leftist predecessor did in terms of dealing with illegal immigration, his failure to move in a more open borders direction is now seen as a grave failing. For critics on the left, it represents something similar to the Thermidorean reaction to the most radical phase of the French Revolution or the fascist reaction in the interwar period to the progress of the European Left. That may be the reason that noting the overlaps between policies pursued by the Obama and Trump administrations is for Trump's enemies unconvincing. From their perspective, Trump halted a multicultural revolution that was seen as in progress before his election.

Part III Social and historical factors in the rise of Trump

Chapter 9 American Exceptionalism on steroids, by David Lotto

In Chapter 9, David Lotto suggests that Trump's slogan "Make America Great Again" symbolizes and embodies a fundamental and central aspect of his appeal to the nation. The success of his movement is seen as primarily the latest manifestation of American Exceptionalism with its glorification of nationalistic and militaristic patriotism that has aspects of a secular religion and is accompanied by a sense of superiority with respect to the other denizens of our planet. The history of American Exceptionalism is briefly examined and the current Trumpian moment is viewed as an expression of long-standing political currents that have been a central aspect of American identity throughout the course of our history.

Chapter 10 What in our politics, history, economy, and culture enabled Trump's rise?, by Ken Fuchsman

While Western European democracies have election seasons of four to six weeks, in the United States in 2016, it lasted 15 months. Our interminable campaigns are an essential element in our civic religion. Presidential candidates have political rallies that resemble revival meetings. Successful nominees frame their appeal in semi-religious terms: we are in dire straits and need a religious-type leader who can redeem us through their inspired personality. Trump played all these political cards well by denigrating existing office-holders and his Republican rivals, and then promising to Make America Great Again. He was aided by the mass media which gave him more attention than any other candidate, by appealing to those most harmed by the 2008 Great Recession and who had yet to benefit from the end of this downturn. In a time of discontent and distrust, his own branding and denigrating others spoke to many who felt disenfranchised.

Chapter 11 A sociologist's view of the Trump phenomenon, by Charles Heckscher

The election of Donald Trump has its roots in social trends that have developed since the 1970s and have spread throughout the Western industrial democracies: most notably, a dramatic decline of confidence in government and other core social institutions. This has come in reaction to the general social and economic "opening" of the past 50 years, which has brought nations and peoples into far closer contact than at any previous historical period, but has also disrupted many established ways of life. From this strain, two contrary movements have developed: populism, which aims to restore traditional values and relations; and

Introduction 7

progressivism, which seeks to broaden inclusion and to reduce historical inequalities. Trump has built an uneasy alliance of populists and traditional conservatives, while progressives have allied with traditional liberals. This divide has fed political polarization, which now constitutes a profound threat to the future and can be resolved only with deliberate efforts at mutual understanding and collaboration.

Part IV Presidential personality and performance

Chapter 12 How Trump's personality influences his policies, by Michael Maccoby

In Chapter 12, Michael Maccoby describes how Trump's policies are shaped by his marketing narcissistic personality. Trump's self-esteem depends on how he is valued by significant others. He must continue to satisfy his base, but he is able to pursue policies that dissatisfy traditional Republicans because he knows they have no alternatives. Trump's narcissism, his grandiosity, and bluffing behavior function as a defense against the vulnerability of his needs for approval and adulation. The chapter also describes the impacts of Trump's policies.

Chapter 13 The president we need, by Michael Maccoby

To recover from a presidency that has increased the distrust Americans have for each other and their national government, in Chapter 13, Michael Maccoby writes that we need a president with the character and competence we can trust to work for the common good. Some of the competencies needed by an effective leader of a democracy were outlined centuries ago by Pericles of Athens. Two of America's greatest presidents, Abraham Lincoln and Franklin Delano Roosevelt demonstrated these competencies in different contexts. They also shared a humanistic philosophy that directed them to work for both the well-being of people and economic progress. In contrast to Donald Trump, these presidents had progressive policies, the ability to express them, and they put the country above self-interest. The chapter ends with a series of questions to be asked of candidates for president.

Chapter 14 Conclusion, by Ken Fuchsman

Ken Fuchsman illustrates how the various perspectives in this book interconnect. Trump is described as a marketing narcissist, a gaslighter, a disruptive demagogue, and a person who makes many false and misleading statements. Each of these characteristics complement and illuminate each other. The authors of these chapters also show that the cultural, sociological, political, and historical factors that enabled Trump's rise connect with the different sides of his personality and public persona. These chapters show the value of combining psychoanalytic, historical, and sociological perspectives to understand the phenomenon of Donald Trump's rise to become President of the United States of America.

Reference

Maccoby, M. (2007). *Narcissistic Leaders: Who Succeeds and Who Fails.* Boston, MA: Harvard Business School Press.

Part I

Who is Donald Trump and why do people follow him?

Chapter 1

Trump's marketing narcissistic leadership in an age of anxiety

Michael Maccoby

Leadership is a relationship between a leader and followers that takes place in a particular context. Someone may gain followers in one context but not in another. Donald Trump's personality, his combination of marketing and narcissistic traits have connected with many voters in this particular historical time.

We are living in an age of anxiety, with fears that are political, social, and individual. We are anxious knowing that weapons of mass destruction are primed to kill millions of people, that climate change and viruses threaten human life, that terrorists can suddenly turn a pleasant outing in places like Paris, London, Barcelona, New York City, and El Paso, Texas, into a bloodbath, that children at school, concert goers, and worshippers in a church or a synagogue can suddenly be murdered by a fanatic.

There are other causes of anxiety. Decades of rapid transition from a bureaucratic-industrial culture to a culture based on information and knowledge have widened the financial and power gap between those able to adapt and those remaining rooted in a vanishing culture. Threats to livelihood and self-esteem have triggered anxiety in people left behind who have been losing industrial jobs due to global competition and automation, and fear they will never catch up.

After Joan C. Williams wrote an article about the white working class in the *Harvard Business Review*, a reader wrote to her:

> Your article deeply articulated the view of my family in a way they never could … They're mostly afraid. Afraid of the brown skin people. Afraid of the day they can't live in their home anymore. Afraid of global economics. Afraid of those who claim their God is not real. Afraid of sexually empowered women. Afraid of the scientific utterances they don't understand related to climate change, so they just reject it outright. Fear manifests itself in many ways, but it's the same route.
>
> (Williams, 2017, 65)

The white working class is not the only anxious group. African Americans (Bahrampour, 2017) and Latinos, including high school students (Rogers et al., 2017). worry about the policies of the Trump administration. A Pew study (Horowitz & Graf, 2019) published in February 2019 reported about 70 percent of U.S. teens see anxiety and depression as a major problem among their peers. Even professionals in the knowledge economy, the so-called elite, are not free of anxiety. Both at work and socially, they are constantly being evaluated as employees and social partners. According to studies by Jean M. Twenge, their children are afraid to grow up in this dangerous world. Twenge also cites reports that increasing numbers of undergraduates suffer overwhelming anxiety (Twenge, 2017). Rather than focusing on living a purposeful life, these young people worry they will become a have-not rather than a have. They worry about paying for education, taking student loans and being saddled with debt, and they worry about getting a job that would make their education a good investment.

The causes vary for different people, but to some degree we are all experiencing chronic and existential anxiety. Because living with extreme anxiety can be unbearable, many people repress it and some escape into drugs, entertainment, and social media. Mechanisms of escape become pathological addictions. Some of the people left behind have joined tribalistic political groups that are vulnerable to demagogues, narcissistic leaders who project power and certainty. These leaders stimulate a regressive transference in their followers. They feed the group's narcissism, blame others for their problems, and promise magical solutions to the causes of their anxiety. This dynamic threatens all of us, the unity of our society, and our ability to work together to address the threats to our wellbeing. It was a key factor in the election of Donald Trump, a leader whose marketing narcissistic behavior increases the fragmentation of society and our existential anxiety. To better understand our national condition, it will help to analyze how the threats to life and livelihood tend to increase narcissism and favor narcissistic leaders.

Narcissism

The concept of narcissism has strayed far from its mythic origin, the story of Narcissus, a beautiful hunter who rejects the love of Echo and is punished by Nemesis who leads him to a pool where he falls in love with his own image and stares at his reflection until he dies. Narcissism has become a household term for all kinds of egoism, arrogance, vanity, and bloated self-esteem. The use of the term has become so broad that the concept has almost lost its value.

The narcissistic personality disorder is well known. It lists symptoms such as entitlement, grandiosity, and paranoia, but doesn't describe their causes. I've thought about the causes and have focused on three different aspects of narcissism other than the narcissistic personality disorder:

1   *Narcissism* essentially combines the survival drive common to all species with specifically human needs for dignity and self-esteem, recognition,

and validation as persons. We all are somewhat narcissistic. If we weren't concerned about ourselves more than others, we'd have less chance of surviving physically and emotionally. Clearly, existential anxiety triggers the narcissistic survival drive. Exaggerated concerns about survival can expand into paranoia, seeing threats everywhere. For the individual as well as for government, overinvesting our energy in defense and security short-changes health, education, and welfare. The extreme need for dignity and self-esteem, recognition, and validation can be a reaction to feelings of humiliation and insignificance. These needs can expand into grandiosity and a pathological need for praise. When the drives for survival and self-esteem dominate the personality, the result is the narcissistic personality disorder. When this is combined with destructive sadism, the result is malignant narcissism.

2   *Group narcissism.* Throughout human history, the group or tribe that shared an identity has been more cohesive, better able to survive against enemies or natural threats. When people with shared identities feel attacked, they are likely to band together. Shared identities can become group narcissism that supports cooperation rather than intra-group rivalry. Cults are a form of group narcissism where people are connected by their identification with a charismatic leader. Malignant group narcissism fuels feelings of group or racial superiority and, in the extreme, results in dehumanization of other groups, leading to violence or even genocide. But group narcissism can also be more benign when it is based on positive shared values. It can motivate people in teams and in companies to collaborate and work harder to prove their superiority.

3   The *narcissistic personality.* Psychiatry focuses on psychopathology, and psychiatrists typically view the narcissistic personality as the narcissistic personality disorder. Psychiatric diagnostic categories describe illness, not personality, and there is no personality disorder without a normal personality which is not described by psychiatrists. Like other personality types, the narcissistic type has strengths and weaknesses. Narcissists can be more or less productive.

In Chapter 2, Otto Kernberg, a psychiatrist and psychoanalyst who is well known for his study and treatment of narcissists, describes a continuum from normal narcissism to extreme narcissistic personality disorders.

The narcissistic personality is one of three normal personality types proposed by Sigmund Freud (Freud, [1931] 1961). They are the erotic, obsessive, and narcissistic types. Erich Fromm added a fourth type, the marketing personality. Both Freud and Fromm proposed that we all express combinations of these types, but that one is usually dominant. Fromm pointed out that each type can be either positive and productive, or negative and unproductive. Erotics can be caring or dependent. Obsessives can be conscientious and reliable or nit-picking and anal. Narcissists can be visionary or just grandiose. Marketing personalities can be adaptive or centerless in need of constant affirmation of their worth. I have added names to these types that indicate their positive qualities: caring (erotic), exacting (obsessive), visionary (narcissistic), and adaptive (marketing). (I have supportive data for these types based on the factor analysis of results of a questionnaire I developed and have tested with hundreds of professionals (Maccoby, 2015)).

Freud, who once described himself as a narcissist to Sandor Ferenczi, describes this type as follows:

> The third type [is] justly called the narcissistic type ... There is no tension between ego and super-ego (indeed, on the strength of this type one would scarcely have arrived at the hypothesis of a super-ego), and there is no preponderance of erotic needs. The subject's main interest is directed to self-preservation: he is independent and not open to intimidation. His ego has a large amount of aggressiveness at its disposal, which also manifests itself in a readiness for activity. In his erotic life loving is pre-ferred above being loved. People belonging to this type impress others as being "personalities"; they are especially suited to act as support for others, to take on the role of leaders and to give a fresh stimulus to cul-tural development or to damage the established state of affairs.

Most of the successful narcissistic leaders I've studied, coached, and treated in analysis shared a developmental pattern. They were men who in childhood did not identify with their fathers either because he was absent (FDR, Barack Obama, Frank Lloyd Wright, Bill Clinton, Steve Jobs), weak (Richard Nixon, Ronald Reagan), or abusive (Abraham Lincoln). Most had strong, supporting mothers. Instead of a strong superego, they developed a demand-ing ego ideal, an ideal self they strived to become. They felt little or no guilt even when they acted in unethical or immoral ways, but they felt shame when they failed to live up to their ideal self-image. Lacking a strong superego, they could be ruthless in their striving to realize their ambitions, attacking those who threatened their self-image.

But those who were gifted not only broke rules, they changed the world in both positive and negative ways, such as FDR's New Deal and Adolf Hitler's Thousand Year Reich. Narcissists have created great companies like Ford, Apple, and Amazon or have destroyed companies like Enron and WorldCom.

Narcissistic leaders are most likely to emerge in times of disruptive change, either in politics, the economy, or technology that transforms society. Their inventions revolutionize the economy, and the narcissistic leader's promise to solve people's problems can inspire hope and dampen anxiety. Because narcis-sists present their inspiring visions with total confidence, they gain followers who either end up participating in their success or drinking their Kool-Aid.

Erich Fromm, in *Escape from Freedom* (Fromm, 1941) described the dynamic of anxious and depressed people becoming vulnerable to the promises of a narcissistic leader. The German lower middle class had a shared social character, a syndrome of character traits that developed as an adaptation to the economic, social, and cultural conditions common to the group. They were hard-working, frugal, patriotic, and submissive to authority. After World War I when Germany fell into a deep depression, these attitudes no longer led to economic success. Inflation made their hard-earned savings worthless. They felt humiliated and resentful. They lost trust in the leaders who had failed them. Hitler promised a return to prosperity and national glory, to make Germany great again. He blamed the people's problems on the Jews, communists, and enemies of Germany. Their obsessive and submissive social character made these people especially vulnerable to Hitler's authoritarian appeal. Hitler also gained support from business leaders who feared the alternative to Hitler was communism.

President Trump

Of course, Trump voters have not experienced the extreme loss suffered by Germans after World War I, but many of them are currently experiencing the results of technological, economic, and cultural changes that have had far-reaching consequences. Some Americans, especially a group that felt dispossessed by cultural and economic changes, supported Donald Trump for president, believing his promises to improve their lives and regain their self-esteem (others supported him for different reasons).[1]

Rather than address the real causes of anxiety due to culture change and threats to life, Trump has encouraged the group narcissism of his base of mainly whites who felt that their culture and livelihood were threatened. He has affirmed their distrust of elites and their prejudices against immigrants and Muslims.[2] Rather than alleviating anxiety, as FDR did when he said, "the only thing we have to fear is fear itself," Trump has increased our anxiety by feeding the flames of political conflict.

What is the difference between Trump's personality and the personalities of visionary narcissists who inspire collaboration for productive goals?

A cottage industry has emerged of mental health experts and commentators diagnosing Donald Trump as suffering from a narcissistic personality disorder. But Trump's personality doesn't fit into a narrow diagnostic category of a narcissistic personality disorder. He is not suffering from a delusion that he is president. He is not disabled. His personality is a variation of a normal narcissistic personality type. Trump has some of the narcissistic traits Freud described, including large amounts of aggressive energy and a weak superego, so he lacks internalized rules to keep his ego in check. He is combative, defensive, and grandiose. He needs constant praise. He makes up stories and facts. He feels no guilt about lying. He can also be seductive, using people and discarding them when they are no longer useful to him.

In Trump's book *Think Like a Billionaire* (Trump, 2004) he claims that the description in my book *The Productive Narcissist* (Maccoby, 2003) (republished as *Narcissistic Leader*s (Maccoby 2007a)) of *productive* narcissists like Steve Jobs and Jeff Bezos fits him:

> Michael Maccoby, a psychoanalyst and consultant, believes that billionaires like Jeff Bezos, Steve Jobs, and Ted Turner are successful in part because they are narcissists who devote their talent with unrelenting focus to achieving their dreams, even if it's sometimes at the expense of those around them. Maccoby's book *The Productive Narcissist* makes a convincing argument that narcissism can be a useful quality if you're trying to start a business. A narcissist does not hear the naysayers. At the Trump Organization, I listen to people, but my vision is my vision.
>
> (Trump with McIver, 2005, xvi)

Trump boasts that he also is a visionary leader, but his type of narcissism and his visions of buildings, gambling emporiums, and golf courses are significantly different from that of Jobs, Bezos, and other productive narcissists in business and politics. So is his relationship to others.

Jobs and Bezos envisioned and produced products and services that have improved the way we live. Subordinates who suffered their demands and insults believed in their visions with almost religious fervor and were rewarded for their devotion. These leaders combined narcissism with a productive obsessive-exacting drive to realize their visions. Unlike Trump, they didn't con people like those who enrolled in Trump University or clip lenders for millions with a series of bankruptcies. Unlike Trump, they didn't demand that their subordinates constantly praise them. They sought competent collaborators, not flattering toadies.

I have puzzled over Trump's variation of the narcissistic personality. How much did he both resent and identify with his jungle-fighting and demanding father who told him he could be either a killer or a loser? Did he both copy and compete with his father, trying to surpass him in riches and prestige? Does he still feel like a victim of paternal abuse who has to continually prove he is not a loser? Unlike his father who tried to avoid publicity, Trump sought the spotlight from an early age. He seems to combine narcissism with a marketing personality. People of this type shape themselves and their products to gain the approval of others. Their sense of self-worth is based not on their human qualities such as caring for others and integrity, but on their perceived value on the market of public opinion. Trump is an extreme example. His marketing orientation makes him vulnerable because he needs constant approval. His grandiose bluff and bluster are parts of a fragile narcissistic self-image defense that must be protected. He dismisses messages and attacks messengers who disparage his self-worth. He seeks constant adulation. The most productive marketing narcissists are innovators with a radar-like sensitivity to the needs of others. Not deeply committed to their products and policies, they can easily drop those that no one is buying. Although they may not be wedded to their policies, they also constantly work to deepen their knowledge to improve their products. Bill Clinton, a more productive marketing narcissist, copiously studied both policy issues and opinion polls and was able to change his policies when he considered it politically expedient. His narcissistic belief that he could get away with his philandering almost destroyed his presidency.

By contrast, Barack Obama has a productive narcissist-caring type of personality. His visions were to help the less fortunate with healthcare, to improve the environment, and end the costly and destructive conflicts in the Middle East. His ego ideal is Abraham Lincoln. He expressed his narcissism when he explained his policies by often coming back to himself, his story, or his feelings. In contrast to Trump's attitude of leaving no attack unanswered, Obama responded to attacks by withdrawing, remaining aloof.

Productive narcissists have convictions that drive their visioning. Jobs produced things he liked that the world then wanted, Ronald Reagan developed strong convictions about the economy when he was spokesman for GE. Trump's set of policies reflect his need to be a winner translated into what he believes will gain him applause from his core supporters. His only conviction is about winning. If his base doesn't like what he is selling, he will sell what he thinks they do like without regard to his ability to deliver it. In 2000, Trump campaigned for President as a liberal under the Reform Party ticket. In his 2016 campaign, he was anything but a liberal. Not even Trump knows what's next. We are anxious about what he might do next because he acts to satisfy his ego or play to his core supporters without regard for the consequences.

Many successful leaders have a strong aesthetic drive. Jobs demanded that his products be beautiful as well as useful. In their article, "Aesthetics of story-telling as a technology of the plausible," Esther Edina and Rafael Ramirez report that leaders with a strong aesthetic drive fashion stories that feel good to them, sometimes denying inconvenient facts (Edina & Ramirez, 2016). Narcissists, even the most productive, typically exaggerate or lie to maintain their self-image, gain an advantage, or manipulate people. Reagan made up a history of his combat in World War II when in fact he was only doing his fighting in movies. I have coached over 30 narcissistic CEOs and executives. Almost all played fast and loose with the truth. One narcissistic CEO in analysis told me that he sometimes lied about his company's products or results, but then he worked hard to make his claims real.

Trump has an extreme aesthetic approach to reality. He needs to make events look and feel good to him so he looks good. His exaggerations and lies beat any I've heard as a consultant to successful narcissists. He habitually bends the truth and makes up stories. In *Commander in Cheat: How Golf Explains Trump*, Rick Reilly documents Trump's habitual cheating and lying about his golf game and the golf courses he owns. When Reilly asked Trump why he was lying about him, Trump answered that what he said "sounds better" than the truth (Reilly, 2019). It's also important for Trump that the key people around him look good and dress well. He even wants his border wall to be beautiful. This toxic brew of aesthetic, marketing, and narcissistic needs that worked for him as an entrepreneur and TV performer makes people distrust everything he says or tweets.

Trump does have productive qualities. He is determined, active, takes calculated risks. He has bounced back from business defeats. He has envisioned and built successful projects and won the presidency because he connected with people who wanted change and those who have felt victims of change. He has raised important issues about military and trade policies, emphasizing that America should not be exploited. He can be an effective performer, but he displays a stunning lack of curiosity about the knowledge needed for productive policy development and organizational implementation in government. He is at his best when he pays attention to experts who persuade him that he will personally benefit from making better decisions.

Narcissistic leaders are more likely to succeed when they partner with people who complement their strengths and keep them from making disastrous decisions. Steve Jobs failed when he tried to run Apple by himself and succeeded when he partnered with Tim Cook and Joni Ives. Napoleon succeeded when he followed the advice of Talleyrand, but failed disastrously when he fired Talleyrand for objecting to his plan to attack Russia.

Trump's marketing orientation treats himself and others as commodities. He values powerful and successful people and treats the weak and vulnerable with contempt as worthless, unless of course they can be useful to him like those who are part of his base whom he seduces with promises and flattery. He respects powerful authoritarian dictators like Vladimir Putin, Xi Jinping, Kim Jong-un, and Mohammed Bin Salman Al Saud but has no respect, much less compassion, for immigrant children or Americans without healthcare.

Trump will sometimes listen to disagreements from people he believes respect him and he respects as successful in their own spheres. He has sometimes been able to listen to generals and the mega rich but these relationships typically don't last. He has no close friends, only collaborators and subordinates from whom he demands loyalty without offering it in return. He is driven to attack anyone who criticizes him personally, and his Twitter feed makes these attacks public. Like all narcissists, he is particularly sensitive to criticism, competition, and threats. As Andy Grove of Intel wrote in *Only the Paranoid Survive* (1996), paranoia, if not severe, serves leaders who have real competitors and enemies. Trump's paranoia is self-defeating, needlessly turning critics into enemies and limiting the input of supporters to what they believe he wants to hear. Trump lacks the sense of humor Lincoln, FDR, and Reagan used to deflate their critics and even make fun of themselves. Personal attacks on Trump will always deafen him to constructive criticism.

The leaders we need

The leaders we need are very different from Trump. We need leaders who will address the causes of our anxiety and work to resolve them. Unlike populist demagogues who promise magical solutions, or leaders who promote special interests, the leaders we need will develop policies and organizations that realistically move all of our society to a better future. Rather than just offering handouts, the leaders we need will inspire social responsibility. We need this kind of leadership on five interrelated levels: global, national, community, organizational, and individual. These leaders may have different types of personality. What is essential is that they are productive and ethical, that they understand the issues and are able to communicate their policies, and that they share a leadership philosophy that makes the wellbeing of the people and the environment their highest priorities. They understand the message of the Spanish philosopher José Ortega y Gasset who wrote, "I am myself and my circumstances and if I do not save my circumstances, I cannot save myself." These are leaders who work collaboratively, who partner with people who complement their strengths and share their philosophy, and who continually learn. They also have a sense of humor, the emotional equivalent of a cognitive sense of reality.

On the global level, no country by itself can deal with the major threats to human life on planet Earth: weapons of mass destruction, climate change, pandemics, and terrorists. We need leaders who develop international collaboration to avoid wars, protect the environment, and care for survivors of wars and disasters. Although global trade has enriched countries, it has also increased inequality, causing the anxiety and resentment that attract populist leaders. This must be addressed globally, nationally, in communities, in organizations, and with individuals.

On the national level, the challenge for the United States is the humanization of capitalism, attacking inequality and putting people before profits. Americans have boasted about their country being a land of equal opportunity, but if that were true in the past, it is no longer true in the knowledge age. Unless the less advantaged have guaranteed healthcare, schools that develop both skills and an adaptive social character, and good jobs, they have no chance of narrowing the income gap.

Lack of healthcare can be a major source of anxiety. Because of the Affordable Care Act, millions of Americans have gained access to healthcare, but millions are still without this benefit. A key challenge, not only for leaders, but also for all citizens who believe that everyone should be entitled to healthcare, is promoting and implementing these policies.[3]

Gaining good healthcare depends on healthcare organizations as well as public policy. My colleagues and I have studied and worked with great healthcare organizations in the U.S., Sweden, and Singapore (Maccoby, Norman, Norman, & Margolies, 2013). They are learning organizations with leadership that continually improves care, cuts costs, and works to improve population health.

The best business and government organizations produce products and services that improve the quality of life. They do not harm the environment. But a product of work is also the people who work in these organizations. Ilene Philipson (2002) writes about patients who look to their workplaces for emotional security, self-esteem, and belonging. But they, like many other employees, are stressed and made anxious in jobs that demand mindless conformity. Gallup surveys report that less than one-third of employees in this country are engaged at work. The majority go through the motions to get paid and get healthcare. The best organizations engage employees and develop their social character. Leaders encourage innovation, collaboration, and respect for individuals and the environment. We need leaders who understand that employees will be engaged when their work has a meaningful purpose, their jobs include continual learning, and they are respected and recognized for their contributions, views, and ideas.

On the level of communities we need to invest in our public schools and teachers. Our schools could and should be models for addressing some of the challenges of inequality, including the skills and social character that equip people for success in this knowledge economy. I have worked with the Knowledge Is Power Program (KIPP) of charter schools that develops school leaders who have been master teachers and who focus on the academic and social character competence of thousands of disadvantaged children, with the result that over 80 percent have qualified for college. The graduates have learned to be collaborative problem-solvers and innovators. KIPP collaborates with public schools in Houston, Texas, to improve college admission and graduation rates. Charter schools like KIPP were established to be laboratories for improving public schools. Some charter schools are less effective than public schools, but public schools can learn from those like KIPP that outperform public schools with disadvantaged children.

Good organizations in terms of both economic and humanistic factors depend on leadership that develops and practices a philosophy that describes the organization's purpose, the practical values essential to achieve that purpose, and how results will be measured to support the purpose and values (Maccoby, 2015). The aim of great organizations is meeting human needs and improving the quality of life. These organizations may have leaders who work interactively with different roles and with different personality types. What is essential is that they share and practice a creative leadership philosophy.

Billions of dollars are spent by companies and governments on leadership development. According to a survey of CEOs by McKinsey, the results have been disappointing, even according to business criteria, much less for the kind of leadership we need.[4] Can the leadership we need be taught? My experience is that it can be developed in people, even some narcissists, who have a positive purpose, strong ethics, passion, and courage. I agree with Samuel Johnson that "courage is the greatest of all virtues because unless a person has that virtue, there is no security for preserving any other."

Treating the causes of anxiety

People can't respond productively to the threats that cause fear and anxiety if they are escaping into drugs, entertainment, and social media. There is alarming evidence that this country is suffering a growing mental health crisis. The Substance Abuse and Mental Health Administration reports an increasing incidence of addictions and they don't even include anxiety meds in their measures. Drug overdoses kill more Americans under the age of 50 than anything else (Financial Times, 2017). Twenge reports that for the generation that has grown up with smartphones, "loneliness, depressive symptoms, major depressive episodes, anxiety, self-injury, and suicide are all on the rise, mostly since 2011" (Twenge, 2017, 302). Twenge blames these conditions on the generation's addiction to smartphones, but it is more likely that the young people suffer from unsuccessful attempts to escape from anxiety. It's good for kids to get limits on their use of smartphones, but that won't cure their anxiety.

We know from psychotherapeutic practice that to deal with existential anxiety without prescribing drugs, people first need to wake up to the fears that are feeding the anxiety. Mindfulness meditation can be better than medication, but neither address the causes of existential anxiety. A challenge for psychotherapists is to help people transform anxiety into productive activity, recognizing that there are rational reasons to be afraid. There are real threats to life and wellbeing.

Can we separate fears that can only be addressed socially and politically from fears that can be overcome by helping people wake up and change their practice of life? To have any chance of doing this, we need to learn more about why so many young people are so afraid of relationships and of growing up. And we need to learn why some young people are living productive lives and are not escaping from anxiety into psychopathology.

Are the parents of the at-risk children transmitting their own fears? Do these children lack models of productive adults? Are the parents marketing personalities who lack purpose or meaning other than making themselves marketable products?

Has this fearful generation displaced their unconscious anxiety onto their demands at college for safe spaces, trigger warnings, and unwillingness to hear challenging speakers?

Why are some people, including many members of the smartphone generation, able to live productive lives, even though they are awaking to the threats we all face in this tumultuous and threatening world? A colleague who is a professor at a university writes that while many undergraduates avoid discussions over issues that would cause conflict and news that would increase anxiety, the most productive are awake to some of the causes of anxiety and are engaged in trying to deal with them. My experience with some very productive young people is based on reviewing hundreds of questionnaires from applicants to become volunteer caregivers in one of the nine Latin American and Caribbean countries served by *Nuestros Pequeños Hermanos* (Our Little Brothers and Sisters) with homes, schools, and healthcare facilities for orphans and disadvantaged children and their families. The applicants are asked to define the meaning of love and how they practice it. They are asked to describe their purpose in life. Their responses show understanding of the difference between sexual and caring love, *eros* vs. *agape*. They describe living purposeful lives with mindsets of continual learning and growth. They have strong ethical and religious values and they want to work with others who share their values and purpose of helping children to develop their potential. They show courage in volunteering to work in challenging cultures and conditions. Can we help children to understand what it takes to transcend anxiety by continual learning and engagement in improving the lives of others?

To conclude, anxiety will not be cured by the false promises of narcissistic, populist leaders or by mechanisms of escape, but only by addressing the causes of anxiety on global, national, organizational, and individual levels. As citizens, we can lead by joining with others to improve our politics and organizations. We can only change political leadership by engaging in the political process and helping to educate the public about the real causes of our anxiety and what it takes to deal with them. As psychotherapists, we should be careful that our patients and clients do not put all the blame for their anxiety on themselves but that they recognize that their mechanisms of escape are more damaging than waking up to the political and social causes of their anxiety.

Notes

1 A study by Emily Ekins describes five different groups that voted for Trump. She names them as American Preservationists (20 percent), Staunch Conservatives (31 percent), Anti-Elites (19 percent), Free-Marketers (25 percent), and the Disengaged (5 percent). The American Preservationists who clinched Trump's win are mainly the white working class who have been left behind economically and socially and who resent the elites who denigrate them.
2 See Chapter 11 for Charles Heckscher's analysis of the causes of distrust in America.
3 The National Coalition on Healthcare, including provider organizations, companies, unions, insurance companies, and non-profits, works with both parties in Congress to promote improvements. It is led by John Rather. I serve on the board.
4 See the work of Jeffrey Pfeiffer: *Leadership BS: Fixed Workplaces and Careers One Truth at a Time* (Pfeiffer, 2010) and *Dying for a Paycheck: Why the American Way of Business Is Injurious to People and Companies* (Pfeiffer, 2018).

References

Bahrampour, T. (2017). Pessimism Grows among U.S. Blacks. *The Washington Post*, September 27, p. 2.

Edina, E. & Ramirez, R. (2016, November). Aesthetics of Story-telling as a Technology of the Plausible. *Future*, 84, 43–49.

Ekins, E. (2017). The Five Types of Trump Voters, Who They Are and What They Believe. Retrieved from www.voterstudygroup.org/publication/the-five-types-trump-voters

Financial Times (2017). US edition, September 12.

Freud, S. ([1931] 1961). Libidinal Types. In *The Standard Edition of the Complete Psychological Works of Sigmund Freud*, vol. XXI. London: The Hogarth Press, pp. 215–220.

Fromm, E. (1941). *Escape from Freedom*. New York, NY: Rinehart.

Grove, A. (1996). *Only the Paranoid Survive*. New York, NY: Currency/Doubleday.

Horowitz , J. M. & Graf, N. (2019). Most U.S. Teens See Anxiety and Depression as a Major Problem Among Their Peers. Washington, DC: Pew Research Center, February 20.

Maccoby, M. (2003). *The Productive Narcissist: The Promise and Peril of Visionary Leadership*. New York, NY: Broadway Books.

Maccoby, M. (2007a). *Narcissistic Leaders: Who Succeeds and Who Fails*. Boston, MA: Harvard Business School Press.

Maccoby, M. (2007b). *The Leaders We Need, and What Makes Us Follow*. Boston, MA: Harvard Business School Press.

Maccoby, M. (2015). *Strategic Intelligence: Conceptual Tools for Leading Change*. Oxford: Oxford University Press.

Maccoby, M., Norman, C. L., Norman, C. J., & Margolies, R. (2013). *Transforming Health Care Leadership: A Systems Guide to Improve Patient Care, Decrease Costs, and Improve Population Health*. San Francisco, CA: Jossey-Bass.

Pfeiffer, J. (2010). *Leadership BS: Fixed Workplaces and Careers One Truth at a Time*. New York, NY: Harper Business.

Pfeiffer, J. (2018). *Dying for a Paycheck: Why the American Way of Business is Injurious to People and Companies*. New York, NY: HarperCollins.

Philipson, I. (2002). *Married to the Job*. New York, NY: Free Press.

Reilly, R. (2019). *Commander in Cheat: How Golf Explains Trump*. New York, NY: Hachette Books.

Rogers, J., et al. (2017). *Teaching and Learning in the Age of Trump: Increasing Stress and Hostility in America's High Schools*. Los Angeles, CA: UCLA's Institute for Democracy, Education, and Access.

Trump, D. J. with McIver, M. (2004). *Trump: Think Like a Billionaire*. New York, NY: Random House Publishing Group.

Trump, D. J. with McIver, M. (2005). *Trump: Think Like a Billionaire: Everything You Need to Know About Success, Real Estate, and Life*. New York. NY: Ballantine Books.

Twenge, J. M. (2017). *iGen, Why Today's Super Connected Kids Are Growing Up Less Rebellious, More Tolerant, Less Happy—and Completely Unprepared for Adulthood*. New York, NY: Atria Books.

Williams, J. C. (2017). *White Working Class: Overcoming Class Cluelessness in America*. Boston, MA: Harvard Business Review Press.

Chapter 2

The anatomy of narcissistic leadership

Interview with Otto Kernberg

Ken Fuchsman and Molly Castelloe

KF: The term "malignant narcissism" is associated with you. You have applied it to Hitler, Stalin, and Saddam Hussein. What do you mean by malignant narcissism in the clinical and the cultural setting?

OK: Clinically, malignant narcissism is a sub-type within the broader category of the narcissistic personality disorder. The narcissistic personality disorder is a frequent type of personality disorder characterized by patients having an attitude of grandiosity, superiority, entitlement, an attitude toward others of devaluation, contempt, depreciation, and at the same time a strong disposition to intense envy, resentment of what others have and they don't have. Envy actually constitutes a major conflict, both consciously and unconsciously. At a deeper level, unconscious envy, discovery of its importance by Melanie Klein, motivates an eager acquisition of things that one would envy not having but then devaluing them, then spoiling them, once one has them. So one ends up empty anyhow.

Greediness, that goes together with entitlement and with a sense of superiority, these are basic characteristics of these patients. In a deeper sense, there is a building up of an abnormal grandiose self-concept, what we call a pathological grandiose self, and a devaluation of the representations of significant others in one's mind. So that one's sense of self exists in an internal vacuum, in contrast to what happens with normal people with an internal representation of the people who are important to them, constituting an internal world of other people that feels like being part of a community, that makes us not feel lonely, even though we may be alone. Narcissist personalities are missing that and need an ongoing admiration from others, as a reconfirmation of their grandiosity. So it's a paradox: they are the greatest, but they need to be admired to confirm it: if they don't get that, there is a basic sense of emptiness.

They are prone to boredom if they don't get ongoing stimulation that replaces their internal world. They generate stimulation by drugs or adventures, dangerous life-styles that give them excitement, sexual adventures, sexual conquests, which lead to sexual promiscuity based on narcissistic dynamics. Additionally, they have problems with their moral consciousness, because the build-up of a normal sense of ethical behavior requires an integration of one's relationships with significant others. It is in one's relationship with significant others that we build up rules and principles of relating to other people beyond what is instrumentally necessarily in discrete interactions in relations with others. In addition to our practical social associations in our daily life, we develop a sense of ethical values that rule our relations with our social environment, and that shows in value systems that, in these patients, often appear as an infantile quality, and lacking adult maturity. These patients want to be loved and admired for basically child-like qualities, like having the best clothing, shiniest cars, the externality of appearance, behavior, and possessions that are a pleasure to everybody. But for them these values are essential and replace those higher values for which we want to be valued, like our ethical integrity, intelligence, human qualities, compassion, empathy. Narcissistic personalities have difficulties in their value systems and difficulties in real empathy, because they have difficulties understanding others whom they tend to devalue to enhance themselves. A price they pay is that others can be judged by their immediate behavior but they have difficulty in assessing other people in depth. So that's the narcissistic personality in a brief way.

There are cases that are more or less ill. The mildest cases seem to have a normal life except they are a little too grandiose, self-affirmative, and have difficulty socially or at work but other than that, everything is fine. At the middle range of severity, they have serious difficulties. At work, they can't get along. They have difficulty, they may be brilliant cognitively, but they are in trouble all the time because of excessive competitiveness in their work environment. They have difficulty with intimacy because they cannot commit themselves to another person whom they value. Typically, there is resentment and envy of the other gender. Men envy women and women envy men. One's sexual partner becomes at the same time one's rival, causing serious couple difficulties, marriage difficulties and sexual promiscuity that tends to ruin their love life. There are serious problems with intimate relations, marital conflicts, serious problems at work, serious problems with social interactions. These patients need treatment. Sometimes narcissistic patients are more severely ill, to such an extent that they either have to be the best or they don't play. They have difficulty learning, have failures at work, they can't engage in stable relationships. They fail in work, social life, intimacy. Their grandiosity is in sharp contradiction to their failures in daily life. They develop severe anxieties, depression, drug abuse. These patients need to be hospitalized. These are narcissistic personalities functioning on an overt borderline level.

Sometimes narcissistic patients are more severely ill, to such an extent that they either have to be the best or they don't play. They have difficulty learning, have failures at work, they can't engage in stable relationships. They fail in work, social life, intimacy. Their grandiosity is in sharp contradiction to their failures in daily life. They develop severe anxieties, depression, drug abuse. These patients need to be hospitalized. These are narcissistic personalities functioning on an overt borderline level.

There are even more severely ill patients, in which lack of development of a moral system leads to severe anti-social behavior. They steal, cheat, write forged checks, become irresponsible with money, and have trouble with the law. If they have an excessive degree of aggression, they may become frankly aggressive, destroying property, attacking people; they become, at worst case, delinquent. A basic category in which there is no remnant of any moral capacity at all constitutes the anti-social personality proper, which we tend to classify separately. These are people who either passively or actively exploit the humanity of everybody else, and get in trouble with the law, or become murderers, serial murderers, or develop dangerous sadistic perversions that bring them also to the law or make them really dangerous. You see it's a very broad spectrum; they all have in common that basic grandiosity and its consequences of deterioration of relations with significant others.

KF: And malignant narcissism?

OK: Malignant narcissism is a specific syndrome that is part of the severe spectrum of this personality disorder, characterized by the fact that intense aggression colors the personality structure to such an extent that the pathological grandiose self gets infiltrated with aggression instead of one's grandiosity, in the milder cases, protecting one from getting too aggressive and too resentful because one is so great and one is above everything, and one has good defenses against envy. Here one's greatness is confirmed by one's power over others, and so malignant narcissism is the infiltration of the pathological grandiose self with aggression. With a manifest search for power, one's control over others, there is also a more severe deterioration of the ethical functioning, a tendency to anti-social behavior, and a tendency to attribute to others the kind of aggression that controls their behavior. In other words, these patients are excessively suspicious, paranoid, and they act in directly aggressive, contemptuous, controlling ways. This behavior is a source of pleasure and shows as a sadistic expression of aggression, severe paranoid tendency, and anti-social behavior. The combination of these four features: narcissistic personality disorder, aggression, anti-social behavior, and paranoid tendencies characterize this syndrome. The syndrome functions along a spectrum in which the more severely ill reduce their relations with reality so much that a total breakdown in the capacity to work and the capacity for sexual intimacy evolves; the grandiosity enters in conflict with this total failure, triggering depression and anxiety. They are usually confused with ordinary borderline patients. Usually the diagnosis is missed because it looks like the total failure of functioning that is typical of borderline patients.

Other patients with malignant narcissism are effective enough to express their narcissistic needs for superiority and for dominance by taking leadership of regressive groups, that, in turn experience group regression into a typical large group. Regressed large groups are united by mutual identification around a common ideology that has a paranoid quality and the leadership of somebody who has sufficiently paranoid features to identify with their paranoia, so that the narcissistic personality becomes the ideal leader because the grandiosity is satisfied by the leadership, the paranoid tendency is satisfied by the common paranoid ideology, the anti-social behavior by providing leadership that permits full expression of hostility without any moral constraints toward selected enemies. The large group identifies with the grandiose leader, is free of moral constraints because the leader represents their morality, and is ready to invest and attack outside enemies. So the paranoid quality, the anti-social quality, the fostering of direct aggression by someone who is self-assured enough to take leadership of groups with these characteristics, that person can become a political leader under conditions of rapid change in society with splitting up into social sub-groups in conflicts, or with a loss of ordinary social structure which threatens their security of daily functioning that one obtains in one's usual status roles. In other words, when one's usually assured roles and status within one's social community and within one's work situation get threatened because society is falling apart, there is a tendency to look for a social community that creates a substitute level of social organization by becoming part of such a regressed group; as Vamik Volkan put it, personal identity is threatened by social disorganization and a second skin is established by being part of a regressed social group. For example, the case of severe conflict between competing social groups and chronic mutual hostility: the Yugoslavian conflicts between Muslims and Christians, in Germany, the Jews constituted a sub-group against which a large group organization could be directed. After the Russian Revolution, the peasantry remnants of the capitalist system were opposed to the revolutionary segment. Pre-existent social sub-groupings get exacerbated by the formation of integrated large groups infiltrated by an ideology that conducts them to take action against enemy groups under the leadership of somebody with such narcissistic characteristics, so that large group regression and this kind of leadership become integrated. Jacques Semelin, comparing the genocides in Rwanda, Yugoslavia, and Nazi Germany showed the similar development of long-standing social sub-divisions, historical crises intensifying them, intellectual development of an ideology that got hold of the dominant group, a malignant narcissistic leader willing to transform it into political action against the enemy group, with the development of socially sanctioned aggression, abandonment of ordinary ethical systems, leading in all three cases to genocide.

KF: Are the conditions that lead to malignant narcissists being in power connected to social regression and also to the leaders developing some sort of ideology that can appeal to social regression?

OK: Yes, he takes up an ideology that speaks to the needs of the particular group.

KF: Your application of malignant narcissism has been, as I said, influential.

OK: I am using the contributions of a number of people. The contributions of Wilfred Bion to small group behavior, Vamik Volkan to the study of large groups; Pierre Turquet, who studied experimentally large groups of 150–300 people when they had no tasks and were forced to interact freely for a period of time. Of course, Freud's theory of mass formation, and the amplification of Freud's theory, by Serge Moscovici, suggesting that contemporary media permit diffusion of information that permits the generalization of an ideological formation, illustrate the hypothesis that Freud made regarding mass movements. Large conglomerates of people who are united by a common pressure to move in a certain direction are an organized large group. Freud pointed out that under such conditions, when an individual feels that he is part of a large group, he shows a tendency to reduce the level of cognitive functioning. In other words, we become less intelligent when we absorb knowledge as part of a large group. If you have an individual teacher who teaches you something and you have the same teacher who teaches you the same thing when you are part of a group of a hundred people, in a lecture, you have more difficulty learning in the large groups that when you are alone. In other words, your capacity for absorbing complexity, for self-reflection, for critical thinking is reduced under such conditions. When we watch people on television, we already have a reduction of our capacity for self-reflection. Through history, the town crier, the invention of the press, the invention of the radio, the invention of television, all increased the possibility of simultaneously organizing mass movements. Multiple large groups may simultaneously evolve because of their adherence to different segments of the internet. By the way, the struggle between Tutsis as opposed to Hutus finally ended up in mass murder in Rwanda. It corresponds to what happened in Bosnia, and of course in Germany, Russia, and the Cultural Revolution in China.

MC: What are your ideas about what is going on here in America at the current time? What are your thoughts about that?

OK: Well, I think there is a certain phenomenon of formation of such a large group situation, in terms of the upsurge of a wish for a synchronized approach to social problems, a certain intensification of a nationalist spirit, which stresses the superiority of one's country, and leads to the fight against potential enemies. Outside enemies—migrants—as well as an inside establishment are to be fought with a combative sense of bring underprivileged, to be corrected in a future ideal state. All of this is formulated in an ideological process, designating an enemy, designating what needs to be done; doing it in a simple, clear style, that corresponds to the cognitive level of absorption of large groups. At the same time, leadership can be admired for assuming moral responsibility for an alternative freedom from moral principles, which induces a sense of liberation as well as the power of identifying with the assured, morally free power of the leader.

KF: Recently some psychoanalysts have applied the idea of malignant narcissism to what is going on in the United States right now. *The Dangerous Case of Donald Trump* discussed this. Are you familiar with that?

OK: I haven't read it.

KF: John Gartner, who identifies himself as one of your former students, talks about malignant narcissism and talks about anti-social personality disorder and applies that to what is going on since Donald Trump was elected. I don't know if you expected that people would use ideas that they say were derived from your writing to something so specific.

OK: There are several questions. First of all, you mentioned psychopathy. The anti-social personality proper usually does not take on leadership functions because they are too disorganized, just as a general statement. Specifically, you deal with the question if Donald Trump should be diagnosed and classified as suffering from malignant narcissism. I have made this point before so I'm going to repeat it. I don't believe in making a diagnosis of any living politician one hasn't seen personally in one's office. From this viewpoint, I'm refusing to make a diagnosis of malignant narcissism applied to Donald Trump. Because theoretically a very astute politician would be able to assume these behaviors, aware of the needs of a regressed large group and assume a public behavior that would correspond exactly to all of this while in his private life show a surprising degree of honesty and depth. It would say something about that person that he is willing to take on such functions, but it is conceivable. So I think that one should not use the diagnosis for political purposes, but judge Donald Trump by his political behavior. The judgment of the man should be done for political reasons and not for diagnostic reasons. In this regard, the psychiatric profession is divided between those who think that we have to diagnose and those who think we cannot apply psychiatric diagnosis to such situations. I don't agree with the first position. If Donald Trump in his public behavior demonstrates an attitude of grandiosity, of inordinate aggression, of frank dishonesty, of paranoid distortion of relationships, if his public behavior is incompatible with what one expects of responsible leadership, then such political rationale should be the basis for saying this is not somebody who has the capacity to be the leader of the nation. That's my viewpoint in that regard. I would distinguish between the characteristics of his public behavior, that may fit nicely the symptoms of "political narcissism" and a clinical diagnosis as a person that could only be assessed by seeing him personally.

When I had dared to use Hitler and Stalin as examples of malignant narcissism, it was because there is so much personal information that is available about both of them. One can reasonably assess, I believe, their personality. Just to give you an example, the quality of personal aggression—cruelty—in Stalin, who invited people for tea, both those he wanted to reward and those he already had decided to condemn, to kill. The invitees were frightened, they did not know which way they were to go, and he enjoyed their fear. Hitler, for weeks, watched the film of the people who tried to kill him and who were condemned to death, to a very slow death that was filmed. He would watch these films for weeks. We have evidence for that and for severe paranoid distortion of external reality by both leaders. In the case of Hitler, his ideas about the supposed conspiracy by Jews to destroy the German culture. Stalin had concerns about people poisoning him. They had little capacity to evaluate people except by their external, perceived behavior. The person whom Stalin trusted most was Beria, who was perhaps psychopathic, and Hitler trusted most Goebbels and Goering; Goebbels was profoundly dishonest. Perhaps the same thing could be said about Mao, but I don't know enough about him. There is a natural collusion between personality structure and a regressed social group. They look for each other, so to speak. But one cannot make the diagnosis of someone who has not been examined clinically. We have to carefully separate out social analysis from psychiatric analysis.

KF: Are you saying that Donald Trump exhibits characteristics of malignant narcissism in his public behavior, but it may or may not be reflective of who he is?

OK: Yes. It may be that he has learned such basic principles that are very effective in mobilizing regressed masses. They were first discovered actually by Stalin, who put radios on the street everywhere so his speeches could be heard. He learned that the repetition of the same simple statements again and again was very effective, if heard enough, to become convincing that they are the truth. Learning to control thought processes by simple repetitive statements: the Nazis picked this up from the communists. Hitler had the same principle; certain basic phrases that were repeated all the time, like "one people, one country, one Führer." Thus, people, nation, and the Führer became one. He was the expression of the German nation and that was felt by each individual, they felt their nationality and Hitler were one. The slogans have a kind of magical quality. "Crooked Hillary" was repeated, "lock her up," "clean the swamp," "build the wall." Each of them implies an entire ideology, but expressed very simply, for members of a large group very convincingly when sufficiently repeated.

MC: In some of the other psychoanalysts writing of the political situation here, there is one who has written about a Trump anxiety disorder. I am wondering if you notice anything different in your patients in the clinical world since he was elected.

OK: Not that I can see.

KF: Have you heard of the Trump anxiety disorder? There is one writer who talks about that. There is another writer who speaks of a Post-Trumpmatic Stress Disorder.

OK: One thing that is very clear is, on the one hand, we have a clear social crisis similar to massive regressions in other countries. At least it seems to me that this has come as a surprise, not a natural evolution of dangerous social situations. It reflects clearly the dissatisfaction and social anxiety of a social sub-group, particularly working-class whites, both in industrial segments and agricultural segments. This was missed by the political elite, the establishment, experts, and explains the large group formation, and why the connection of Trump was facilitated. Given his manifest behavior, he harmonized with the large group's needs. Yet, it is still surprising that it happened at this point in this country, although a counter-argument, parallel movements have recently occurred in other parts of the world. But the United States has not suffered from extreme challenges, such as Eastern Europe, Poland. The strengthening of such tendencies in Germany has followed a huge immigration that has brought a large foreign group into Germany. France has had similar problems. There may be some more general sociological factors that I don't know whether we understand sufficiently at this point, rather than an exclusive cause affecting this country. That is an open question, at least for me.

MC: Do you have certain thoughts about American culture just generally?

OK: You raised one question which you sent me, that in the year 2000 I said "paranoid" about this country. I believe I said litigious. I may be wrong. Did I say paranoid?

MC: In the interview it was printed as paranoid. Maybe you meant litigious.

OK: Litigious, which of course has a paranoid quality. It's a very specific one, a tendency to try to resolve conflicts legally. It has created a kind of legal structure fostering an excessive use of legal means for settling disputes. Everybody sues everybody much more easily here than in the rest of the world.

KF: That has been the case in the United States going back to the colonial period.

OK: It is my thought that this is a very open culture, except the problem of the racial bias against blacks, which had to do with the importation of blacks at a certain point and who really were a very different social group. Other than that, there has been a remarkable capacity to bring in people from many cultures and religions. Even regarding the discrimination against blacks, I think there has been a positive development in the last 20 to 30 years. In general, we're much more open than most African or Asian countries. The increase in discriminatory feelings about immigrants coming from Mexico is part of large group regression and leadership stimulation. It is not a general custom of our culture, I believe.

MC: I wanted to ask about your reference to *Rhinoceros*. Did you see the play or read the play? Your feelings about the play. How you understood the metamorphosis of the people into rhinoceroses.

OK: It appears to be one of the greatest plays of the Theatre of the Absurd, that wave during the 1960s. I think it illustrates how easily self-affirmative regression reflects the temptation of raw power, aggression, throwing off civilization's restrictions. How easily that is triggered under certain social situations. That is what happens in large group regressions. It shows that underneath our civilized cultural surface there is a lot of deep, buried aggression that under certain circumstances is mobilized, and much more available than we believe. These large group regressions are a demonstration of that. The fact that the assertion of free, raw aggression and enjoyment of making others suffer can be so tempting to imitate can be seen in the reaction to Isis. How many people were attracted to Isis because of their cruelty? No doubt about that. What was horrible for most people, the videos of decapitation, was sexually exciting for many. The Milgram experiments indicate how easily we accept aggression. The case of sadistic men who commit sexual murder: While they are in prison, they get hundreds of letters from women who want to get involved with them. We see many instances of patients being tempted to identify with sadistic behavior and to become the victims. We have become familiar with the victimization of women who are mistreated by husbands. There are also men who are mistreated by women and go for it. They don't talk about it but we see those cases. So it's universal.

KF: Makes me think of the Stockholm syndrome.

OK: Yes.

KF: There is a great struggle to not have too much social aggression so that some of the darker sides of feeling beings do not create a catastrophe, such as Hitler, Stalin, Rwanda, Yugoslavia.

OK: Henry Dicks did a study of 28 Nazi concentration camp guards in prisons in Great Britain. They were severe personality disorders, but there were no more attempts to carry out sadistic torture and murder once they were out of the social situation of Nazi Germany. Those kind of people, plus the right kind of indoctrination, were willing to be employed in the concentration camps to murder, torture without any feelings of guilt. There are the letters of the director of a hospital in Austria when occupied by Germany. He was committed to killing psychiatric patients, mentally retarded children and adults. While he was organizing all this killing, he was sending warm letters to his family and was a loving father. Auschwitz prison guards with their families, there were able to have a good family life. Individuals with the capacity to split off severely aggressive tendencies may be mobilized by large group regression to express that ordinarily suppressed aggression.

KF: I have something that doesn't quite relate to all this, but relates in some way. You talk about regression and say there is rage and the next level is hatred. I am interested in sequences such as going from attachment, to cooperation, caring, bonding, loving. I wonder if you think if there are sequences from rage to hatred and then it may go somewhere else that is more along those lines.

OK: Yes, of course. Freud's theory was of the libido and the death drive. I think that this is clinically highly relevant. I don't think there is an inborn libido, an inborn death drive, but inborn positive and negative affect systems. I'm following Panksepp in that regard. It seems to me that the disposition to fight–flight affects expresses itself with rage. When attachment needs are frustrated, rage is the first response, and activation of separation panic follows, which is a major fear of disaster, of threat to survival. Chronic excessive stimulation of rage leads to the internalized relationship between an enraged self and an enraging other that is experienced as a danger to self. Then a chronic disposition follows to try to destroy whatever emerges as dangerous others. In so far as this becomes a structured behavior pattern and a derived, destructive attribution of aggression to the external reality, it fosters the consolidation of permanent enemies, and so rage is transformed into hatred, a chronic disposition to attack and destroy an enemy rather than be destroyed, a profound disposition to hatred. Only under circumstances when loving relationships dominate, can the integration of the positive and negative segment of affective experience neutralize the aggressive predispositions. Under severely pathological circumstances, the split between persecutory and idealized relations remains and this becomes the territory for the development of hatred, which can then be socially fostered, located, and distributed and then you have the conditions of permanent violence and hatred. Going back to the first question about cultural hatred, there are culturally fostered negative dispositions that under ordinary circumstances don't have much weight. At the time of the Second World War the Japanese were the bad guys until 20 years later we became friends again. There are normal narcissistic temptations that the industrial world uses in marketing: looking more beautiful, getting what everybody is going to envy you, infantile features that are fostered by advertisements. These normal narcissistic features don't have the profound individually based roots in pathology that the narcissistic personality has. There isn't a simple continuity between social conditioned bias and paranoid structures that are deeply built into the disposition of the narcissistic personality.

Chapter 3

The allure of Trump's narcissism

Elizabeth Lunbeck

Grandiose, entitled, arrogant, and hungry for admiration, Trump appears to many professional and amateur diagnosticians the very embodiment of the malignant narcissist, a "world-class" exemplar of this miserable personality type—the greatest narcissistic president that God ever created. He has long envisioned himself a king, "a ruler of the world," according to his second wife Marla Maples, and now he actually is—though whether he is more George III (MSNBC; *The New Republic*) than Henry VIII (*The Economist; Newsweek*) is an open question. Favoring the latter is a steady stream of reports leaked from the White House suggesting that it's gone full Tudor court, with rampant backstabbing, treachery, and organized paranoia.

Focusing on Trump's character can shed some light on one of the puzzles stumping commentators, namely, how it is that a staggering 63 million American citizens voted for this man with no political experience, a man roundly judged to be unfit to hold office, who broke just about every political norm? And why have a goodly proportion of his supporters stuck with him, driven not only by expediency—though expediency is certainly in play—but more interestingly by what is by all accounts an utterly implacable, unperturbable belief in him and what he represents?

I will focus here on his narcissistic appeal—and not, as does almost all of the commentary on Trump, on the liabilities of narcissism. Trump mobilizes his narcissism, I'll argue, to connect to his followers, thereby eliciting their willing submission and unwavering loyalty. The bonds forged with these supporters afford him—a master exploiter of opportunities embedded in a rapidly changing media environment—a steady stream of adulation. What does he promise in return? Participation in his greatness. The deal thus struck, many of the nation's most disenfranchised and aggrieved have sworn allegiance to this larger-than-life figure who, they feel, understands them and their struggles. Unfazed by his performance in office, notably his occupying rather than draining the Washington swamp, they continue to declare their unwavering support to puzzled print and television journalists.

Neither psychiatrists' *Diagnostic and Statistical Manual of Mental Disorders*, a.k.a. the DSM, nor research psychologists' construals of narcissism

The allure of Trump's narcissism   35

can help us understand this phenomenon—precisely because they focus on the condition's liabilities to the exclusion of its upsides. And yet it is precisely these upsides that hold the key to making sense of what Trump's character means for his followers and the country in general.

But, first, let's consider the many ways in which even psychiatric and psychological experts have been stumped by Trump. Some argue that labeling him a narcissist offends not only ethical precepts prohibiting diagnosing at a distance but also common clinical sense. Sure, he looks and acts like a narcissist, but he's not suffering, nor is he impaired—after all, as he's reminded us, he's the president and we're not. Distress is a key criterion in diagnosing personality disorder, according to the DSM, and, these clinicians argue, while we might be feeling it, Trump most certainly is not. However much he looks like the stock narcissist, we'd therefore be wrong, they argue, to label him as such. Clinicians' reasoning varies. Psychiatrist Allen Frances, who wrote the DSM criteria for narcissistic personality disorder (NPD), argues that Trump is a narcissist but doesn't meet the criteria for diagnosing NPD because he's neither stressed nor impaired—a distinction without a difference in the public debate (Frances, 2017). And psychologist W. Keith Campbell, who in his co-authored 2009 best-seller, *The Narcissism Epidemic* (Twenge & Campbell, 2009), blithely brands an entire generation of millennials as selfish, entitled, navel-gazing narcissists, demurs when it comes to the celebrity-obsessed billionaire president on the grounds that "he's functioning pretty highly."

Many a layperson, consulting the DSM, has surmised that Trump's behavior and temperament conform to psychiatric descriptions of pathological narcissism. More than a few articles have presented the DSM's nine criteria for the diagnosis using side-by-side examples drawn from Trump's actions, speeches, and Twitter feed. This exercise is almost too easy, especially given Trump's extensive record of over-the-top self-assessments as well as his preoccupation with fantasies of unlimited success and power, his interpersonal exploitativeness, his conviction that others envy him, and his lack of empathy. By such DSM criteria, Trump is a living, breathing textbook of character disorder, meeting just about every criterion in the literal book—Frances's objections notwithstanding.

Yet: The DSM narcissist is an altogether repugnant character. Reference to it can't help us understand why anyone—let alone all those voters—would be drawn to such a person. Pompous, entitled, devaluing, boastful, exploitative—what is the attraction? The DSM's narcissistic personality disorder can certainly account for why people might fear Trump, but not why so many Americans would flock to him with abject devotion.

My point here is that focusing on narcissism's disabilities leaves a lot of what's most useful about the category on the table. The fact is that narcissism is actually a remarkably protean concept. In clinicians' hands, it refers to a broad range of behaviors and dispositions, encompassing traits both desirable and supportive of worldly success (ambition, self-confidence), on the one hand, and despicable and undermining of that success (ruthlessness, a lack of empathy), on the other. It is an epithet in popular parlance, used synonymously with "selfish" and "self-involved." But it can also refer to a neutral quantity of self-feeling (akin to self-esteem) as well as, confusingly, to a seriously disturbed yet often high-functioning type of person. Confusing indeed—and yet everyone's an expert on narcissism in an age when a Google search of the term will yield you 10 million hits, when you can take a 40-question test on the internet (the Narcissistic Personality Inventory) that will tell you in a flash just how narcissistic you are, and when you can play amateur psychiatrist, tallying Trump's symptoms alongside the DSM checklist.

Everyone may be an expert, but all this expertise—including that found in the DSM—does not explain Trump's appeal. What we need to do is acknowledge the often considerable charisma and charm that enable some high-functioning and successful narcissists to extract from adoring acolytes the admiration that sustains their sense of self. This understanding of narcissism is rooted in psychoanalytic thinking and, while now found throughout the literature on leadership, it is missing from popular discussions. It is indispensable to understanding Trump. After all, unappealing narcissists pose little threat in a democratic political system; few voters will willingly tie their fortunes to a monster. It's the successful and beguiling narcissist, the one who flatters, seduces, and finally enslaves you into mirroring his (most of these narcissists are men) greatness and feeding his bottomless appetite for approval who is dangerous. The psychoanalyst-turned-leadership guru Michael Maccoby usefully calls such individuals "productive narcissists," and Trump places himself in their ranks. Maccoby argues that Trump's personality is similar to those of "charismatic leaders who emerge in times of turmoil and uncertainty, when people are ready to follow a strong leader who promises to lead them to greatness"—Make America Great Again. Freud took note of this type more than 80 years ago, writing that such individuals are aggressive, not easily intimidated, and primed to "take on the role of leaders." They "impress others as being 'personalities,'" Freud continued, warning they were capable of damaging "the established state of affairs." These narcissists are appealing but they can also be dangerous visionaries. You won't find them in the DSM. Then again, psychiatry and the DSM don't own narcissism.

The question then becomes less "is Trump a narcissist?"—and more "how does Trump mobilize his narcissism to connect with his followers?" Many studies of leadership start from the premise that a successful leader will be, by definition, narcissistic—capable of crafting a vision of change and transformation and charismatic enough to attract acolytes yet ruthlessly prepared to sacrifice anyone and anything in pursuit of his own aims. Trump is this leader. A figure of fascination, obsessive interest, and intrigue, he conscripts others to join in his outlandish visions and then lulls them into submission, extracting from them ongoing awe and devotion. Journalists are busy charting Trump's shrinking base, reporting that his approval rating has taken a hit as it's become clearer that he has no intention of honoring his campaign promises to protect the most vulnerable among them. Yet despite the changed sentiments of voters like the Kentuckian originally drawn to Trump sensing that "he had a kind of charisma about him, something different," who now rues his support, saying that "he played me for a fool," approval still hovers at around 40 percent. That's a lot of ongoing devotion.

The news media itself routinely falls victim to Trump's charisma, even as various outlets engage in self-flagellation for doing so. During the campaign, they could hardly take their collective eyes off of Trump, which meant that he enjoyed, it is estimated, around $2 billion in free coverage. Happily exploiting this fascination, Trump explained in an interview with Bloomberg in 2016, "I just don't think I need nearly as much money as other people need because I get so much publicity. I get so many invitations to be on television. I get so many interviews, if I want them" (Sutton, 2016). Virtually every day he threw the media a bone—in the form of an outrageous or offensive claim—and virtually every day the media gnawed on it, lamented it, analyzed it, and, most important, showcased it.

There are of course no leaders without followers. And it is Trump's gift to make others feel that he values them—even as he flew around the country in his own 757 and sat atop Fifth Avenue in his own little Versailles. Charismatic leaders excel at apprehending and even exploiting the often unarticulated needs of those they would dominate, and we can see in this quality something of Trump's success. Any successful leader reflects back what people need, the analyst of narcissism Heinz Kohut proposed, with the charismatic narcissist more dangerously endowed with "the uncanny ability to exploit, not necessarily in full awareness, the unconscious feelings" of subordinates. Perhaps no narratives were more ubiquitous throughout the campaign than, first, Trump cares about me and, second, he is offensive, to be sure, but only saying what others think. As one supporter recently explained her vote for Trump, "he says the things out loud that I say to myself."

How, then, did Trump convince the proverbial little person that he actually cared about him or her? Consider how Trump invites people to identify with him and thus share in his omnipotence and power. His braggadocio and rule-breaking incite envy among those who have little to boast of and feel imprisoned by their circumstances. His offer is of, course illusory—no amount of speechifying will launch the little guy into the economic stratosphere Trump inhabits. But Trump has some awareness of what he is doing. "I play to people's fantasies," Trump writes in his best-selling *The Art of the Deal* (Trump & Schwartz, 1987).

People may not always think big themselves, but they can still get very excited by those who do. That's why a little hyperbole never hurts. People want to believe that something is the biggest and the greatest and the most spectacular. I call it truthful hyperbole. It's an innocent form of exaggeration—and a very effective form of promotion.

Trump projects and promises self-transcendence. "I think he touched something inside of a lot of people, maybe even something that they didn't know what it was," an 86-year-old woman from small-town Pennsylvania told a reporter after the election. "I don't like authority," she added. "I don't like people breathing down my neck." To her, he promises something intangible yet powerful: a sense of autonomy and freedom. He routinely offers himself as a remedy for powerlessness. First, he points to his followers' marginalization and humiliation: "We're tired of being the patsy for, like, everybody. Tea Party people ... You have not been treated fairly." Then he declares himself their tribune: "At least I have a microphone where I can fight back. You people don't!" Finally, he shares his power with them, telling the crowd, "You don't know how big you are. You don't know the power you have." Trump's speeches are full of fights won and clowns and losers humiliated by his take-no-prisoners combativeness. He promises respect to those who have none.

Trump is also a master at performing intimacy. His engagement with his followers is direct, whether at mass events or by way of Twitter, which he's likened to having his own free newspaper. Disdaining the media as corrupt and dishonest, he skirts them by connecting at all hours with his followers through a barrage of tweets, by turns bombastic, hyperbolic, and pugilistic, filled with unsubstantiated claims and outright lies and expressive use of intense negative emotion ("Sorry losers and haters, but my I.Q. is one of the highest-and you all know it! Please don't feel so stupid or insecure, it's not your fault"—from 2013). "I mean, he's so authentic," said Donald Jr., speaking of his father's tweets, adding that the fact he writes them himself is "actually what makes him the great candidate that he is." Trump sees "genius" in his tweets: "I mean, you will get—you will read some of the stuff, there is genius there. You have to find the right genius. But it is a powerful thing." There is genius in this.

Trump's fantasies and primal emotions are openly on display in a way no other American president's emotions have been. This is another aspect of his pull on his followers—the ways in which he links his own emotions and fantasies of total and absolute control to those of his followers, their own narcissistic strivings tempered as life has beaten them down and passed them by. Bound together by the vague but powerful ideal of "Making America Great Again," they become "susceptible to his commands and directives." Consider how he uses anger. "The people are angry," Trump proclaims, but so is he. "I will gladly accept the mantle of anger," he says, explaining that he doesn't have time for therapy. Throughout the campaign, he positioned himself as the change and anger candidate: anger at the federal government, at Obama and about Obamacare, about illegal immigration, and about the direction in which the country is headed. Think here of his repeatedly engaging his crowds in symbolic acts of expulsion, as he yells, variously, "Get him out," "Knock the crap out of" protesters and "take their coats," and "Throw them out into the cold"—directives that crowds at his rallies fulfilled. This is all straight out of the analytic textbook: in the words of one analyst, the followers "submit in order to preserve their love of the leader, and whatever esteem they experience comes from the sense of devotion to the ideals and causes established in the leader's image."

Trump's apparent authenticity—his lack of the usual filters—is likely both a sign of his cluelessness and profoundly strategic, meant to distract and inflame. His constant rule-breaking is engaging and dramatic, and invites his followers' identification with him as sharer of secrets and speaker of truths that cannot otherwise be expressed. The analyst Kohut understood how powerful this sense of direct access to the mind of another—the feeling of being part of its intimate workings—could be in nurturing identification of the sort we can see among Trump's followers.

It's been said that "he's a poor person's idea of a rich person" and that his lifestyle exemplifies "beer taste on a champagne budget." But a more significant dimension of this aspirational appeal can be seen in the abandon with which he asserts his dominance and the ease with which he inhabits power. He invites others to identify with his aggression and independence from constraining norms. Explaining his bankruptcies, he told a crowd: "You have to use the laws to your advantage. What I did to that bank? ... I should get credit for having vision that things were on the decline ... I made a lot of money in Atlantic City." Many of his supporters are eager to interpret his record of bankruptcies as evidence of his independence and dominance. As one middle-aged woman put it, "the important thing is he doesn't need their money."

In sum, it's a mistake to overlook the intensity of the connection he has forged with his enthusiasts—even to those of them who know, as one supporter put it, that "Trump doesn't give a shit about me, or almost anyone else." Many of his supporters don't care that his relationship with truth is shaky and opportunistic. They don't care that he trades in anger and hate, and that he invites violence against his enemies. They don't care that he as much as admitted to sexual assault. The difficulty in explaining Trump and his appeal lies in the fact that he has prevailed not despite but because of all of his lies, anger, contempt toward losers, intolerance of dissent, and bombastic grandiosity. His flouting of just about every political, social, and sexual norm has only enhanced his appeal to his devotees. In short: His narcissism is a resource for—not an impediment to—his electoral and political success.

Acknowledgments

Originally published as "The Allure of Trump's Narcissism," *Los Angeles Review of Books*, July 8, 2017. Available at: https://lareviewofbooks.org/article/the-allure-of-trumps-narcissism/

References

Frances, F. J. (2017). Trump Isn't Crazy: I Wrote the DSM Criteria and He Doesn't Meet Them. *Psychology Today*, January 31, 2017. Retrieved from www.psychology today.com/us/blog/saving-normal/201701/trump-isnt-crazy

Sutton, K. (2016). Trump: No Need to Raise Much Money Because 'I Get So Much Publicity'. *Politico*, June 8, 2016. Retrieved from www.politico.com/blogs/on-media/2016/06/trump-i-get-so-much-publicity-224076

Trump, D. & Schwartz, T. (1987). *The Art of the Deal*. New York: Ballantine Books.

Twenge, J. M. & Campbell, K. W. (2010). *The Narcissism Epidemic*. New York: Free Press.

Part II

How Trump leads

Chapter 4

Probing Trump's disruptive narcissistic personality

Paul H. Elovitz

Introduction: The Great Disrupter

Donald John Trump's presidency has disrupted Washington, the country, the western world's alliance system, international economics, and his own administration. It is marked by his attacks on what he calls the dishonest press, Democrats, NATO allies, illegal immigrants, trade agreements, and not much success in terms of legislative policy, which he focuses on less than his personal vendettas. His greatest successes are as a disrupter of the status quo.[1] What he disagrees with is labeled as "fake news." He appears quite un-pre-sidential due to this combativeness, which is an integral part of his person-ality. Personalizing virtually every disagreement induces combativeness in others, resulting in low approval ratings. Thus, as president it took him only eight days to achieve majority disapproval, as compared to 1,205 for George W. Bush, 1,136 for George H.W. Bush, 936 for Barack Obama, 727 for Ronald Reagan, and 573 for Bill Clinton (williamjordann, 2017). Never-theless, while maintaining a negative approval rating of over 50 percent since his first week in office, he consistently maintains overwhelming support among Republicans, with strong supporters who will usually vote against any Republicans in the primaries who dare to openly criticize their "Make America Great Again" president; Trump clearly dominates the Republican Party as I write this.[2] President Donald Trump's intense need for conflict interferes with his ability to function effectively as leader of the world's greatest superpower, which has traditionally maintained close alliances with countries around the world and sought stability at home. As Jeb Bush said in 2016, Trump's a "'chaos candidate' and he'd be a 'chaos President'" (Boot, 2018). There are times that it seems the most predictable thing about Trump is his unpredictability.

When a new occupant moves into the White House, allies need reassurance that the United States will be with them supporting NATO, checking Chinese expansionism and North Korean nuclear threats, and generally being a sta-bilizing force. However, in his own words, Trump, "who likes [to] play to people's fantasies" and "test people" (Trump & Schwartz, 1987, 58), is busy picking fights and then having to backtrack in many cases. In public and private he shows evidence of not understanding proper boundaries. He does not understand the difference between presidential and personal power, thus he sees the Attorney General and the Justice Department as his personal lawyers and is enraged when they don't act accordingly. He regularly condemns the chairman he appointed to the Federal Reserve system when the stock market goes down because "he views the stock market as a report on his presidency" (Rappeport, 2018, 14). On a personal level, he once told talk show host Howard Stern that it was alright to call his daughter Ivanka a "piece of ass" (Nelson, 2016). All of this is extraordinarily disruptive and destabilizing for both America and the world order. These tendencies may be traced back to Trump's early childhood and are ultimately self-defeating for his policies and unsettling for our country.

Disruption as an early and basic part of the president's personality

Donald John Trump's need for disruptive conflict is an integral part of his personality and can be traced back to his early schooling, which, like all his other schooling, was private rather than public. As a child, he delighted in being bad and being the toughest kid on the block. To satisfy his craving for attention, Donny Trump became the family troublemaker, even if it sometimes meant a paddling with a wooden spoon, "time outs," and ultimately being sent away to military school at age 13. As a "very aggressive" "troublemaker" (his own words), he disrupted school by testing the rules, throwing spitballs, talking without permission, passing notes, and even, so he claims without confirmation, giving his second-grade music teacher a black eye (Kranish & Fisher, 2016, 35).[3] Some classmates called detention "DT" since Donny had it so often. At birthday parties he was inclined to raise a ruckus by throwing water balloons, stink bombs, and even cake.

He says he was growing into a "pretty tough kid" who "wanted to be the toughest kid in the neighborhood, and had a habit of mouthing off to everybody, while backing off to no one." At summer camp he was described as "an ornery kid" who "figured out the angles." His eldest sister said that "He was a brat" (Elovitz, 2016b, 95). Talking tough as the bad boy of American politics worked for Trump in winning the 2016 election, but so far it is not working well in the actual presidency. Before probing this issue, I will focus some more on the childhood of our 45th president to deepen the reader's understanding about the development of his personality and worldview.

Donald idealized his father Fred, an ambitious workaholic businessman who made no time to play with his children, but would sometimes take the boys to work where Donny remembers picking up bottles and cans for the deposit money. The first biographer of the Trump family reports that, like his father and grandfather, Donald would ultimately share the characteristics of being "energetic," having "a range of solid, practical skills," doing "almost anything to make a buck," and having "a certain ruthlessness" and "a free and easy way about the truth" (Blair, 2015, 456). There is absolutely no question that Donald absorbed his father's message that he should be "a king," a winner, and "a killer" (Trump & McIver, 2004; D'Antonio, 2015, 9). However, the bad reports from school, talking back, and his general rebelliousness strained Donald's relationship with his parents. They decided drastic action had to be taken when they discovered that as a 12-year-old, with a wealthy playmate, Donald was secretly taking the subway to Manhattan and buying switchblade knives.

Trump's narcissism and splitting of the world into good and bad

Trump lives in a world of good and bad. Something that serves his purpose is good, such as leaks during his campaign, and bad when it impacts negatively on him, such as leaks once he became president and he does not do the leaking himself. Throughout his career the future president was well known as a leaker, sometimes on the telephone claiming to be his own spokesman named John Barron. Denial and projection are mechanisms of psychic defense that he uses even more than splitting. Projection, taking something within oneself and attributing it to others, Trump does to an extraordinary extent. In studying him since the summer of 2015 when I realized he was a significant contender for the Republican presidential nomination, I quickly learned that when he labels someone, there is a good chance he is projecting his own thoughts and behaviors. Thus, when he called James Comey, a man with a reputation for integrity and discretion, a "showboat," a "grandstander," and a "nut job," these characteristics were much more apropos to him than to the former FBI Director who was fired after he refused to swear personal loyalty to the President (Stromberg, 2017).[4] Another example is when Trump, who never served his country's military through evasion of the draft, repeatedly insisted that Senator John McCain was "not a war hero," but rather "a loser" because he was captured in Vietnam. His splitting into good and bad turned out to be an advantage with his electoral base. Wherever he was at his rallies, he told people "I love you" since his supporters were the "good people" and lashed out at the "bad people"—the news media, any demonstrators who showed up, and of course, Hillary Clinton, who was so bad that she "should be in jail." At his rallies his adherents could and can feel his love and those he branded as his enemies could and can feel his contempt. As Michael Maccoby points out, "narcissistic leaders are quite dependent on their followers—they need affirmation and preferably adulation" (Maccoby, 2004, 5).[5] This is why as president he consistently goes to his followers' rallies since he feeds off their support.[6] Without it he feels like a man dying of thirst in the desert.

The narcissism of Donald John Trump is one of his most outstanding characteristics; indeed, it is tempting to call him a narcissist on steroids.[7] While most people in the public arena reject labels such as narcissism, he embraces them, most explicitly in *Trump: Think Like a Billionaire*. In it, he justifies this quality by quoting the psychoanalyst Michael Maccoby's statement that narcissism can be a useful quality when starting a business. Thus, "'a narcissist does not hear the naysayers.' At the Trump organization, I listen to people, but my vision is my vision."[8] Trump then proceeds to write: "Almost all successful alpha personalities display a single method determination to impose their vision on the world, and a rational belief in unreasonable goals, bordering at times on lunacy." He then proclaims his own "alpha personality," determination, and "very large ego" (Trump & McIver, 2004, xviii). This embrace of narcissism, near lunacy, and alpha-male type leadership helps to explain why candidate Trump kept defying his advisers when they wanted him to sound more like a typical presidential aspirant and why as president he has had an unprecedentedly high turnover rate of his staff and Cabinet members. As a narcissist, he is "acutely aware whether or not people are with ... [him] wholeheartedly" (Maccoby, 2004, 6). What it means for his presidency is being determined at the present time, but there is great danger in having a self-absorbed leader with poor impulse control who feels besieged and seeks to strike fear in those who are not his supporters. As an emotionally isolated, incredibly thin-skinned, narcissistic personality, Trump gets lost in his grandiosity and narcissistic rage. Added to the enormous burdens and pressures of the presidency are the special difficulties with aging that narcissists face since they are less realistic about their declining physical and perhaps mental problems than their contemporaries. There is also the danger that, like his father Fred and President Reagan, Donald will succumb to Alzheimer's disease.

Walls in the life, mind, and politics of Donald Trump

Walls are enormously important to Donald John Trump and have been throughout his life. This significance is reflected in his choosing to have a Christmas government partial shutdown over the funding of his border wall, rather than compromise at a time when Republicans still controlled the House and Senate. After 35 days of the longest-ever government closure in the face of Congressional opposition under Nancy Pelosi, he reopened the government without achieving his funding for the wall. Yet, because of the importance of the wall to him, he opted to risk a constitutional crisis by declaring a national emergency as a justification for diverting money Congress had allocated for other purposes to his "wall."

In his childhood, when the neighboring kid's ball landed in the walled yard of his 23-room house in Queens, instead of throwing it back, young Trump's response was to keep it and threaten to call his Dad or the police. This is one of the first references I've come across of a physical walling out of the "other" with walling off southern immigrants being a central tenet of his presidency. In his presidency the news media are a primary enemy; at his campaign rallies, reporters were kept separate—walled off—from his supporters. This is the same media that made his rise in politics possible by their intense focus on him during the election, resulting in well over a billion dollars of free publicity. Candidate Trump promised to build an "impenetrable, physical, tall, powerful, beautiful wall" that Mexico would pay for (*The Economist*, 2016).[9] I have heard him refer to it as a "Great Wall" and declare that "nobody knows walls like me." His proposal to build a wall (my term) in the sky "to ensure that we can detect and destroy any missile launched against the United States anywhere, any time, any place" (Sanger & Broad, 2019, A9) is really an unrealistic fantasy. As a boy identifying with his father, he loved to build with blocks, as a young man, he made his reputation as a builder, and as president, he sees building the southern wall as achieving a major campaign promise.[10] He lives in a world of walls that serve to split off the bad from the good (Ward & Singhvi, 2019, A1).[11] When it is convenient for him, he sees bad Mexicans, Muslims, and terrorists behind those walls, while he as a "good" person can travel the world doing business wherever he sees the potential for a profit. The work on some of his construction projects was carried out by low-paid, and sometimes never paid, illegal Polish workers, and two years into his presidency some illegal workers at his properties have stepped forward to expose his hypocrisy (Blair, 2015, 314–316).

As a psychoanalytic psychobiographer, I wonder about the internal and physical walls in Trump's psyche. Ted Levine, his one-time roommate at the New York Military Academy (NYMA), declared that "it was like he had this defensive wall around him, and he wouldn't let anyone get close." When Levine mocked the "insanely neatness" of the classmate he called "Mr. Meticulous," they got into a physical fight and Trump tried to push the much shorter boy out the window until restrained (Elovitz, 2016c, 279). The external border wall Trump so desperately wants to build to wall off Mexico with "its bad honchos" is psychologically fascinating. External walls usually unconsciously symbolize internal walls.[12]

We do not have a full picture of when and how Donald Trump first developed his psychic walls during the crisis of his early life. The full details of Trump's early childhood are far from clear, but there are strong indications that he had to turn inward to himself at age 26 months when his younger brother was born and his mother had a hysterectomy, followed by life-threatening peritonitis and more surgeries. Subsequently, Mary Anne Trump's health remained precarious and she had little time for Donald, her second son and fourth child (Blair, 2015, 226).[13] As a result of this crisis, young Donald turned inward. Two striking elements about his personality are that he craves constant attention, but that he defiantly acts as if he doesn't need the world. Since childhood, he has persisted in saying erroneous things despite repeatedly being told of his error. To Trump, it is his inner world that counts more than the reality of the external world. As a young child, feeling physically and emotionally abandoned by his mother, he responded to this hurt by denying his own vulnerability. From early in his life he has had a fearless, "I can do anything" quality, and a disregard for the feelings of others. Biographer Michael D'Antonio thinks that Mary Anne Trump "as a mother who had known true hardship in her childhood ... terribly spoiled her son ... [who] had everything he wanted and never had much taken away from him" (Blair, 2015, 230–231; D'Antonio, 2015, 236).[14] As stated above, the bottom line was that she was not there emotionally for her toddler who demanded attention. He, in turn, was demanding and angry, expressed in his bullying his younger brother and expressing anger, at age 5 or 6, by wandering into a neighbor's yard and throwing stones at her toddler, who was in a playpen (Kranish, 2016, 33).[15] Trump thinks that he is the same person now that he was at age 5 and I am inclined to agree with him. The internal walls of the inadequately emotionally cared for young child are expressed by his 73-year-old presidential self as a demand for $5.7 billion from Congress to wall off our southern border from the needs of others (Kranish, 2016, 33).[16] Trump's insatiable needs sometimes take the form of what feels like presidential temper tantrums tweeted to the world. His profound sense of grievance helps to connect him to millions of his voters who feel aggrieved that they are left behind economically and emotionally in America. He wants to wall in his supporters and wall off those who vote for Democrats or criticize him.

The president of early morning tweets and "my generals"

The unprecedented turnover of the President's staff and cabinet is a continuation of what occurred in his business career (Lu & Yourish, 2019). There has been a record turnover of personnel both within the Cabinet and among White House staff of a leader who expects complete loyalty while, in typical fashion for a narcissist in charge, not granting loyalty to his subordinates (Maccoby, 2004, 8). When something does not go as he wants it to, it is always the other person's fault, never his. Long ago an employee noted that he had an unusually short attention span that was timed as 26 seconds (Hurt, 1993, 18). He has become an isolated leader, muttering about his staff as "freaking fools," "idiots," and declaring that "it's war every day" (Baker & Haberman, 2018, 1A, 25A). Trump, who has a long-standing pattern of sleeping only four or five hours a night, wakes up to tweet whatever is on his mind, typically setting the news agenda for the day. These early morning tweets reflect primary process, rather than critical thinking that has been examined in the light of day, and has the benefit of the insights of knowledgeable advisors and diplomats who can predict some of the impact on the country and the world. Trump calls himself a counterpuncher, which means that, with the Democrats in control of the House of Representatives and eager to attack the occupant of the Oval Office, who for two years controlled both houses of Congress, he faces much tougher scrutiny than he previously had and he is focusing more on attacks on him rather than on his own agenda. This raises the issue of Trump being a self-defeatist. Although his actions induce contempt and numerous attacks on him, I do see him as reckless and determined to be a winner at the expense of others, but not necessarily self-defeating, although one of his former employees told Harry Hurt otherwise (Hurt, 1993, 245).[17] Ultimately, his erratic, reckless, and unpresidential behavior is likely to catch up with him.

The New York Military Academy temporarily disciplined 13-year-old Donny Trump, who held the military in high regard. Over a half century later came his proud appointment of "my generals": four-star Marine generals Jim ("Mad Dog") Mattis as Secretary of Defense and John Kelly as Secretary of Homeland Security and subsequently chief of staff, and as national security advisors three-star Army officers Michael Flynn and, after Flynn's firing for lying to the Vice President, H.R. McMaster. The President had declared that "the generals are going to keep us so safe." Many Washington insiders and the press hoped the former generals would be able to keep Trump focused and the country safe from his erratic behavior. There was considerable talk of ill-advised presidential orders being removed from his desk as, with his short attention span, he moved on to other concerns. These hopes were dashed as the President fired, forced out, or made the position of "my generals" untenable. The generals could not control Trump any more than his family could when he was a rambunctious child. Trump was also never subjected to actual military discipline since, as a young, healthy, athletic man, he used student deferments and then an alleged heel spur to avoid the draft during the war in Vietnam (Eder, 2018, A1, A12).[18]

Defense Secretary Mattis resigned on principle when, against his advice, Trump decided to remove all American troops from Syria and spoke of removing them from the entire region (although Trump subsequently backed down). This was the first time in 40 years that a cabinet-level official had resigned on principle. The President, who had been dictating a tweet of glowing praise for Mattis resigning "with distinction," changed his tune when he heard news reports of Mattis' letter and declared that he had fired Mattis—who had actually already quit—two months before Mattis' intended resignation date. The Secretary of Defense's letter of resignation indirectly criticized his commander-in-chief when he wrote "that our strength as a nation is inextricably linked to the strength of our unique and comprehensive system of alliances and partnerships" and went on to rebuke the "authoritarian model" of "China and Russia" (Mattis, 2018, 10). Mattis' concerns resonated with Senator McConnell and other Republican allies of the 45th President (Fandos, 2018, A12). Working for a disruptive narcissist is extremely difficult for any man of integrity who values his country more than the temporary resident of the Oval Office once the luster of serving the president wears off.

Probing additional roots of Donald John Trump's combativeness, narcissism, and personality

At age 13, while in summer camp just prior to his being exiled to military school, Donald had to face parental rejection. When feeling down, he would sprawl on his bed staring at the large words—a precursor of his name plastered on buildings—he had painted on the inside of the cabin door, which read "Trump 59." Donald's answer to his early adolescent angst seems to have been to strengthen his grandiose self.[19] Therein lies the genesis of Trump Airlines, Trump Plaza, Trump Place, and a multitude of other things he has put his name on. To my mind, this represented a defense when feeling unloved and abandoned by his parents. He would be better than everyone else, and in the process, not let others get close to him.

At the NYMA, his narcissism would be challenged. An ex-combat soldier used physical, social, and psychological force to impose discipline on the young Trump and get him to literally stand tall—thus his excellent posture. Donald soon fell into line and is reported to have "learned respect for other people ... [and] self-discipline," while still striving "to be number one, in everything" (Elovitz, 2016a, 95). He would do anything to win and this made him very coachable.

Psychoanalysts find that grandiosity is a reaction to feeling inadequate. Thus, buried deep below Trump's almost lifelong grandiosity I suspect there is a sad and vulnerable boy who is terrified of being called a loser, a label he likes to project onto others, including the war hero John McCain. He is unable to make close friends because he is in need of the instant gratification of feeling superior to others. Trump is too competitive to allow anyone to be truly close to him emotionally, as described by a military academy roommate, who said Donald "wasn't that tight with anyone. People liked him, but he didn't bond with anyone. I think it was because he was too competitive, and with a friend you don't always compete" (Blair, 2015, 237). Looking good and being surrounded by good-looking people was important to him; thus at NYMA he dated only very attractive girls—subsequently, all three of his wives would be beautiful models. He prized his father's mantra to be a winner, king, and killer; his striving covered over his vulnerability and neediness. To me, Trump comes across as a hollow man, lacking in compassion, empathy, and real friendship. He attempts to compensate for these human failings by accumulating billions, fame, and the presidency. People like the late Roy Cohn, more recently Steve Bannon, and "my generals" have filled the void in his values; thus he was enamored of them—for a while. Trump's need for things and the applause of others is insatiable, which is why D'Antonio chose his title of *Never Enough* and writes "Donald Trump came to express a personality that was practically all id, all the time" (D'Antonio, 2015, 10). Trump craves attention, which can be negative as well as positive.[20] He is at war with his critics and this state of war is virtually life-long. Trump calls himself a "counterpuncher," and thus he gets his energy from responding to the criticisms of others. More than most competitive people, Trump defines himself by his enemies. This reminds me of the discredited Richard Nixon declaring: "I just get up every morning to confound my enemies" (Elovitz, 2008, 42).

The President's insatiable need for adoration runs counter to his intense combativeness. While many conservatives and voters in red states clearly approve of his attacks on the political establishment, for all but his most devoted followers it is not easy to adore someone who is constantly picking fights with a wide variety of people and institutions. Moreover, while he ran as an anti-establishment populist, he is governing as a conservative who surrounds himself with the very wealthy. My impression is that a significant part of the American establishment, including the bureaucracy, is (often quietly) becoming a counterpuncher to the constant attacks emanating from him and his administration. When Trump tweets to his over 50 million followers, he feels they are on his side. But for how long? When he issues a hiring freeze, those who voted for him and had hopes of bettering themselves, now find that their path may be blocked. Those who will have worse or no health care if the Affordable Care Act is repealed will have their loyalty tested. When his voters realize the extent to which the world fears and distrusts America under Trump's leadership, their support for him will quite likely weaken.

The essence of being presidential is to have your own long-term objectives and long-term interests of the country as your main priorities. Being presidential requires prudence and forming alliances with disparate groups rather than antagonizing them. It involves consoling the nation in the face of tragedies, such as Hurricane Katrina or shocking domestic terrorism shootings in El Paso and Dayton in August 2019. Our 45th occupant of the White House simply does not know how to do this because his need for adoration and constant turmoil gets in the way of sober consideration. It remains unclear if Trump has the ability not to act when there are strong societal pressures to go to war or take other dangerous actions.

It should be kept in mind that in his business ventures, Donald Trump has had at least as many failures as successes, all of them bearing the name Trump.[21] Yet he does not seem to have been daunted by these disappointed ambitions any more than by his two failed marriages. He has used a "shotgun" approach in starting many different things, some of which have been successful and most of which have spread like buckshot at a distance, missing their target. His attitude toward failure has been to deny it by claiming victory, blaming it on a system being rigged, or simply ignoring it. Ultimately, none of these methods are likely to be successful in the media hothouse of the presidency, where the eyes of the world are on Trump and American policies. This may be part of his reason for going to war against the media, calling it "the enemy of the [American] people" (Davis, 2018).

Trump's use of racism

"The Great Disrupter" has a long history of being racially insensitive and using racial divisions to gain attention. Under the guidance of his mentor Roy Cohn, he fought the Nixon's Justice Department's condemnation of his family's racial prejudice in housing, but ultimately had to settle the case. Trump demanded the death sentence for five black and Hispanic teenagers wrongfully convicted as the Central Park rapists, and came to political prominence as a birther denier of Barack Obama's legitimacy to be president based on the false claim that he was born in Africa or Asia. He uses the Muslim ban, prejudices against Central Americans, and others as political instruments. He calls some African nations "shithole countries." When four American Congresswomen, named "the squad," called for his impeachment, Trump said that they should "go back" to the countries they come from even though all are U.S. citizens and only one was born outside the U.S. (Baker et al., 2019, 1, 21).

Simultaneously, Trump has befriended black athletes, politicians, media celebrities, and hip-hop stars who were in the public spotlight. He flew to Japan in 1990 for the fight of his friend, heavyweight, undefeated champion boxer Mike Tyson; but when the boxing world was shocked by the champion's upset defeat, Trump surprised his entourage by not going to console his black friend because of his fear that losing might rub off on him. Instead he went to the winner's locker room. Trump hires blacks in his administration and proudly declares that the African American unemployment rate has never been so low. At his campaign rallies, two black sisters and Internet stars sometimes warmed up the crowd and went on to become Fox News hosts. Staffers positioned Michael "the black man" holding up signs saying "Blacks for Trump" in camera range behind the candidate's podium as further evidence that Trump is not a racist (ibid.). In America, it is not politically correct to be openly racist and the President declares that "I am the least racist person you have ever met." Although he insists he is not a racist, Trump, who once on *The Apprentice* TV show wanted to have an all-white blond team compete with an all-black team to increase ratings, has relied on the racial fears of white Americans to further his political objectives (ibid.).

The President is a racist of the type who uses race opportunistically. Trump is a man who thinks in stereotypes, thus he is quoted as saying, "Black guys counting my money! I hate it. The only kind of people I want counting my money are short guys that wear yarmulkes every day." Trump is the kind of racist who can say "some of my best friends are black." (But does an extreme narcissist really have friends?) While he may like orthodox Jews counting his money, he also says that Jews who vote for Democrats "show great disloyalty" (Sullivan, 2019). Donald Trump's unfettered narcissism leads him to utter one outrageous statement after another!

Conclusion

The Great Disrupter Trump seems incapable of following a steady course, except in his rhetoric and some actual conservative policies, beyond what he perceives to be his personal self-interest, like lower taxes on the rich. One of the great dangers with Trump as president is that he will pick fights with other countries as a way of showing that he is in control and because conflict is second nature to him. His lifelong inclination to disrupt and create enemies is likely to manifest itself as his agenda and that of his Republican allies diverge. Although thus far he has focused on withdrawing U.S. forces and military commitments abroad, foreign military action is an arena in which he can feel strong. It remains to be seen where the Great Disrupter will take our country.

In his seventh decade, does Trump have the energy or the political skill to go against his conservative Republican allies to endanger our democracy? Despite his authoritarian inclinations leading him to admire dictators like Putin, it is my guess that he is likely to be seen in the end as an American Silvio Berlusconi, who is now viewed more as a bombastic Italian clown, rather than as a Mussolini or Hitler. Even if he has the instincts or inclinations of the two fascist leaders, our democracy is not as fragile as was that of Italy in the aftermath of World War I and Germany during the Great Depression. Nor does Trump have a disciplined army of party members ready to intimidate the opposition. As a historian, I can vouch for America having survived some bad presidents.

It is Trump's disruptive narcissism that is the greatest danger to his presidency and America. As an extremely thin-skinned, distrustful, and grandiose narcissist, he is becoming emotionally isolated at his moment of greatest success—the presidency. He has become more distant from his own children. Not having subordinates he could respect for any length of time, a sidekick he could trust, nor a psychoanalyst who could help him understand and control his grandiosity and rage (Maccoby, 2004, 7–8), leaves Trump in a vulnerable position in the White House, where he is less grounded in reality than he was as a businessman and television star. Furthermore, with Democratic Congressional Committees eager to expose that which the President would like to keep hidden, his vulnerabilities are becoming more apparent. The fear of failure strengthens his grandiosity, leading Trump to state that "I am the one"—with religious overture of godlike power, annoyance that Denmark does not want to sell Greenland to the U.S., and to tweet that American business must stop dealing with China—something he does not control. While our 45th President has weathered Special Counsel Robert Mueller III's probe, it remains to be seen if he can survive his own lack of grounding in reality.

Acknowledgments

A rudimentary part of this chapter was published in "The Implications of Trump's Need for Conflict on His Presidency," *Clio's Psyche*, Vol. 24, No. 1 (Summer 2017), pp. 63–71.

Notes

1 As is always the case with politicians, and especially the showman Trump, one must carefully look at the reality behind the appearance. In his presidency, Trump has accomplished little beyond weakening the governmental structure protecting ordinary Americans and the environment from the worst excesses of unfettered capitalism. His legislative victory of tax reform is for the rich and will cause a further ballooning of the national deficit as well as pressure to reduce entitlements. The placement of two Supreme Court judges is a major long-term victory for conservatives. The reform of NAFTA is more of an update than a radical change in favor of the U.S. After provoking a nuclear crisis with North Korea, he has done little to change the nuclear standoff on the ground. The late 2018 Criminal Reform Bill is a bipartisan legislative success, of which there are very few.

2 The fear of being "primaried" led critical Republican Senators like Jeff Flake and Bob Corker to retire rather than run for re-election. (A number of moderate Republican Congressmen have announced that they are not running again because Trump is anathema in their suburban districts that are now voting for Democrats as a protest against Trump.) As of the mid-term 2018 elections, the Republicans became Trump's party. For how long this will continue is an open question.

3 While in a hospice before his death in 2015, the teacher involved called young Trump "a pain" as a kid who "needs attention all the time" and even as a 10-year-old "a little shit."

4 I do not mean to justify Comey's action late in the 2016 campaign regarding Hillary Clinton's emails.

5 While Maccoby's article is about the pros and mostly cons of business leaders, what he writes applies very well to Donald Trump. I first became interested in his application of psychoanalytic ideas to leadership in 1979–1980 when I was studying the economic leadership of the English Industrial Revolution and I read Maccoby's (1976) book, *The Gamesman*. Maccoby (2003) references numerous businessmen, celebrities, and politicians—Trump is not included in his index.

6 The motivation of Trump's intense supporters and voters generally is a complex issue, which would require a separate chapter.

7 As a psychoanalytic presidential psychobiographer since 1976 who has published 43 articles and chapters on the subject, my research and publications have been governed by three principles: (1) no statement of my political preference; (2) the avoidance of psychological/psychoanalytic terminology; and (3) empathizing with my subjects, especially in the formation of their personality and values in childhood. My intensive research on Trump prior to his election resulted in my writing "A Presidential Psychobiographer's Countertransference to Trump" (Elovitz, 2016b) and the suspension of my first two principles in covering Trump. In presenting and teaching about the 2016 election, I simply could not maintain a neutral position regarding Trump due to his lack of qualifications and disruptive, narcissistic personality.

8 His claim that as a narcissist he does not hear the naysayers is exactly the opposite of how the President responds to disapproval; his nightly tweets reflect his extreme sensitivity to criticism.

9 To most people, walls are not beautiful, none can be impenetrable, and Mexico will not pay for Trump's wall. As a wealthy boy and man, Trump feels protected by walls.

10 In the face of overextending himself as a builder to the point where he faced a number of corporate bankruptcies, had to be bailed out by his family and banks

(as too big to fail), Trump turned away from actually building to selling his name and making a career as a TV celebrity. As a businessman he prided himself as "the king of debt" and as president this tendency is reflected in adding two trillion dollars of national debt in the first two years of his administration. Trump's fascination with walls extended to his purchase of 40 Wall Street in Manhattan, which was once very briefly the tallest building in the world and which he bought at a bargain price. He reports that as a young man "I was mesmerized by its beauty and its splendor" and refers to his "love for this grand building" (Trump & Bohner, 1997, 46, 50). I assume the association with the riches of Wall Street, having been the tallest building in the world, having wall in its name, and being a bargain he could buy during a period when he was on the verge of total bankruptcy, were all part of its attraction.

11 Illegal immigration is close to a 50-year low, but this is the reality which Trump and most of his supporters do not seem interested in as they strengthen their identity in opposition to those they see as dangerous outsiders.

12 Psychogeography provides important insights and the March 2001 issue of *Clio's Psyche* had a special issue on it with nine articles.

13 His father, Fred Trump, was a total workaholic who made little time for his family and was not a help to his wife. There was a Scottish maid named Emma and a black chauffeur who drove the family's two Cadillacs.

14 Blair provides testimony from a neighbor that gives a picture of young Donald needing to go next door to have cookies, play with pets, and throw dirt bombs. She gave Donny strong toy trucks for his birthday and Christmas which her daughter said he took apart at the parties. To me this fits the picture of an angry destructiveness that seems not to have been corrected by his parents.

15 Kranish and Fisher (2016, 33). Also, Anthony Schwartz, who spent hundreds of hours with and around Donald Trump while writing *The Art of the Deal* (Trump & Schwartz, 1987) with him, thinks that "There are two Trumps. The one he presents to the world is all bluster, bullying, and certainty." Tony Schwartz also concluded "I wrote *The Art of the Deal* with Trump. He's still a scared child" (Schwartz, 2018).

16 Trump's father had a clear disdain for neighbors, which Donald emulated.

17 "Donald had his death wish. He wanted to get caught. It was like he wanted to keep taking risks he knew he shouldn't take and leave it to the rest of us to fix it for him. He'd start one project and then go off and start something else. He'd say, 'Look at all the people who want to give me money. Look at Citibank.' But he knew we'd fooled Citibank ..."

18 During the presidential campaign, Trump did not remember if the alleged heel spur was in his right or left foot. The family of the podiatrist diagnosing the spur remembers it as a favor to the doctor's landlord, Trump's father. It is clear to me that the Trumps have a tradition of draft avoidance with Donald's grandfather avoiding the draft in Germany and then being refused citizenship as a draft dodger when he sought to return because of his wife's homesickness.

19 In a January 5, 2019 email, Michael Maccoby pointed out the extent to which adulation, which Trump craves, strengthens the grandiosity of narcissists.

20 In our era of celebrity culture, negative publicity can be equal to or even more valuable to a celebrity than positive publicity, since more people pay attention to it. Donald Trump has taken the showmanship and prevarication of celebrity culture into the White House. Trump's lie regarding Obama being born outside of the U.S. was an important basis of his building a political following.

21 Pulitzer Prize-winning journalist David Cay Johnston provides numerous examples of Trump's failures, lying, and grandiosity in his business career.

References

Baker, P., et al. (2019). Trump Turns to Old Tactic: Using Race for His Gain. *New York Times*, July 19, 2019, pp. 1, 21.

Baker, P. & Haberman, M. (2018). Isolated Leader Sees 'a War Every Day'. *New York Times*, December 23, 2018, pp. 1A,25A.

Blair, G. (2015). *The Trumps: Three Generations of Builders and a Presidential Candidate*. New York: Simon & Schuster.

Boot, M. (2018). Jeb Bush Was Right, Trump Really Is the Chaos President. *Washington Post*, March 12, 2018. Retrieved from www.washingtonpost.com/news/global-opinions/wp/2018/03/12/jeb-bush-was-right-trump-really-is-the-chaos-president/?noredirect=on

D'Antonio, M. (2015). *Never Enough: Donald Trump and the Pursuit of Success*. New York: St. Martin's Press.

Davis, W. P. (2018). 'Enemy of the People': Trump Breaks Out This Phrase During Moments of Peak Criticism. *New York Times*, July 19, 2018. Retrieved from www.nytimes.com/2018/07/19/business/media/trump-media-enemy-of-the-people.html

Eder, S. (2018). A Foot Doctor's 'Favor' May Have Helped Trump Avoid Vietnam. *New York Times*, December, 26, 2018, pp. A1,A12.

Elovitz, P. H. (2008). Presidential Responses to National Trauma: Case Studies of G.W. Bush, Carter, and Nixon. *The Journal of Psychohistory*, Vol. 36, No. 1, pp. 36–58.

Elovitz, P. H. (2016a). A Psychobiographical and Psycho-Political Comparison of Clinton and Trump. *Journal of Psychohistory*, Vol. 44, No. 2, p. 95.

Elovitz, P. H. (2016b). A Presidential Psychobiographer's Countertransference to Trump. *Clio's Psyche*, Vol. 23, No. 1, pp. 1–8.

Elovitz, P. H. (2016c). Reflections on Trump's Celebrity Politics and Psychobiography. *Clio's Psyche*, Vol. 22, No. 4, p. 279.

Elovitz, P. H. (2017). The Implications of Trump's Need for Conflict on His Presidency. *Clio's Psyche*, Vol. 24, No. 1, pp. 63–71.

Fandos, N. (2018). Fresh Concerns Divide G.O.P. and the President. *New York Times*, December 21, 2018, p. A12.

Hurt III, H. (1993). *Lost Tycoon: The Many Lives of Donald J. Trump*. New York: W. W. Norton & Company.

Johnston, D. C. (2016). *The Making of Donald Trump*. New York: Melville House Publishing.

Kranish, M., & Fisher, M. (2016). *Trump Revealed: An American Journey of Ambition, Ego, Money, and Power*. New York: Simon & Schuster.

Lu, D., & Yourish, K. (2019). The Turnover at the Top of the Trump Administration is Unprecedented. *New York Times*, January 14, 2019. Retrieved from www.nytimes.com/interactive/2018/03/16/us/politics/all-the-major-firings-and-resignations-in-trump-adm inistration.html?mtrref=www.google.com&gwh=67E9616B5E6D3E4CE8B4C4DBD DD1286D&gwt=pay&assetType=REGIWALL

Maccoby, M. (1976). *The Gamesman*. New York: Simon & Schuster.

Maccoby, M. (2003). *The Productive Narcissist: The Promise and Peril of Visionary Leadership*. New York: Broadway Books.

Maccoby, M. (2004). Narcissistic Leaders: The Incredible Pros, the Inevitable Cons. *Harvard Business Review*, January–February, p. 5.

Mattis, J. (2018). Read Jim Mattis's Letter to Trump: Full Text. *New York Times*, December, 21, 2018, p. 10.

Nelson, L. (2016). Trump Told Howard Stern it's OK to Call Ivanka a 'Piece of A–'. *Politico*, October 8, 2016. Retrieved from www.politico.com/story/2016/10/trump-ivanka-piece-of-ass-howard-stern-229376

Rappeport, A. (2018). Trump Attacks Fed as Mnuchin Seeks to Halt Free Fall. *New York Times*, December 25, 2018, p. 14.

Sanger, D. E., & Broad, W. J. (2019). At Pentagon, Trump Shares His Ambitions to Lift Missile Defenses. *New York Times*, January 18, 2019, p. A9.

Schwartz, T. (2018). I Wrote The Art of the Deal with Trump. He's Still a Scared Child. *The Guardian*, January 18, 2018. Retrieved from www.theguardian.com/global/commentisfree/2018/jan/18/fear-donald-trump-us-president-art-of-the-deal

Stein, H. F., *et al.* (2001). Psychogeography Special Issue. *Clio's Psyche*, Vol. 7, No. 4, pp. 167–189.

Stromberg, S. (2017). Trump's 'Nut Job' Comment Says More about Trump than Comey. *Washington Post*, May 21, 2017. Retrieved from www.washingtonpost.com/blogs/post-partisan/wp/2017/05/21/trumps-nut-job-comment-says-more-about-trump-than-comey/

Sullivan, E. (2019). Trump Again Accuses American Jews of Disloyalty. *New York Times*, August 21, 2019. Retrieved from www.nytimes.com/2019/08/21/us/politics/trump-jews-disloyalty.html

The Economist (2016). In Trump They Trust. September 3, 2016. Retrieved from www.economist.com/united-states/2016/09/03/in-trump-they-trust

Trump, D., & Bohner, K. (1997). *Trump: The Art of the Comeback*. New York: Times Books.

Trump, D. & McIver, M. (2004). *Trump: Think Like a Billionaire: Everything You Need to Know about Success, Real Estate, and Life*. New York: Ballantine Books.

Trump, D. & Schwartz, T. (1987). *The Art of the Deal*. New York: Ballantine Books.

Ward, J. & Singhvi, A. (2019). What's Really Happening at the Border. *New York Times*, January 15, 2019, p. A1.

Williamjordann. (2017). Days until achieving MAJORITY disapproval from @Gallup [Twitter post], January 29, 2017. Retrieved from https://twitter.com/williamjordann/status/825781634330980352?lang=en

Chapter 5

Is Donald Trump competent and fit to be president?

Ken Fuchsman

President Donald J. Trump, to some, is like a straight-talking Lone Ranger whose audacious leadership is bringing back prosperity, taking big government off our backs, and restoring American greatness at home and abroad. To others, he is the Emperor with no clothes, an ill-informed, impulsive, pathological liar who is more interested in twittering against perceived foes than faithfully performing his constitutional duties.

In a politically polarized nation, Trump has exacerbated our differences, while keeping public attention riveted on himself. Since he declared his presidential candidacy in June 2015, no political or entertainment figure in the entire history of the U.S. has so dominated public discourse as has Donald Trump. He is truly a phenomenon.

Yet, for all his skill in drawing attention to himself, his competency, temperament, and character are often criticized. His ability to astound and outrage even extends to those whom he appointed to office. Rarely, if ever, has a former Secretary of State called the President he served undisciplined, uninformed, disinterested in policy details, and who frequently wanted to do illegal things (Blake, 2018). Nor has there been precedent for the Secretary of Defense, when resigning, to castigate his President for not showing loyalty to our allies and failing to take sufficient action against our foes (Mattis, 2018). Republican Bob Corker, the former Senate Foreign Relations Chair, after a series of Trump tweets, declared that the "White House has become an adult day care center. Someone obviously missed their shift this morning" (Rucker & DeMirgian, 2017).

The characteristics that these one-time government officials pointed out about Donald Trump are not revelations. Even during the 2016 presidential campaign they were evident. He was ignorant of the laws and the Constitution, uninformed on policy, criticized our allies while praising Vladimir Putin, changed his positions regularly and made many false and misleading statements. This does not include the way he cleverly demeaned fellow Republicans during the primaries and called for Hillary Clinton to be locked up. Still, 46 percent of those who cast ballots in the presidential election did so for Donald Trump. Many did so believing that he would make America great again, and his demeaning others, ignorance of government, frequent changes of opinion, and his false and misleading claims did not deter them from voting for the man who promised to make America great again. Though it has become a national pastime for some to disparage this President, his Electoral College triumph is as much about his fellow Americans as it is about him. What in American politics, culture, economics, and history set the stage for his rise and election?

These are complex and controversial questions. In this chapter I will look at what in the campaign and in his business career showed that Trump's actions might have disqualified him as a viable candidate. Then, in Chapter 10, I will examine what in our own national traditions and recent trends led his strong appeal to so many of the electorate.

We hope Presidents are honest, but going back decades, they have sometimes deceived the electorate. In Donald Trump's case, making false and misleading statements has been a way of life. Does this make Trump incompetent?

During the campaign, according to *The New Yorker*'s Amy Davidson, "Trump spreads lies the way terrorists plant bombs: one goes off, and when the first responders rush in, there's a second, or even a third" (Davidson, 2016). *Politifact* kept a scorecard of Donald Trump's campaign statements. They found that over 29 percent were true, mostly true, or half-true, while, over 70 percent were mostly false, false, or pants on fire (*Politifact*, 2020). In September, 2016, Trump spoke one untruth every 3.25 minutes, according to *Politico*, and in the 33 days following September 15, 2016, journalist Daniel Dale counted 253 false Trump statements (Cheney et al., 2016; Dale, 2016).

Times reporters Maggie Haberman and Alexander Burns, examining the same week as did *Politico*, found that Trump's various remarks were peppered "with untruths so frequent that they can seem flighty or random—even compulsive." There was a reason behind these falsehoods. "Virtually all of Mr. Trump's falsehoods directly bolstered a powerful and self-aggrandizing narrative depicting him as a heroic savior for a nation menaced from every direction" (Haberman & Burns, 2016).

Trump also specialized in denying what he had distinctly said, as when he claimed to have been against the Iraq War from the beginning, or his assertion that he had not tweeted about Miss Universe Alicia Machado's sex tape when it is in black and white that he did.

Trump rashly declared that North Korea is no longer a nuclear threat to the U.S., when there was ample evidence to the contrary. Similarly, he proclaimed that Isis has been defeated in Syria, though his military advisers told him this was not so. His inaccuracies have not slowed down since he took the oath of office. From his inauguration to August 5, 2019, according to the *Washington Post*, the President has made over 12,000 false or misleading statements. In his first nine months in office, Trump averaged five false or misleading statements a day, in the seven weeks prior to the 2018 mid-term elections that rose to an average of 30 a day, and for all of 2018 made 15 untrue declarations a day (Kessler, 2018; Kessler, Rizzo, & Kelly, 2018; Kessler, Rizzo, & Kelly, 2019).

At the end of 2018, the *New York Times* wrote not only about the "scale of the president's mendacity" but what have been the patterns of his inaccuracies. He both repeats and then inflates his untrue claims, such as falsely saying over 100 times that his tax cuts are the biggest in American history. Trump shifts and deflects from his inaccurate statements without admitting he lied, including the various permutations about his knowledge of payments to women who claimed sexual connection to him. He gives fanciful details and can be vague when making unverified claims, such as claiming that one of Judge Kavanaugh's accusers said she never met him, without giving the name of any such accuser. Trump also invents straw men and then makes false statements about them, his targeting of the so-called fake news is a frequent example (Qiu, 2018). It is not always clear if Trump recognizes his misstatements or believes them, but he is more than willing to publicly proclaim them.

For instance, on a December 26, 2018 visit to American troops in Iraq, Trump proclaimed to the assembled soldiers that the U.S. military had not seen a pay raise in a decade, but he has implemented a 10 percent increase this year. Sitting in the audience the troops would know that what the President said is false, as they received 2.6 percent higher that year, and some may know that the military has received wage hikes each year for the past three decades (Papenfuss, 2018).

What do these men and women feel when face to face with them their Commander-in-Chief makes an obvious falsehood? Could it be that Trump's intended audience were not the soldiers but his civilian followers in order to brag that he has made our military great again, or that he may be trying to elevate himself to himself? In any case, why would a 72-year-old-man who has reached the pinnacle of electoral success wish to lie to others and himself about this or any other issue? Trump's incessant lying while he retains the allegiance of so many Americans is one of the puzzles of our time.

Trump did not get the falsehood habit when he first ran for office. It was part of his standard operating procedure all through his real estate career. Gwenda Blair discusses his modus operandi of entering a room to make a pitch, and bowl people over with his drive and determination, but his audience usually knew he was distorting facts left and right (Blair, 2015).

There is the story of Trump and what eventually became the Manhattan Javitz Center. Trump had an option on the property where, in 1978, New York City officials announced they were going to construct a convention center. Trump claimed he was entitled to a commission of $4 million, but would waive the fee if they named the center after his father. Municipal officers seriously considered the offer for a month until one of them reviewed Trump's actual contract with New York and found he had multiplied what the city owed him by more than ten times (Kranish & Fisher, 2016, 73).

No question that during his checkered business career Trump indulged in big lies, including excuses for his multiple bankruptcies. Billionaire businessman, Michael Bloomberg, declared "Trump says he wants to run the nation like he's running his business? God, help us, I'm a New Yorker, and I know a con when I see one" (Fox, 2016). In the 2016 campaign, many Americans did not perceive or give much weight to the fact that Trump was gaslighting them. But then again, Trump is not the first successful presidential candidate to construct an imaginative narrative in order to sell himself to the American people.

Central to Trump's image is that he presents himself as the strong, decisive, stable leader who can turn this country around. Yet, during and after the 2016 campaign, he often changed his mind. Between June 2015 and July 2016, NBC News tracked Trump's statements on 20 major issues, and found 117 policy shifts, including three contradictory statements on abortion in eight hours (New York Times Editorial Board, 2016; Timm, 2016). How could Donald Trump make America great again if he could not make up his own mind?

This trait of being indecisive continued as President, where he would frequently promise one thing to one group, then either meet with his advisers or see something different on Fox News or somewhere else, then reverse his position. A prime example is after the school shootings in Parkland, Florida, he said one thing on gun control to members of Congress, then took it back after meeting with the National Rifle Association. Given the number of mass shootings in the U.S. during Trump's term of office, this pattern of saying he is interested in legislation on gun control and then changing his mind has happened more than once.

More than most anything, Trump strives to project an image of unmovable strength, yet in practice he publicly reverses himself all the time. This is so characteristic of Trump that in Washington many do not put much faith in the President's word. Yet his frequent wobbling has not yet undermined his image as a strong leader among his adherents, though it is certainly not a sign of competency.

His many alterations in course are often preceded by grandiose declarations. One of Trump's heroic predictions in April 2016 was that he could get rid of the $19 trillion national debt in eight years (Kapur, 2016). This was one of the few instances where Trump actually followed up a fantastic claim with a policy proposal. It got him in hot water.

This initial policy would have raised the debt by $11.5 trillion over ten years, according to the nonpartisan Committee for a Responsible Federal Budget (Nussbaum & Weyl, 2016). Recognizing that this increase would not do, Trump made another attempt at getting rid of our indebtedness. In September 2016, he again presented a tax and fiscal initiative. This time, the same Committee said Trump's proposals would raise the debt by $5.3 trillion in the first decade, while Hillary Clinton's proposals would show a $200 billion increase for the same period of time (Shahidi, 2016). There was clearly a wide disparity between Trump's extravagant promise on making America great and what his deficit policies would deliver.

Not surprisingly, once President, Trump's pledge to eliminate the debt went out the window. He followed recent Republican tradition and supported legislation that cut taxes, which passed and will substantially increase the debt. The annual deficit the fiscal year Trump took office was $585 billion. In his first full fiscal year of 2018, it was $779 billion, is projected to be $984 billion for FY 2019, and a little less than $1 trillion for the next few years, and leveling out to $800 billion by 2023 (Chantrill, 2019). If these deficit predictions are on the mark, and if Trump is re-elected, he will either increase the debt more than any other President in history or come in second after President Obama. Between his inauguration on January 20, 2017, and February 11, 2019, there was over $2 trillion added to the national debt, pushing it to over $22 trillion (Bryan, 2019).

In the 2016 election season it was not only Trump's honesty and steadfastness that were questioned, so were his competency and temperament. He is the first President in American history without prior government experience. When running for office, he was not interested in obtaining the knowledge a President needs. When a CEO of a major company offered to present a report of over a hundred pages on China to him, Trump said send either three pages or do it orally for "I have a lot of common sense and I have a lot of business ability." He claimed to be so busy he had no time to read books, although he had plenty of time to watch television (Kranish & Fisher, 2016, 347).

Trump gave few speeches with detailed proposals; nor were many policy statements displayed on his website. His focus was on political rallies, slogans, branding and demeaning his opponents, speaking off the cuff, and tweeting at all hours. At campaign appearances he made provocative statements, which pleased his supporters but led many former senior foreign policy and intelligence officials to state Trump was unfit to be Commander-in-Chief.

As President, questions of his competency remain. Secretary of State Tillerson said Trump regularly proposed illegal actions. It was reported that White House counsel, Don McGahn, warned Trump that his wish to order the Justice Department to criminally investigate Hillary Clinton and former FBI chief James Comey could lead to impeachment (Fleishman, 2018). When former White House adviser Steve Bannon mentioned the 25th Amendment to the President, Trump asked, "What's that?" (Sherman, 2017). There are still few, if any, signs that the Commander-in-Chief has knowledge of the nation's statutes. Evidence that he is taking care to make sure the nation's laws are being faithfully executed is completely absent. Since President Trump does not like to read the CIA's written daily intelligence briefings, he has started receiving oral briefings supplemented with photos, videos, and graphics designed for a President "with a famously short attention span" (Leonnig et al., 2018). Aides and friends of former Trump Defense Secretary

James Mattis say that the four-star general found Trump "to be of limited cognitive ability" (Goldberg, 2019). If a President cannot long concentrate on complex issues, can he or she actually be competent?

During the 2016 campaign and while in office, Trump has been seriously uninformed about central issues. He shows few signs of wishing to be accurate and knowledgeable. Then there is the fact that the President regularly does not appear in the Oval Office until late morning or noon, in what has been labeled executive time. He does not usually return to the office after dinner. No one can fully document what he does while in the residential section of the White House, still it is reported that both in the morning and evening he is glued to cable news and calling his acquaintances to vent and get feedback on how he is doing. In December 2017, the *New York Times* reported that Trump watches between 4 and 8 hours of television a day (Haberman, Thrush, & Baker, 2017). Will we ever know whether this President spends more of his day watching television and chatting with friends than performing his actual constitutional duties?

Another question about Trump concerns his temperament and character, and how they might impact his fitness for office. At his 2016 rallies, Trump approved violence. On February 1, 2016, in Cedar Rapids, Iowa, Trump told the crowd, "If you see somebody with a tomato, knock the crap out of them." He also pledged to pay the legal fees of those who acted on his directives (White, 2016). In late February 2016, in Las Vegas, he told his audience about a protestor, "I'd like to punch him in the face." He said he missed the "good old days" when you could treat people at rallies differently and disrupters would "be carried out on a stretcher" (Diamond, 2016b).

Trump embraced the notion that his female Democratic opponent should be locked up. He repeated an allegation that Ted Cruz's father had something to do with John Kennedy's assassination. Never had a major party candidate incited such disruptive behavior, aroused such fury in his followers, and was so vile so often. Some were repelled by such talk while others jumped on the Trump bandwagon.

Trump is notoriously thin-skinned. When criticized, he tries to discredit the critics rather than deal with the substance of the matter. From time to time, he becomes so preoccupied that he seems immature. "Part of growing up is developing self-control. Trump never has," asserts columnist Ruth Marcus (Marcus, 2016). She was referring to the numerous times Trump interrupted Clinton in the first Presidential debate on Monday, September 26, 2016, and to his response to a topic discussed there. Hillary Clinton brought up 1996 Miss Universe, Alicia Machado, whom Trump disparaged, particularly about her weight. Ms. Machado seemed to stick in his craw. Instead of moving on, he dumped on her the next day. Then that Friday morning between 3:00 a.m. and 5:30 a.m. he posted a flurry of seething tweets on the former Miss Universe. He is "the impulse-control-deficient-Republican nominee," said *Politico*'s Louis Nelson (Nelson, 2016).

He was also the pot who called the kettle black. He regularly castigates others for what he himself does. During the primaries, over and over again Trump criticized his opponents for being beholden to large money interests. He said both Ted Cruz and Hillary Clinton were totally controlled by Goldman Sachs. Speaking about the big banks, he proudly proclaimed: "They have no control over Donald Trump. I don't want their money. I don't need their money." Then it was revealed that he is indebted to large financial institutions for $650 million, including Goldman Sachs (Flores, 2016). It turns out Trump has needed, wanted, and taken their money.

He repeatedly criticized Hillary Clinton because she voted for the Iraq War resolution, acquiesced in the later withdrawal of most American forces from Iraq, and advocated intervention in Libya. But he took the same positions. Trump is on record as supporting invading Iraq, then later saying we should pull out all our troops, and also advocated overthrowing Libyan leader Gaddafi.

Then there is Trump on others' sexual lives. After he falsely claimed there was a sex tape of Miss Universe Alicia Machado, it turned out that Trump himself had been featured in several soft-core Playboy videos.

Discussing Bill Clinton's numerous infidelities was a Trump campaign preoccupation. Being faithful to one's spouse is not an area where the thrice-married Trump's record is stellar. During his first marriage, he carried on an extended affair with Marla Maples, shamelessly bringing her to public events where his wife was present. When, in September 2016, he was asked by reporters if, like Bill Clinton, he had ever been unfaithful to any of his wives, Trump responded, "No – I never discuss it, I never discuss it. It was never a problem." A follow-up question specifically asked about committing adultery with Ms. Maples; he repeated, "I don't talk about it" (Healy & Haberman, 2016). Trump had to know that his discussing Bill Clinton's sexual escapades would inevitably lead to his own infidelities. Given his history, why would he venture into territory where he was so vulnerable himself, especially as in the next month he paid women who had sexual contacts with him to remain silent?

These payments occurred soon after a recording of Trump describing his sexually assaulting women came out on October 7th. He tried to divert attention from himself by showing how Bill Clinton was much worse. As if President Clinton's actions meant we should ignore his. This is the defense of a man who commits manslaughter and claims he should not be prosecuted because this other guy committed first-degree murder. Trump lives in a glass house and cannot stop throwing stones.

Some say he is projecting his faults onto others. In psychoanalysis, projection and projective identification are phenomena that are largely unconscious. In these pot and kettle examples, Trump's motivation may be unconscious, but he is not unaware of his own actions, even though he denies, evades, or tries to divert attention from what he has done. As his own conduct is so often uncovered, it is peculiar that time and time again he goes on the offensive to harshly criticize someone, and time and time again it comes out that he is criticizing others for what he himself does.

Trump is either a shameless hypocrite, is setting himself up, or does not feel he will be held accountable, or some combination of them all. Trump does sometimes think he is immune from being held responsible. As he said in 2005 in a different context, "when you're a star ... You can do anything" (Revesz, 2016). In the same vein, in January 2016, he proclaimed, "I could stand in the middle of 5th Avenue and shoot somebody and I wouldn't lose voters" (Diamond, 2016a).

Trump often acts as if he will not suffer negative consequences, but not always. At the same time as he feels above it all, he is almost begging to be discovered. Trump is like a mischievous boy who telegraphs his misconduct so he can be caught and punished. Once discovered, he then denies he is guilty, counterattacks, says that the system is rigged against him, that it is fake news, a witch hunt, or presidential harassment. Trump seems unaware that he both wants to get away with things and to be punished for his transgressions. This preoccupation with blaming others for what he does and his response once caught was one of the more bizarre phenomena in an election overloaded with absurdity. This behavioral pattern has not decreased since he was inaugurated. Jim Mattis's aides and friends also asserted that Mattis thought Trump was of "generally dubious character" (Goldberg, 2019).

Trump's melodramatic psychodramas include the ways he slanders others. Here are just a few examples. In early May 2016, Trump forwarded a false *National Enquirer* story linking Ted Cruz's father to Lee Harvey Oswald and the JFK assassination, and also went on Fox News to link Rafael Cruz and Oswald. Accusing anyone of being involved with Lee Harvey Oswald is serious, and involves fact checking. Trump, of course, was not interested in verifying the quickly debunked *Enquirer* claim. Right after the Republican Convention, Trump defended the aforementioned supermarket paper (Farley, 2016). He said that "in many respects" the *National Enquirer* "should be well respected" (Spinelli, 2016). To find this publication reputable is to live in a tabloid world, which is not infrequently the case with Donald Trump.

Trump often acts like a gossip columnist spreading dirt about people; he relishes demeaning those who offend him. This practice long precedes his presidential bid. On May 14, 1990, a *Forbes* article said that Trump was not worth the $1.7 billion the magazine had previously claimed, but $500 million. He was furious, and blamed the piece on owner Malcolm Forbes, though Forbes had died three months before the article was published. Still, without looking into things, he retaliated. Trump added a section to a forthcoming book revealing that Forbes was homosexual (Kranish & Fisher, 2016, 112–113). Trump made no effort to check his assumption that Forbes inspired the article, and went below the belt to get even.

To Trump, those who criticize him must have ulterior motives. He tries to expose them, without looking before he leaps. As President, Trump has continued this impulsive practice of leaping without looking, as when in March 2017, without evidence, except from a Fox news report he had just watched, he accused President Obama of wiretapping him during the campaign. Of course, President Trump could easily have asked his intelligence officials about the accuracy of these charges, but as usual he assumed rumors were true, and acted accordingly. While Trump almost always exempts himself from having vile motives, he regularly assumes the worst about those who criticize him.

"Man is the most vicious of animals," Trump declared, "and life is a series of battles ending in victory or defeat ... You just can't let people make a sucker out of you" (Kranish & Fisher, 2016, 94). Much of his 2016 campaign rhetoric was about how other nations were making suckers out of the U.S., and he vowed to remedy that situation. In Iraq, in December 2018, Trump said he had fixed this problem, "We're not the suckers of the world. We're no longer the suckers, folks. And people aren't looking at us as suckers" (Li & Clark, 2018).

There is at minimum a tinge of paranoia in Trump's view of this dog-eat-dog world of winners and losers, of the savvy and the suckers. To prevent others from getting an edge on him, Trump has initiated over 1,900 lawsuits (Kranish & Fisher, 2016, 300). This figure does not include all the times he has merely threatened to sue reporters or authors who are looking into his actions.

Some people who play in the rough and tumble worlds of business or politics can maintain their equanimity, and some cannot. Without a doubt, the thin-skinned Trump falls into the latter group. To many, Trump's lack of steadiness and willingness to fly off the handle made him unsuited for the Presidency. Little he has done as President has led many to a change in that assessment.

Another aspect of Trump's paranoia is his belief that the political system is rigged, and, of course, rigged against him. His belief that things are stacked is the other side of his grandiose belief in his being immune from harm. When things do not go his way, he falls back on things being fixed, there is a conspiracy of fake news out to get him, the Democrats on Mueller's staff are conducting a witch hunt, and congressional investigations are presidential harassment.

As Hillary Clinton pointed out after Trump claimed that the federal judge of Mexican descent was biased against him, and when his TV show lost the Emmy's three years in a row, he tweeted that these awards were rigged. Clinton said, "This is a mindset. This is how Donald thinks" (Clinton, 2016).

On September 24, 2012, he did tweet, "The Emmys are all politics, that's why ... The Apprentice never won" (Gajanan, 2016). Another campaign example of things being stacked against him: on September 19, 2016, Trump claimed that the Presidential debate moderators "are all Democrats," including that NBC's Lester Holt "is a Democrat." To Trump, "It's a very unfair system." Lester Holt is a registered Republican, and the only actual Democrat among the moderators is Fox News' Chris Wallace (Haberman & Burns, 2016). As President he has continued this pattern of inaccuracy. By the end of 2018, he had made over 250 inaccurate claims about the Mueller investigation (Qiu, 2018).

For Trump, there is no reason for facts to invalidate his often-paranoid tinged narratives, or for him to investigate what is true before he asserts something. Trump has created his own melodramatic world in which he is both besieged on all sides and yet will emerge triumphant. To himself, he is a heroic leader who will rescue himself and the rest of the unfairly treated silent majority from these unfair betrayals, this corruption from within by the likes of Lyin' Ted, Crooked Hillary, and all the corrupt, biased FBI and Mueller officials.

This grandiosity, living in the political gutter, and self-deception characterize him, his campaign and presidency. He went farther into the depths than any major party candidate in our already squalid history of campaigning. During the campaign and while President, Trump has successfully played out this psychological melodrama to cheering crowds, many of whom often appear to share a similar paranoid style, resentful anger, viciousness, and disinterest in factual accuracy.

To cap off his playing to the darkest impulses, he presents the first woman to be a major party Presidential nominee as the devil who should be imprisoned (Murphy, 2016). Also, racism and sexism have been central to his presentation of self in everyday life. These prejudices are often accompanied by paranoia in Trump and others. Some deep anxiety and anger in the American soul have been encouraged by Donald Trump. These traits indicate that he is unfit to be President of the United States.

Acknowledgments

This chapter is based on Fuchsman (2017a; 2017b).

References

Blair, G. (2015). *The Trumps: Three Generations of Builders and a President*. New York: Simon & Schuster.

Blake, A. (2018). Rex Tillerson on Trump: 'Undisciplined, Doesn't Like to Read' and Tries to Do Illegal Things. *Washington Post*, December 7, 2018. Retrieved from www.washingtonpost.com/politics/2018/12/07/rex-tillerson-trump-undiscipline d-doesnt-like-read-tries-do-illegal-things/?noredirect=on&utm_term=.3027cc4f36be

Bryan, B. (2019). The US National Debt Just Pushed Past $22 Trillion—Here's How Trump's $2 Trillion in Debt Compares with Obama, Bush, and Clinton. *Business Insider*, February 20, 2019. Retrieved from www.businessinsider.com/trump-nationa l-debt-deficit-compared-to-obama-bush-clinton-2019-2

Chantrill, C. (2019). What Is the Deficit? U.S. Government Spending, January 2, 2019. Retrieved from www.usgovernmentdebt.us/federal_deficit

Cheney, K., *et al.* (2016). Donald Trump's Week of Misrepresentations, Exaggerations, and Half-Truths. *Politico*, September 25, 2016. Retrieved from www.politico.com/magazine/story/2016/09/2016-donald-trump-fact-check-week-214287

Clinton, H. (2016). The Final Trump-Clinton Debate Transcript, Annotated. *Washington Post*, October 19, 2016. Retrieved from www.washingtonpost.com/news/the-fix/wp/2016/10/19/the-final-trump-clinton-debate-transcript-annotated/

Dale, D. (2016). Confessions of a Trump Fact-Checker. *Politico*, October 19, 2016. Retrieved from www.politico.com/magazine/story/2016/10/one-month-253-trump-untruths-214369

Davidson, A. (2016). Trump Still Lying about Birthism. *The New Yorker*, September 20, 2016. Retrieved from www.newyorker.com/news/amy-davidson/trump-is-still-lying-about-birtherism

Diamond, J. (2016a). Trump: I Could 'Shoot Somebody and Wouldn't Lose Voters'. *CNN*, January 24, 2016. Retrieved from www.cnn.com/2016/01/23/politics/donald-trump-shoot-somebody-support/

Diamond, J. (2016b). Donald Trump on Protestor: 'I'd Like to Punch Him in the Face'. *CNN*, February 23, 2016. Retrieved from www.cnn.com/2016/02/23/politics/donald-trump-nevada-rally-punch/index.html.

Farley, R. (2016). Fact Check: Trump Defends Claim on Oswald and Cruz's Father. *USA Today*, July 23, 2016. Retrieved from www.usatoday.com/story/news/politics/elections/2016/07/23/fact-check-trump-lee-harvey-oswald-rafael-cruz/87475714/

Fleishman, G. (2018). Trump Wanted to Prosecute Comey and Hillary Clinton, Report Says. *Fortune*, November 20, 2018. Retrieved from http://fortune.com/2018/11/20/trump-impeachment-charges-comey-clinton-white-house-counsel/

Flores, R. (2016). Report: Donald Trump's Companies at Least $650 Million in Debt. *CBS News*, August 20, 2016. Retrieved from www.cbsnews.com/news/report-donald-trump-companies-at-least-650-million-in-debt

Fox, E. J. (2016). Bloomberg on Trump: "I Know a Con When I See One." *Vanity Fair*, July 27, 2016. Retrieved from www.vanityfair.com/news/2016/07/bloomberg-dnc-trump-con

Fuchsman, K. (2017a). The Presidential Campaign that Astounded the World: A Psychohistory of Donald Trump and the 2016 American Election. *Journal of Psychohistory*, Vol. 44, No. 4, pp. 292–309.

Fuchsman, K. (2017b). The Return of the Ghost of Thomas Dewey in 1948: Hillary Clinton and the 2016 Election. *Journal of Psychohistory*, Vol. 45, No. 1, pp. 23–40.

Gajanan, M (2016). Yes, Donald Trump Said Even the Emmys Were Rigged. *Fortune*, October 19, 2016. Retrieved from http://fortune.com/2016/10/19/presidential-debate-donald-trump-rigged-emmys/

Goldberg, J. (2019). The Man Who Couldn't Take It Anymore. *The Atlantic*, October. Retrieved from www.theatlantic.com/magazine/archive/2019/10/james-mattis-trump/596665/

Haberman, M. & Burns, A. (2016). A Week of Whoppers from Donald Trump. *New York Times*, September, 24, 2016. Retrieved from www.nytimes.com/interactive/2016/09/24/us/elections/donald-trump-statements.html?hp&action=click&pgtype=Homepage&clickSource=story-heading&module=first-column-region&region=top-news&WT.nav=top-news&_r=0

Haberman, M., Thrush, G., & Baker, P. (2017). Inside Trump's Hour-By-Hour Battle for Self-Preservation. *New York Times*, December 9, 2017. Retrieved from www.nytimes.com/2017/12/09/us/politics/donald-trump-president.html

Healy, P. & Haberman, M. (2016). Trump Opens Up New Line of Attack on Hillary Clinton: Her Marriage. *New York Times*, September 30, 2016. Retrieved from www.nytimes.com/2016/10/01/us/politics/donald-trump-interview-bill-hillary-clinton.html?hp&action=click&pgtype=Homepage&clickSource=story-heading&module=photo-spot-region&region=top-news&WT.nav=top-news&_r=0

Kapur, S. (2016). Trump Makes Dramatic Turnaround on Eliminating National Debt. *Bloomberg Politics*, April 22, 2016. Retrieved from www.bloomberg.com/politics/articles/2016-04-22/trump-makes-dramatic-turnaround-on-eliminating-national-debt

Kessler, G. (2018). A Year of Unprecedented Deception: Trump Averaged 15 False Claims a Day in 2018. *Washington Post*, December 30, 2018. Retrieved from www.washingtonpost.com/politics/2018/12/30/year-unprecedented-deception-trump-averaged-false-claims-day/?noredirect=on&utm_term=.8e7439037c31

Kessler, G., Rizzo, S., & Kelly, M. (2018). President Trump Has Made 6,420 False or Misleading Claims over 649 Days. *Washington Post*, November 2, 2018. Retrieved from www.washingtonpost.com/politics/2018/11/02/president-trump-has-made-false-or-misleading-claims-over-days/?noredirect=on&utm_term=.c326fcdc6e2e

Kessler, G., Rizzo, S., & Kelly, M. (2019). President Trump Has Made 12,019 False or Misleading Claims over 928 Days. *Washington Post*, August 12, 2019. Retrieved from www.washingtonpost.com/politics/2019/08/12/president-trump-has-made-false-or-misleading-claims-over-days/

Kranish, M. & Fisher, M. (2016). *Trump Revealed*. New York: Scribner.

Leonnig, C., Harris, S., & Jaffe, G. (2018). Breaking with Tradition, Trump Skips President's Written Intelligence Report and Relies on Oral Briefings. *Washington Post*, February 9, 2018. Retrieved from www.washingtonpost.com/politics/breaking-with-tradition-trump-skips-presidents-written-intelligence-report-for-oral-briefings/2018/02/09/b7ba569e-0c52-11e8-95a5-c396801049ef_story.html?noredirect=on&utm_term=.509c904c4737

Li, D. & Clark, D. (2018). Trump to American Troops in Iraq: U.S. No Longer 'the Suckers of the World.' *NBC News*, December 26, 2018. Retrieved from www.nbcnews.com/politics/politics-news/trump-makes-surprise-visit-u-s-troops-iraq-his-first-n952081

Marcus, R. (2016). Most People Grow Out of Middle School, Not Donald Trump. *Washington Post*, September 30, 2016. Retrieved from www.washingtonpost.com/opinions/most-people-grow-out-of-middle-school-not-donald-trump/2016/09/30/f8de0d7e-8732-11e6-a3ef-f35afb41797f_story.html?hpid=hp_no-name_opinion-card-c%3Ahomepage%2Fstory&utm_term=.301e607b338b

Mattis, J. (2018). James Mattis' Resignation Letter. *CNN*, December 21, 2018. Retrieved from www.cnn.com/2018/12/20/politics/james-mattis-resignation-letter-doc/index.html

Murphy, T. (2016). Trump's Call to Imprison Hillary Was More than a Year in the Making. *Mother Jones*, October 10, 2016. Retrieved from www.motherjones.com/politics/2016/10/hillary-for-prison-slogan-origins

Nelson, L. (2016). Trump Jumps into the Gutter. *Politico*, September 30, 2016. Retrieved from www.politico.com/story/2016/09/trump-early-tweet-storm-alicia-machado-228947

New York Times Editorial Board. (2016). Why Donald Trump Should Not Be President. *New York Times*, September 25, 2016. Retrieved from www.nytimes.com/2016/09/26/opinion/why-donald-trump-should-not-be-president.html?utm_source=huffingtonpost.com&utm_medium=referral&utm_campaign=pubexchange&_r=0

Nussbaum, M. & Weyl, B. (2016). Trump's Budget: Making the Deficit Great Again. *Politico*, July 11, 2016. Retrieved from www.politico.com/story/2016/07/donald-trump-budget-deficit-225389

Papenfuss, M. (2018). Rep. Adam Smith, Incoming Head of Armed Services Committee, Vows to Challenge Trump's Lies. *Huffington Post*, December 28, 2018. Retrieved from www.huffingtonpost.ca/entry/adma-smith-warns-trump-on-falsehoods_us_5c25c8dfe4b05c88b6fef06a?utm_hp_ref=ca-us-politics

Politifact. (2020). Donald Trump's File. Retrieved from www.politifact.com/personalities/donald-trump/

Qiu, L. (2018). Deciphering the Patterns in Trump's Falsehoods. *New York Times*, December 29, 2018. Retrieved from www.nytimes.com/2018/12/29/us/politics/trump-fact-check.html

Revesz, R. (2016). Full Transcript: Donald Trump's Lewd Remarks About Women on Days of Our Lives Set in 2005. *The Independent*, October 8, 2016. Retrieved from www.independent.co.uk/news/world/americas/read-donald-trumps-lewd-remarks-about-women-on-days-of-our-lives-set-2005-groping-star-a7351381.html

Rucker, .P. & Demirgian, K. (2017). Corker Calls White House 'An Adult Day Care Center' in Response to Trump's Latest Twitter Tirade. *Washington Post*, October 8, 2017. Retrieved from www.washingtonpost.com/news/post-politics/wp/2017/10/08/trump-attacks-gop-sen-corker-didnt-have-the-guts-to-run-for-reelection/?noredirect=on&utm_term=.283bcd5bd531

Shahidi, J. (2016). Trump Would Beat Clinton by Trillions When It Comes to Driving Up Debt. *CNN Money*, September 22, 2016. Retrieved from http://money.cnn.com/2016/09/22/news/economy/hillary-clinton-donald-trump-taxes-spending/

Sherman, G. (2017). "I Hate Everyone in the White House!": Trump Seethes as Advisers Fear the President Is Unraveling. *Vanity Fair*, October 11, 2017. Retrieved from www.vanityfair.com/news/2017/10/donald-trump-is-unraveling-white-house-advisers

Spinelli, D. (2016). Trump Revives Rumor Linking Cruz's Father to JFK Assassination. *Politico*, July 22, 2016. Retrieved from www.politico.com/story/2016/07/trump-ted-cruz-jfk-assassination-226020

Timm, J. (2016). The 141 Stances Donald Trump Took During His White House Bid. *NBC News*, July 7, 2016. Retrieved from www.nbcnews.com/politics/2016-election/full-list-donald-trump-s-rapidly-changing-policy-positions-n547801

White, D. (2016). Donald Trump Tells Crowd to 'Knock the Crap Out Of' Hecklers. *Time*, February 1, 2016. Retrieved from http://time.com/4203094/donald-trump-hecklers/

Chapter 6

Gaslighting and beyond

Robin Stern and Judith Logue

Part I

ROBIN STERN

These days you can hardly go more than a day or two without seeing the word gaslighting appearing in a newspaper. *The Urban Dictionary* has defined gaslighting and even our President has been called a gaslighter. But when I wrote the book *The Gaslight Effect* over ten years ago, the term was virtually unknown, although the phenomenon itself was widespread.

Gaslighting, I wrote, is a type of emotional abuse where the intention on the part of the gaslighter is to plant seeds of doubt in an individual or members of a group, hoping to make the target question their own memory, judgment—sometimes their character and even their sanity. In gaslighting, the gaslighter tries to convince you that you are misremembering, misunderstanding, and misinterpreting your own motivation, behavior, or character, thus creating doubt in your mind about your own reality.

Gaslighting, I wrote in 2007, is always a co-creation of two people. The gaslighter who is the 'more powerful' person in the dynamic, engages in an ongoing systematic knocking down of the confidence in the gaslightee, sowing the seeds of doubt in his or her reality. The gaslightee, is the other 'less powerful' player in what I call the *gaslight tango*. In order to keep the relationship going, the gaslightee allows himself or herself to be knocked down and experiences a growing shakiness of self as he or she begins to doubt and question his or her own perceptions and reality. This dance they do, the gaslight tango, is a co-created dynamic that requires the active participation of two people.

When I wrote the book, my hope was that it would land in the hands of everyone who needed help with a gaslighting relationship. I wanted to write a popular book rather than a scholarly paper or series, because I wanted the information to be accessible to people all over the country at every level. I used terms and language that were less clinical and more accessible to describe gaslighting—how to spot it, survive it, change the dynamic or make the choice to leave—all in the service of feeling whole and taking back your reality.

"You're so careless," a gaslighter might say—then, instead of, for example, simply smiling and replying, "I guess that's how you see it," in the trenches, a gaslightee ultimately would feel compelled to insist "I am not." A gaslightee cares deeply how her gaslighter would see her ... often she couldn't rest until she could convince him that she was right and that she was not careless. "I don't understand how you can be so extravagant with your money," the gaslighter might say. A non-gaslightee could reply casually that "everyone is different," and go on about her life. A gaslightee might spend hours locked in miserable self-reflection, ruminating desperately about whether her gaslighter might in fact be right.

As I wrote in my book, the *gaslight effect* describes what happens to you when you begin to second-guess yourself because you have allowed another person to define your reality and erode your sense of self, your confidence, and judgement. The gaslight effect is a consequence of a relationship that is co-created between two people when the gaslighter needs to be right in order to preserve his sense of self and having power in the world, and the gaslightee is the target of the gaslighting, who has allowed the gaslighter to define her sense of reality because she idealizes him and seeks his approval. This mutual participation is alterable because it means the gaslightee holds the key to her own prison. Once she understands what is happening, she can find within herself the courage and clarity to refuse the gaslighter's story about her, and the crazy-making distortions that undermine her self-perception.

How did I discover the gaslight effect? The book was inspired by the prevalence of gaslighting in the lives of women I knew who were otherwise powerful and strong and decision-makers. And yet somehow they were questioning and second-guessing themselves by someone who was more powerful in their lives. So when somebody shows up with the scars of name-calling, it is easy to blame the other person. But somehow when the insidious undermining of who you are, that more gradual chipping away at your sense of reality, many people I saw, mostly women, blame themselves. At its mildest, gaslighting leaves women uneasy, wondering why they always seem to end up in the wrong. At its worst, gaslighting leads to major depression, with formerly strong, vibrant women reduced to misery and self-hatred. Either way, I was continually astonished both as a therapist and in my personal life at the degree of self-doubt and paralysis that gaslighting can induce.

How did I coin the term gaslight effect? I have been in private practice in New York for 30 years, trained at the Postgraduate Center for Mental Health in New York, and have been seeing couples and women for these many years. I witnessed this "dance" happening over and over again. One night I was watching the movie with Ingrid Bergman and Charles Boyer called *Gaslight*. Particular moments in the movie connected me instantly with moments I was hearing from my patients. In the movie, Ingrid Bergman as a young girl watches as her aunt is murdered. She grows up and falls in love with someone who is a very charming charismatic who wants to take her back to her home town in London. We, the audience, begin to figure out that the guy whom she falls in love with is actually the person who murdered her aunt. Charles Boyer tries to drive his wife crazy so that he can hospitalize her, then steal her jewels and get all her money. The process he used to drive her crazy—his insistence that she didn't know what she was talking about, didn't see or hear clearly, was forgetful and losing things, was ill (all not true) was effective over time in causing her to believe she was ill and not mentally well. The 'effect' of constant gaslighting was devastating and, reminiscent of what I had witnessed in my personal life. I knew I had to write about it. Especially because gaslighting is not always consciously intended, and the gaslighter not always diabolical, but it always takes its toll, and always ultimately can be named and dealt with. And, importantly, gaslighting is not just about men targeting women, it can happen between parents and children, friends, and siblings; both men and women can be gaslighters.

In my private practice the pairing I saw most often was women coming into therapy because they didn't even know they were being gaslighted, but they knew there was 'something wrong' with a romantic relationship they were involved in and couldn't put their finger on what was happening. After I wrote my book, people kept coming into my office asking me how I knew exactly what was happening to them. Most had looked in self-help books for a description of what they were going through and nothing fit the dynamic exactly. At the time, there really wasn't anything around that detailed the progression into gaslighting from the moment where it seemed like your partner was making a silly comment (Stage 1) to the feeling that you are being driven crazy by his certainty—and, where you need to defend yourself all the time (Stage 2), to where you begin to take on his perception, own it, and think that 'I *am* too sensitive,' 'I *am* really crazy in this way,' and 'he *is* right.'

In between the years that I published in 2007 and probably as close to 2016 as I remember, gaslighting would occasionally pop up when there was a review of the movie *Zero Dark Thirty*. They talked about how the interrogation techniques were really undermining people's realities. My colleague, Dr. Marc Brackett and I worked with Facebook for a while, where we were reporting on bullying and doing focus groups. I noticed that among teens and young adults gaslighting was an experience when somebody online said something to you and then 30 or 40 people saying the same thing was even more horrific and now you had 30 or 40 people at a time were acknowledging that there was something wrong with you. It was hard enough to stand up to one person, what do you do if you are on the internet and on Facebook? So, we created a downloadable online *bully prevention hub* where we give helpful advice to kids, parents, and educators to help them manage and have words for situations where they were part of bullying and psychological abuse, or where they witnessed or heard about their child or student being part of such situations.

Then, in 2016, gaslighting was really catapulted into the popular press. John Oliver, the HBO comedian and show host, claimed that Donald Trump had gaslighted him. Donald Trump had tweeted out that he was invited four or five times to be on John Oliver's show. In fact, John Oliver had never invited him. But Trump was so certain and so insistent that after a while that listening to that *one channel* of information, that *one channel* of certainty, John Oliver went back and asked his producers, "Hey, wait a minute, did I forget something? Did I actually invite Donald Trump?" Of course, he hadn't. He knew he was right. But the experience of somebody coming at him with that kind of certainty, when he had the humility enough to say to himself maybe I forgot, caused him to second-guess himself.

What I realized in that moment was that unlike the women in my practice who were in gaslighting relationships with someone they were close to, Oliver was second-guessing his reality and, he wasn't even in a personal relationship with Trump. John Oliver *wasn't* invested in Donald Trump; yet he had the experience of being gaslighted by him. So maybe the concept of gaslighting was becoming more a socio-political phenomenon and not just a personal one.

Part 2

JUDITH LOGUE

Gaslighting: the personal to the political: a psychoanalytic and psychohistorical perspective

"Sunlight is the best disinfectant," comedian Bill Maher once quipped, a statement he borrowed from Louis Brandeis, Associate Justice on the Supreme Court from 1916 to 1939, who borrowed it from James Bryce, British Ambassador to the United States from 1907 to 1913 (Brandeis, 1914). Who knew that Maher (or perhaps one of his writers) was such a student of history?

With this in mind, I want to shed some light on Robin Stern's conclusion that the concept of "gaslighting" extends from individuals into the social, cultural, and political arena.

First, I shall define and describe "gaslighting" and the *gaslight effect* and apply them to the current social and political climate. I believe there are historical precedents going back to at least the 1960s, and that understanding some of the similarities and differences is worth exploring.

Then I want to review the cultural factors and historical antecedents that have fostered the current chaotic political milieu. I shall also suggest that the current wave of populism evoked in the Trump era has taken us beyond gaslighting.

What is most relevant to the psychoanalytic community is how the personal and intrapsychic inform the sociopolitical. This allows us to take a close look at Donald Trump—the man. It enables the application of contemporary psychoanalytic theory to express our professional views about his character, his psyche, and how and whether they relate to his fitness for his leadership as United States President.

Finally, I want to suggest some options to preserve democracy and stop authoritarian and "gaslighting" techniques.

Defining and describing gaslighting

The Gaslight Effect, Robin Stern's book, defines gaslighting as the systematic manipulation of another's reality with the unwitting cooperation of the victim (Stern, 2007). The gaslighter insists that his or her version of reality is true. Consequently, the gaslight victim begins to believe this and doubts herself or himself.

Briefly, the gaslight effect is the consequence of allowing another person to undermine your judgment about reality—which distorts the relationship and causes you to question the validity of your own feelings, perceptions, and experiences.

The term was inspired by the 1938 British play by Patrick Hamilton and then the 1944 American movie starring Charles Boyer, Ingrid Bergman, and Joseph Cotton. *Gaslight*, the movie, tells the story of a charming, powerful man, Gregory, who almost convinces his new bride, Paula, an heiress, that she is going crazy. He does this so he can steal her murdered aunt's jewels, which are in their attic. Gregory wields great power over Paula, because she desperately wants to please him and win his love and approval. He continually tells her that she is ill, weak, and fragile. He manipulates the gas lamps in the house so that she sees the lights dim for no apparent reason.

The Trump administration and the 2016 election extend this sinister concept into the social, cultural, and political arena. The Trump slogan, "Make America Great Again," seared the weakness of America into the group unconscious. President Trump's description of the "carnage of America" in his inaugural address left America with only one way to go but up (Trump, 2017a). His message was that he would take us there by Making America Great Again.

It was especially heard by those whose frustration and anger were insufficiently recognized by the Hillary Clinton campaign. They felt duped by the political establishment—dubbed the "swamp" by Donald Trump.

This is not a sudden manipulation or brand-new phenomenon or occurrence. Public opinion was manipulated during WWII and the McCarthy era, and after. Robert David Steele, author of *Intelligence for Earth* and a former clandestine CIA officer, is dedicated to exposing the Deep State in America. He argues that the lack of transparency, truth, and trust in our social and political climate is not new. In his opinion, this loss of integrity goes back at least to the early 1960s with the FBI leadership of J. Edgar Hoover, and the assassinations of President John Kennedy and Martin Luther King, Jr. (Steele, 2010).

However, Trump's gaslighting is unique. It is transparent and extensive. President Trump insisted that he would make Mexico pay for a border wall to stop immigrants, that he would eliminate the national debt in eight years, and that he could negotiate a pact with Kim Jong Un to stop North Korean nuclear armament.

Instead, President Trump now uses his executive powers to work around Congress for the American government to fund the border wall, although he had repeatedly promised roaring crowds that Mexico would pay for the wall. Despite a promise to eliminate the national debt, he has added over $2 trillion to the national debt in his first two years in office (Bryan, 2019). In 2019, the North Koreans resumed testing ballistic missiles. This casts doubt on the ability of Trump's public declaration of love for Kim Jong Un to reverse the steps toward war (Denyer, 2019).

He proudly directs people at rallies to believe what he says rather than what respected investigative researchers report. The distortion of accurate truth and reality is in plain sight. For example, on July 24, 2018, President Trump drew comparison to George Orwell's book, *1984*, in an attack on the media during a speech at the Veterans of Foreign Wars National Convention. He defended his decision to put tariffs on trading partners. He said the farmers will be the biggest beneficiaries. Mr. Trump told the group that "It's all working out," and he warned the audience against believing what they see in the news. "What you're seeing and what you're reading is not what's happening" (Trump, 2018). In contrast, *The Washington Post* found that in his first 928 days as President, Trump made over 12,000 false or misleading statements (Kessler et al., 2019).

Charles Lewis, author of *935 Lies: The Future of Truth and the Decline of America's Moral Integrity* (Lewis, 2014)—a book about presidential and government deception—says we are living in an era when "up is down and down is up and everything is in question and nothing is real." As psychoanalytic psychohistorians, it is helpful to look beyond the role of government.

Referring to President Trump, Allen Frances, a physician who is former editor of the *Diagnostic and Statistical Manual of Mental Disorders* (DSM) IV, and opponent of the process leading to DSM V, suggests that we must analyze the societal sickness that gives someone so flawed the power to determine the fate of the world (Politi, 2019).

An important question is whether presidential deception over the past 50 or so years has increased gradually, and/or changed, along with a decline of America's moral integrity. I wonder if we have evolved from an Age of Narcissism to an Age of Sociopathy and Psychopathy (or what a patient of mine prefers to call The Age of Apathy and Greed), and now, more than ever, long for an Age of Integrity.

Gaslighting and beyond   77

Historical antecedents: review and analysis

Cultural factors

Ken Fuchsman, in Chapter 10, has a most cohesive and integrated answer to the question of Allen Frances: What in our society gives someone so flawed the power to determine the fate of the world? Fuchsman outlines four points:

1   Our governmental structure— the separation of powers and Electoral College—has led to the election of a candidate with a majority vote in the Electoral College, but not the popular vote, five times.
2   The United States has a cultural pattern of long, almost endless, political campaigns. These resemble sporting contests—like the Super Bowl—that focus on how things play politically more than policy details or the complex process of governing.
3   Campaigning and governing are quite different. The candidate has to know how to get and keep media attention and hold spirited rallies. Campaigners, not just Trump, point out the nation's problems, but are long on promises and short on specifics. Fuchsman describes the importance of arousing audience emotions, as well as the use of religious overtones. A competent POTUS, of course, needs to have knowledge of the issues, work with Congress and conduct foreign policy. I also note that President Trump blends the advantages and rhetoric of campaigning with the role of governing. Because he filed to run in 2020, he may hold campaign rallies, use Air Force One for campaigning, and solicit campaign donations.
4   The degradation of the previously high standards and accuracy of the print and broadcast media—and the focus on contest and personality rather than the issues—play a central role. Strongly connected to the changes in the news business is that we became a "celebrity culture." Entertainment values now supersede accuracy and truth. Cable news networks keep our interest, even creating dependency and addiction for some. Fuchsman points out that Trump has no compunction about exploiting our rituals or about going to the gutter and the sensational when the spirit moves him. He is a master of political publicity. A genius, some—especially Trump—would say. And he would be right (Fuchsman, 2017).

Derek Thompson, senior editor at *The Atlantic*, in a January 28, 2017 *New York Times* opinion article, "Live from the White House, It's Trump TV," explains that there are three rules of popular entertainment. Each of them applies to Mr. Trump.

First, every successful franchise has a mythical hero—whether a brave firefighter or a sociopath.

The second rule is that distribution is more important than content. President Franklin Roosevelt reached tens of millions of people with his radio fireside chats, and TV presidential addresses became blockbuster events. But as entertainment options grew, President Reagan's and President Bill Clinton's star power diminished. It "ended a golden age for the bully pulpit," writes Thompson.

Twitter in the hands of President Trump has combined the old-fashioned direct line to voters with a major twist. His chief audiences are newspapers and television, not the public. He deftly blends a direct line to the voters with consistent amplification by the largest broadcasters. A 2019 Pew Research Center analysis estimates one-in-five adult Twitter users in the U.S. (19 percent) follow Mr. Trump's personal account on the platform, @realDonaldTrump (Wojcik, 2019).

Last and worst, but not least, the third rule of popular entertainment is that President Trump works to establish political media dominance. He seeks dominion over his own set of facts by demonizing critical and traditional news companies and sources in and outside the government. He promotes sycophants loyal to his view of reality and labels anything that disagrees with him as "fake news." Kellyanne Conway, Rudy Giuliani, Alan Dershowitz, and William Barr are among the ongoing parade of loyalists who promote and devalue whatever political agenda is currently relevant.

Two more weapons in Trump's gaslighting arsenal are his daily use of Twitter and his repeating that investigative reporting is "fake news."

The hope of optimists, and those who care, is that the distorted news will lead the public to want and require investigative journalism and renewed civic engagement. President Trump has paradoxical instincts to condemn news companies while seeking their approval, and to elevate popularity over politics and policy. He broadcasts a separate media reality, and, so far, remains the hero of many of the people. Derek Thompson writes: "If he succeeds, the Trump Show will be worse than reality television. It will not be reality at all." I believe this is our new reality.

Beyond gaslighting: populism and the creation of yearning for strongman rule

A thought-provoking 2017 prediction of Melik Kaylan is that clues about the psychology evoked in the Trump Era are found in populist regimes around the world. He predicted that Trump would appoint new chiefs ... who would fight with their rank and file... and try to downsize and defund; and that there would be "pushback." He expected that confusion and uncertainty would create a yearning for strongman rule, and that institutions themselves would be eroded (Kaylan, 2017).

Kaylan's prediction was accurate. The yearning for strongman rule is demonstrated by those who support the praise of strongmen such as Vladimir Putin and Kim Jong Un. Degrading and devaluing our allies in Canada, Mexico, Britain, Europe, Scandinavia, and elsewhere have become the "new normal."

President Trump has downsized the administration and government agencies. He has dismantled positions by firing department heads without filling vacant positions. He has removed consumer and environmental regulations in the interest of free enterprise (Trump, 2017b). This has engendered movements from the left and political adversaries who fight for progressive change with legislation and lawsuits (Renae & Tracy, 2018; Popovich, 2019).

Certainly, it seems that relevant factors are the computer revolution's impact on manufacturing and international trade, the reduction of the middle class from 62 percent in 1970 to 43 percent in 2014, and beginning with September 11, 2001, the start of suicide bombing terrorist attacks. These are important factors in our so-called "societal sickness," which lead to choosing a strongman like Trump to be in charge of the nuclear codes.

Middle-aged males, those without college degrees, and the middle class felt disenfranchised and became more conservative, sexist, nativist, and enraged. The hostility toward Congress, people of color, Jews, immigrants, and "the other," along with envy and contempt toward high achieving women, enabled Trump to successfully stereotype and exploit these feelings for his personal advantage. There are many such examples of his denigrating others for his advantage. When announcing his candidacy in June 2105, he said "When Mexico sends its people," they are "sending people that have lots of problems" who are "bringing crime. They're rapists. And some, I assume, are good people" (Trump, 2015). In July 2019, he asked about four freshman Democratic Congresswoman of color, "Why don't they go back" to "the totally broken and crime infested places from which they came" (Rogers & Fandos, 2019).

The end goal is the deadlock of due process while the strong leader takes the strategic heights of state power, as done by Putin in Russia, Erdogan in Turkey, Chávez in Venezuela, and Bolsonaro in Brazil. According to Kaylan, populists take over by excluding and arresting journalists. Trump threatened, then eliminated the traditional White House press briefings, and it has been reported that he told former FBI Director James Comey to put in jail those journalists who report classified information. He has declared war on journalists. One of his most often used mantras is what the President calls facts that reporters print "fake news." He once tried to banish CNN White House Reporter Jim Acosta, and in August 2019, pulled the credentials of another reporter (Bauder, 2018; Gerstein, 2019). Populists create oligarchs who are loyal and indebted to them. And, they ally with media rulers who have money and political influence.

The personal and intrapsychic inform the sociopolitical: a psychoanalytic modern conflict theory and dimensional diagnostic perspective

Physical health

Before I discuss or speculate about Donald Trump's psychological make-up, defenses, or temperament, it is essential to consider that neurological or organic factors, especially in a man who as President is in his seventies, may contribute to his unique and unusual behaviors and actions. It is possible that what we are seeing are signs of one of the dementias or a type of brain disorder. You may recall, however, that during the campaign his physician, Dr. Harold Bornstein, said his health is "astonishingly excellent," along with "extraordinary" physical strength and stamina. Dr. Bornstein later reported that Mr. Trump directed the content of this medical report (Parker & Bernstein, 2018).

Verbatim reports about President Trump's tortured syntax, mid-thought changes of subject, and apparent trouble formulating complete sentences or coherent paragraphs in unscripted speech are frequent. He was not so linguistically challenged in the past.

The differences since his inauguration are "striking and unmistakable." Statements include those with missing words, or that do not make sense, as at a press conference when he said: "We'll do some questions, unless you have enough questions." In an NBC interview with Lester Holt, he explained:

> When I did this now I said, I probably, maybe will confuse people, maybe I'll expand on that, you know lengthen the time because it should be over with, in my opinion, should have been over with a long time ago.

"From the time I took office til now, you know, it's a very exact thing. It's not like generalities" (Vitali & Siemaszko, 2017).

Neurolinguistics and cognitive assessment experts who compared Trump's speech from decades ago to that in 2017 agreed there had been a deterioration. In the 1980s and the 1990s interviews with Tom Brokaw, David Letterman, Oprah Winfrey, Charlie Rose, and others, he spoke articulately, used sophisticated vocabulary, inserted dependent clause into his sentences without losing his train of thought and put together sentences into a polished paragraph—even when asked tough questions about his divorce, bankruptcies, and housing for working-class Americans. In years past, Trump spontaneously used words and phrases such as "subside," "inclination," "discredited," "sparring session," and "a certain innate intelligence." He spoke sentences such as, "It could have been a contentious route," and offered thoughtful, articulate aphorisms: "If you get into what's missing, you don't appreciate what you have," or "Adversity is a very funny thing."

As Sharon Begley has documented, today his vocabulary is simpler with frequent repetition and lurching from one subject to an unrelated one (Begley, 2017).

Whether or not deterioration in the fluency, complexity, and vocabulary of spontaneous speech indicates diminished brain function due to normal aging or neurodegenerative disease and/or stress, frustration, the effects of anger and fatigue remain questions.

Gaslighting and beyond 81

Some controversies

Diagnosis

So much has been blogged, posted on my psychoanalytic listservs, and presented at conferences on life in The Age of Trump, it is hard to keep up with it. My goal is to highlight some of the psychological, psychiatric, and psychoanalytic controversies.

We psychoanalysts fight among ourselves about the ethics of diagnosing outside the consulting room. We argue about applying the Goldwater Rule, which prevents psychiatrists from diagnosing public figures or taking a position in elections and political events. We disagree about which psychoanalytic theories are the best, about whether psychoanalysis and psychoanalytic psychotherapy are qualitatively different or on a continuum, and about who is entitled to use the title, "psychoanalyst."

Isolation is a most important tool in the gaslighter's kit. Keep victims away from anyone who, or anything that, can provide a reality check—the Goldwater Rule!

Some background about diagnosis for those who are not in the mental health field: At the risk of offending many if not all analysts, and satisfying none, I'll try to keep things relatively simple. It is helpful to differentiate the dimensional and psychological approach of Nancy McWilliams in her book, *Psychoanalytic Diagnosis* (McWilliams, 2011), and in the *Psychodynamic Diagnostic Manual* (PDM), co-edited with Vittorio Lingiardi (Lingiardi & McWilliams, 2017) from the medical and categorical approach in the American Psychiatric Association's *Diagnostic and Statistical Manual of Mental Disorders* (DSM) (APA, 2013).

The *Psychodynamic Diagnostic Manual* (PDM) is dimensional. It is psychological. It indicates the spectrum covered, such as personality, anxiety, or depressive disorder. It is explicitly in-depth with a psychoanalytic framework. The *Psychoanalytic Diagnostic Manual*, Second Edition, published in 2017, includes etiology, psychological mechanisms of each disorder, and effective treatment strategies.

The DSM categorically assigns individuals to diagnostic classifications based on observable clusters of symptoms and attributes. It is descriptive and superficial. It is used for medical coding, insurance reimbursement, prescription medicines and polypharmacy. Though the manuals differ, psychoanalysts may use both.

Based on President Trump's public statements and behaviors, which often distort reality or change facts, are erratic and impulsive, and which have been consistently documented in video and taped interviews, many psychoanalysts diagnose him from afar. We know that professionals in other fields, as well as non-professionals and lay people of any political stripe, also frequently diagnose and describe Trump psychologically whether in the media or in conversations.

82 Robin Stern and Judith Logue

My analytic training in the late 1960s and 1970s rigidly emphasized that diagnosis is for treatment, not for hostility or social disapproval. But my personal frustration and human imperfections sometimes cause a lapse. My primary care physician called Trump "schizophrenic" and "psychopathic" and "sociopathic" the week before the 2016 election. He said he'd have to leave the country if Trump were elected. In spite of my classical training and admonitions about diagnosis, I agreed with him! Neither of us evaluated or treated Trump, and our diagnoses were politically motivated, whether or not we were accurate. And neither of us left the country. Where to go?!

The Goldwater Rule

Lance Dodes, MD, was the lead writer of a *New York Times* letter of February 13, 2017, signed by 35 psychoanalysts and has been interviewed on major TV shows. As a physician psychoanalyst, he is less concerned with breaking the Goldwater Rule than that mental health professionals stand against and stop Trump's authoritarian and irrational behaviors because they have harmful and damaging consequences.

He strongly believes that Trump's well-documented traits require that mental health professionals exert our "duty to warn," which overrides the Goldwater Rule not to diagnose *in absentia*. Dodes believes that publicly diagnosing enduring character traits is different from endorsing a particular label in the DSM, which changes every few years. He believes that Trump is clinically and significantly impaired and that he is dangerous especially, but not only, because he is in charge of the nuclear codes. It is important to note that a number of psychoanalysts vehemently disagree with him. In 2017's *The Dangerous Case of Donald Trump*, Dodes declares that "Donald Trump's speech and behavior show that he has severe sociopathic traits" (Lee, 2017, 91).

Application of contemporary psychoanalytic theory

Modern Conflict Theory based on Freud is the framework for my perspective. Without a semester to teach it, I can briefly mention only a few dynamics that may fit a psychoanalytic case formulation of an insecure, unlikable child who is now our president.

Tony Schwartz, Trump's co-author of *The Art of the Deal*, and a staff member who worked with him, as reported to his analyst friend, asserted that Trump is childish, hyperactive, with hardly any attention span, and a braggart who is quick to attack. He needs approval and adulation, and to control people. Best one can tell, Trump exhibits a "primitive" nature, little self-control or discipline, and is preoccupied and self-absorbed. His history includes a tough, dominating, harsh, if not abusive, father, and a traditional mother in the background (Schwartz, 2018).

Paul Elovitz speculates that early maternal abandonment at age 2 due to his mother's life-threatening illness had traumatic effects on his character (Elovitz, 2017, 2018). It is also of psychological interest that two of Trump's three wives are immigrants like his mother. Interestingly, all of them are Caucasian, have a work history, and they have entered the country legally.

Mr. Trump is obsessed with gold and all things grand. He strongly believes he can save us from WW III and achieve world peace. Most of us are familiar with Trump's bad character and behaviors. Regardless, according to most of the analysts on my professional listservs, this is a man who is untreatable, with character armor that is impervious; and he would never end up in the consulting office of a psychoanalyst.

Conclusion: some options to preserve democracy and stop gaslighting and authoritarian techniques

Policy vs. character focus

One of the most interesting op-eds on this subject is "The Right Way to Resist Trump" by Luigi Zingales (Zingales, 2016). He says he already saw this movie in Italy when Silvio Berlusconi was prime minister for nine years between 1994 and 2011. Zingales integrates this psychohistorical analysis by reporting success when there is a focus on policy, issues, and accurate journalism instead of personality, contest, and tabloid news.

Zingales writes that "the Italian experience provides a blueprint for how to defeat Mr. Trump." He demonstrates that eventually a focus on the issues, not character, wins the day. He argues that it adds to the opposition's credibility to find points in common, not just differences. In his opinion, ridiculing a leader's behavior, and/or denying a legitimate win, provides free advertising.

I agree that policy, issues, and accurate journalism are critical instead of the elevation of celebrity culture. But we also need to elevate psychology and psychohistory. Character, personality, temperament, motivation, and defenses, and the psychology of our leaders have long been ignored as if they are irrelevant. For the most part, we have paid dearly for this omission. The Joe McCarthy, President Richard Nixon, President Bill Clinton, and Secretary Hillary Clinton scandals and characterological theories about them are but a few examples.

Strategies for individuals applied to systems and groups

From Robin Stern's recommendations for individuals, some common-sense strategies that may also be applied to systems and groups include:

1. "Be willing to leave." This means acting against psychopathic and sociopathic modes of functioning as distinct from moral and ethical modes of

functioning. An example was to attempt to minimize partisan bias by appointing a Special Counsel to head the investigation into Russian activities against the United States after the firing of James Comey. This was achieved when former FBI Director Robert Mueller was named special counsel. However, the Trump Administration made partisan attacks on the investigation, threatened to end it, and declared it a witch hunt. Attorney General William Barr presented an early partisan public summary of the 400-page Mueller report that omitted or de-emphasized relevant information. Trump used the complex and detailed report to declare a partisan victory. Congressional hearings demonstrated division without bipartisanship. As of this writing, investigation into Russian activities, criminal obstruction of justice, and possible misconduct are ongoing.

2. Just as important, we must stand firm against what Fuchsman calls "the abandonment of civility." In early May 2017, journalists were able to expose the legal, but unethical and uncivil, breach by Trump of confidential information from an ally. He shared with Russia highly classified "code" information about ISIS from Israel. It is his prerogative as POTUS, and legal, to de-classify information. But Trump's judgment, wisdom and the implications were questioned. Experienced security experts are appropriately concerned that Russia will share secrets with their allies (Syria and Iran) and harm Israel.

Conclusion

Ultimately, like it or not, President Trump's supporters do not care whether he is a disordered gaslighter. They think the left is hysterical, crazy, and more menacing than Trump. Trump maintains that the left is on a witch hunt, and myriad other accusations. Trump's supporters maintain that he is doing what he said he would do: bring back jobs, keep out the Mexican murderers, rapists, and the radical Muslims. Trump has made it okay to be a traditional man, sexist, and racist. He is anti-Constitutional. His publicly stated goal is the deconstruction of the administrative state (Michaels, 2017).

To quote a Hillary Clinton supporter: "Trump says, 'The Hell with civil rights or anything inconvenient about equal protection under the rule of law.'" In contrast, Trump loyalists disagree. They also do not see Trump's lies as lies. And when they do, they do not care.

A loyalist Trump activist told me in 2019, "The ends justifies the means." Is Trump playing head games with the elite? If so, is it conscious? Just like the condescending and sneering liberal left, the conservative right snickers that Trump is "getting one over" on the elites and moderates and leaving them in the dust.

In the movie *Gaslight*, Paula eventually comes to realize what her husband has been doing to her. How did this happen? An external third party from Scotland Yard, played by Joseph Cotton, who is investigating her husband for the murder of her aunt, steps in. He is well aware that her husband is tricking her and validates her perceptions of reality. Her husband is trying to gain possession of her aunt's jewels. She is not going crazy.

Many hoped that Special Counsel Robert Mueller, the man whose investigation, like Joseph Cotton's, would reassure us that facts are facts, not lies or "alternate facts." The Mueller report was not blocked by President Trump, despite cliff-hanging concerns. In 2019, Mueller appeared before Congress and reassured us that we are not crazy—in a step toward a bipartisan focus on our democratic process. But it did not end the ongoing division, chaos, and "craziness." Mueller followed the law which requires Congress to evaluate the facts, and then decide on further steps, such as impeachment or legislation to limit or support the Trump Administration.

Using a simple psychoanalytic lens, and our classical metaphors, one might say that our culture, society and individuals—not just Trump and his administration—appear to lack sufficient "ego." I define this concept as the part of the mind that mediates between the conscious and the unconscious; it is responsible for reality testing, judgment and cognitive functioning. I define the concept of the "id" as the part of our psyche that initiates talk and behavior based on immediate gratification and impulse. I think of this part of me as "I want what I want when I want it."

A capacity for "mentalization"—the ability to understand other people have minds—and the ability to translate understanding and insight into rational and reasonable speech and behavior, is the opposite of functioning based on impulse—or "id" functioning.

Bemoaning what I perceive as our current and pervasive social and individual fragmentation, lack of integration and cohesion, I'm reminded of what Freud wrote in 1933: "*Where id was, there shall ego be. It is a work of culture—not unlike the draining of the Zuider Zee*" (Freud, 1931, 91). Sound familiar?!

Whether you agree with my historical and psychoanalytic perspectives, I think you will agree that the people of the United States—of any color, race, ethnic group, religion, class or political party—do not have to accept lies in our time, or from the past, or in the future. We do not have to live an existence where facts and reality are insignificant –and in which someone adjusts the gaslights to achieve his or her own ends.

References

APA (2013). *Diagnostic and Statistical Manual of Mental Disorders*, 5th edn. Washington, DC: APA.

Bauder, D. (2018). White House Bans CNN Reporter After a Confrontation with Trump. *Associated Press*, November 8, 2018. Retrieved from www.apnews.com/a 211dd90113847a59c5c01487035ee72

Begley, S. (2017). Trump Wasn't Always So Linguistically Challenged. What Could Explain the Change? *STAT*, May 23, 2017. Retrieved from www.statnews.com/2017/05/23/donald-trump-speaking-style-interviews/

Brandeis, L. (1914). *Other People's Money and How the Bankers Use It*. New York: Frederick A. Stokes.

Bryan, B. (2019). The US National Debt Just Pushed Past $22 Trillion — Here's How Trump's $2 trillion in Debt Compares with Obama, Bush, and Clinton. *Business Insider*, February 20, 2019. Retrieved from www.businessinsider.com/trump-national-debt-deficit-compared-to-obama-bush-clinton-2019-2

Denyer, S. (2019). North Korea Has Been Testing Ballistic Missiles. So Why Won't Trump Use the B Word? *Washington Post*, May 27, 2019. Retrieved from www.washingtonpost.com/world/asia_pacific/when-is-a-north-korean-ballistic-test-not-a-test-when-trump-and-moon-say-it-didnt-happen/2019/05/23/dd2e3dca-7c89-11e9-a66c-d36e482aa873_story.html

Elovitz, P. (2017). Trump's Disruptive Personality and Need for Conflict. Paper presented at 40th International Psychohistorical Association meeting at New York University.

Elovitz, P. (2018). *The Making of Psychohistory: Origins, Controversies, and Pioneering Contributors*. New York: Routledge.

Freud, S. (1931). *New Introductory Lectures*. In *The Standard Edition of the Complete Psychological Works of Sigmund Freud*, vol. XXII. London: The Hogarth Press.

Fuchsman, K. (2017). The Presidential Campaign That Astounded the World: A Psychohistory of Donald Trump and the 2016 Election. *The Journal of Psychohistory*, Vol. 44, No. 4, , pp.292–309.

Gerstein, J. (2019). Judge Questions White House Standards for Revoking Playboy Reporter's Press Pass. *Politico*, August 27, 2019. Retrieved from www.politico.com/story/2019/08/27/white-house-playboy-reporter-press-pass-1476136

Kaylan, M. (2017). Hidden Clues in the Trump-Comey Drama. It's Worse Than You Think. *Forbes*, May 11, 2017. Retrieved from www.forbes.com/sites/melikkaylan/2017/05/11/hidden-clues-in-the-trump-comey-drama-its-worse-than-you-think/#16f1 1ededfda

Kessler, G., Rizzo, S., & Kelly, M. (2019). President Trump Has Made 12,019 False or Misleading Claims over 928 Days. *The Washington Post*, August 12, 2019. Retrieved from https://beta.washingtonpost.com/politics/2019/08/12/president-trump-has-made-false-or-misleading-claims-over-days/

Lee, B. (Ed.). (2017). *The Dangerous Case of Donald Trump*. New York: Thomas Dunne Books.

Lewis, C. (2014). *935 Lies: The Future of Truth and the Decline of America's Moral Integrity*. New York: PublicAffairs.

Lingiardi, V. & McWilliams, N. (2017). *Psychodynamic Diagnostic Manual*. New York: Guilford Press.

McWilliams, N. (2011). *Psychoanalytic Diagnosis*. New York: Guilford Press.

Michaels, J. (2017). How Trump Is Dismantling a Pillar of the American State. *The Guardian*, November 7, 2017. Retrieved from www.theguardian.com/commentisfree/2017/nov/07/donald-trump-dismantling-american-administrative-state

Parker, A., & Bernstein, L. (2018). Political Stress Test: Trump's Medical History Becomes Another Divisive Issue. *Washington Post,* May 2, 2018. Retrieved from www.

washingtonpost.com/politics/political-stress-test-trumps-medical-history-becomes-ano
ther-divisive-issue/2018/05/02/eaed3926-4e17-11e8-af46-b1d6dc0d9bfe_story.html

Politi, D. (2019) Psychiatrist on CNN: Trump "May Be Responsible for Millions More Deaths" than Hitler, Stalin and Mao. *Slate,* August 25, 2019. Retrieved from https://sla te.com/news-and-politics/2019/08/psychiatrist-cnn-trump-responsible-for-deaths-hitler. html

Popovich, N., Albeck-Ripka, L., & Pierre-Louis, K. (2019) 84 Environmental Rules Being Rolled Back Under Trump. *New York Times*, August 29, 2019. Retrieved from www.nytimes.com/interactive/2019/climate/trump-environment-rollbacks.html

Renae, M. & Tracy, J. (2018). Trump Is Systematically Backing Off Consumer Protections, to the Delight of Corporations. *Washington Post*, March 6, 2018. Retrieved from www.washingtonpost.com/business/economy/a-year-of-rolling-back-consumer-protect ions/2018/03/05/e11713ca-0d05-11e8-95a5-c396801049ef_story.html.

Rogers, K. & Fandos, N. (2019), Trump Tells Congresswomen to 'Go Back" to the Countries They Came From. *New York Times*, July 14, 2019. Retrieved from www. nytimes.com/2019/07/14/us/politics/trump-twitter-squad-congress.html

Schwartz, T. (2018). I Wrote The Art of the Deal with Trump. He's Still a Scared Child. *The Guardian*, January 18, 2018. Retrieved from www.theguardian.com/ global/commentisfree/2018/jan/18/fear-donald-trump-us-president-art-of-the-deal

Steele, R.D. (2010). *Intelligence for Earth: Clarity, Diversity, Integrity, & Sustainability.* Okton, VA: Earth Intelligence Network. Retrieved from www.oss.net/dynamaster/ file_archive/100302/71ca06a92bf1fc3598e7140ed12ba4fd/INTELLIGENCE%20for% 20EARTH__version%20008.pdf

Stern, R. (2007). *The Gaslight Effect: How to Spot and Survive the Hidden Manipulation Others Use to Control Your Life.* New York: Harmony.

Trump, D. (2015). Here's Donald Trump's Presidential Announcement Speech. *Time,* June 16, 2015. Retrieved from https://time.com/3923128/donald-trump-announcem ent-speech/

Trump, D. (2017a). The Inaugural Address. The White House, January 20, 2017. Retrieved from www.whitehouse.gov/briefings-statements/the-inaugural-address/

Trump, D. (2017b). Executive Order (EO) 13777, Titled "Enforcing the Regulatory Reform Agenda." The White House, February 24, 2017. Retrieved from www. whitehouse.gov/wp-content/uploads/2018/06/EO13777_EnforcingRegulatoryReform Agenda.pdf

Trump, D. (2018) Remarks by President Trump at the Veterans of Foreign Wars of the United States National Convention, Kansas City, MO. The White House, July 24, 2018. Retrieved from www.whitehouse.gov/briefings-statements/remarks-president- trump-veterans-foreign-wars-united-states-national-convention-kansas-city-mo/

Vitali, A. & Siemaszko, C. (2017) Trump Interview with Lester Holt: President Asked Comey If He Was Under Investigation. *NBC News*, May 11, 2017. Retrieved from www. nbcnews.com/news/us-news/trump-reveals-he-asked-comey-whether-he-was-under-inves tigation-n757821

Wojcik, S., Huges, A., & Remy, E. (2019). About One-In-Five Adult Twitter Users in the U.S. Follow Trump. Pew Research Center, July 15, 2019. Retrieved from www. pewresearch.org/fact-tank/2019/07/15/about-one-in-five

Zingales, L. (2016). The Right Way to Resist Trump. *New York Times*, November 18, 2016. Retrieved from www.nytimes.com/2016/11/18/opinion/the-right-way-to-resist- trump.html

Chapter 7

Trump the demagogue

Michael Signer

President Trump's crude performance at an annual gathering of conservatives—he physically embraced the American flag, called the Mueller probe "bullshit" and referred to Rep. Adam Schiff as "shifty"—was an affront to the decorum we expect from presidents, and plenty of critics pointed this out. Trump was "not merely undignified as a leader; he is committed to stripping away the dignity possessed by others," Michael Gerson wrote in *The Washington Post* (Gerson, 2019). One Twitter commenter described the speech as "an undignified mess of slop," and another labeled Trump "the most undignified President in history."

But this was the same Trump who as a presidential candidate referred to the size of his manhood during a Republican debate. He said about protesters at his campaign events, "In the good old days, this doesn't happen, because they used to treat them very, very rough." He asserted that "Islam hates us" and that Mexicans are "rapists." Not only did he get away with those offenses, but they somehow made him stronger. And he's gone even further as president. After each episode, Trump's critics have been as scandalized as they have been ineffective, just as they were after the speech at the Conservative Political Action Conference in March 2019. During the campaign, Sen. Marco Rubio (R-Fla.) called Trump "the most vulgar person to ever aspire to the presidency," and see how far that got Rubio.

In fact, demagogues like Trump are almost always undignified. That is a feature, not a bug, of their politics. When Hillary Clinton infamously described his supporters as a "basket of deplorables," Trump swiftly converted the comment into a badge of honor. It turned out that he wanted his followers to trumpet themselves as "Les Deplorables", because that was already his argument. While their critics think demagogues hurt themselves politically by violating the standards of polite society, they're doing the opposite: They're doubling down on an unorthodox but potent politics.

In other words, we must understand why Trump's CPAC performance was rational from his perspective before we can begin to understand how to deal with it. And that means taking Trump, his supporters and his "undignified" performances seriously.

Trump the demagogue   89

A textbook demagogue meets four tests. First, he identifies as a man of the masses, usually by attacking elites. Second, he creates great waves of passion. Third, he uses that passion for political benefit. Fourth, he tests or breaks established rules of governance. Taken together, this approach enables the demagogue to create a state within a state—a massive cult—that follows him alone.

Trump is the first demagogue to actually become president, but American history has seen a lot of them, whether the segregationist Alabama Governor George Wallace, the Wisconsin Senator and communist-chaser Joseph McCarthy, the Louisiana Governor and Senator Huey Long, or the Detroit "radio priest" Father Charles Coughlin. World history has seen Mussolini and Hitler and, more recently, Hugo Chávez in Venezuela and Alexander Lukashenko in Belarus.

All of these figures were called undignified by critics who thought their antics could not succeed because they should not succeed. For Chávez, for instance, vulgar language and insults were a trademark, not a flaw. He talked to national audiences about having sex with his wife, called Americans an obscene term, described his bowel movements on television and named the first cellphone made in Venezuela after a popular slang term for penis. Opponents said his talk was crude and made them ashamed. In 2009, a 70-year-old Venezuelan social worker lamented to a reporter, "A president needs to project a good image." But Chávez's power only grew. Only cancer stopped his political career.

Whether you call it decency or decorum or dignity, these old-fashioned standards provide cold comfort when they are the very things demagogues want to blow up as they seek domination. The fact is that demagogues thrive at the lowest common denominator. That is why they relish their status as political bad boys, vulgarians who say things they really shouldn't. That "Oh, no he didn't" sense of daring lets them play the hero in a drama in which they take on the naysaying establishment.

This renegade behavior easily satisfies the demagogue's four tests: attacking elites, stirring massive emotional power, converting that emotion into politics and, most important, obliterating the rules that allow normal governance. Put another way, what so many critics of demagogues have trouble getting their minds around is also the most necessary to understanding them: It's rational for a demagogue to seem irrational.

Trump methodically, over a period of two hours, intensified his support among his base through a series of precise inflammations, while carefully steering his audience toward the new norms and institutions he's creating. It's the same as when he delights in leading his supporters to angrily chant, "CNN sucks!" The United Nations' Human Rights Chief called those attacks on the press "close to incitement to violence." The accused Florida mail bomber was at one of those Trump rallies, holding up one of those signs.

Most normal people would assume that vulgar, crude people would fail in politics. So how do they succeed, practically speaking? In the ancient world, they were still fairly new, so philosophers were interested in studying them. Aristotle observed that it was easier for demagogues than statesmen to use enthymemes—proofs or analogies dependent on collective past experience—because they shared more in common with the people they were addressing. While educated speakers used "commonplaces and generalities," Aristotle observed, demagogues "speak of what they know and of what more nearly concerns the audience."

What Trump understands is that millions of Americans feel left behind by our politics. They are frustrated by everything about conventional politics, including the expectation that traditional rules like decency and dignified behavior will help solve their problems. They are ripe for a demagogue.

The problem of how elite critics miss the demagogue's strategy, hiding in plain sight, is as old as democracy itself. In ancient Athens, the well-born playwright Aristophanes attempted to undermine a demagogue named Cleon through a series of satirical plays, staged before thousands. Cleon was a colorful figure who said, "As a general rule states are better governed by the man in the street than by intellectuals." After a generation of statesmanlike leaders, Cleon took joy in demolishing decorum. While making speeches, he would do things like suddenly shout, dramatically throw open his tunic and slap his thighs for emphasis. So Trump was following an old playbook when he wrapped his body around an American flag—or when he mimicked a disabled reporter during the presidential campaign. For his followers, these antics are intoxicating.

Aristophanes depicted Cleon in his plays as a vulgar sausage-seller. He mocked the "pig's education he has had." He wrote, "You possess all the attributes of a demagogue: a screeching, horrible voice; a perverse, cross-grained nature; and the language of the market-place." None of this worked. Athenians continued to elect Cleon as general. The plays may have heightened his celebrity.

This pattern has also played out in American history. Consider how the ruling class mocked Long, the folksy Louisiana Governor, as he rose to the U.S. Senate. H.L. Mencken dismissed him as a "backwoods demagogue of the oldest and most familiar model—impudent, blackguardly, and infinitely prehensile." In 1931, the new senator cheerfully greeted a visiting German naval commander in a pair of green silk pajamas and a bathrobe. After the German consul's office issued statements of outrage and protest, Long met the commander the next day in a formal striped suit and tails. Long's antics created a sensation of nationalistic defiance, and one historian wrote that Long learned the "value of buffoonery in winning national publicity" and would continue to "cultivate a reputation as a country bumpkin and a clown."

This "bumpkin" was also described by a woman in 1935 as an "angel sent by God." Before he was assassinated by the son-in-law of a political rival in 1935, Long created hundreds of nationwide chapters of his Share Our Wealth Society. He very well could have defeated Franklin Delano Roosevelt in the 1936 Democratic primary for president.

Chávez, too, adopted tactics that were so outrageous, so unthinkable, that they seemed impossible just up until the moment they became successful. As president, Chávez became so audacious in his demagoguery that he made a speech that was literally 10 hours long. But there was method to his madness. He was taking over the state, in plain view.

Demagogues have been with democracy from the beginning. It's not over-stating things to say the demagogue represents the battle between darkness and light—between our prejudices and our reason—that's at the heart of democracy itself. After all, Alexander Hamilton worried in the very first of the Federalist Papers about those who would pay "obsequious court to the people; commencing demagogues, and ending tyrants."

In his CPAC speech, Trump told the crowd: "I'm in love, and you're in love, we're all in love together … There's so much love in this room, it's easy to talk." Faced with the threats of impeachment from Congress and evidence of law-breaking in the Mueller report, he demanded that his supporters choose sides.

As Democratic presidential candidates debate whether to "go low" or "go high" in countering Trump, I'm not one who believes in mirroring Trump's indignities. That won't work for any non-demagogue. After their ruinous experience with demagogues like Cleon, Athenians ultimately addressed the reign of demagogues not through plays but through constitutional punishments. Under a system enacted several years after Cleon's death, a politician charged with "having proposed a measure contrary to democratic principles and to Athens' laws" could be ostracized by a majority of the voters for 10 years.

It's not a far leap to "high crimes and misdemeanors."

Acknowledgments

This chapter was originally published as Signer (2019).

References

Gerson, M. (2019). Trump Boldly Asserts that He Has Learned Nothing These Past Two Years. *Washington Post*, March 4, 2019. Retrieved from www.washingtonpost.com/op inions/trump-boldly-asserts-that-he-has-learned-nothing-these-past-two-years/2019/03/ 04/e85aa238-3eb8-11e9-922c-64d6b7840b82_story.html

Signer, M. (2019). Yes, Trump Is Undignified. Demagogues Have to Be. *Washington Post*, March 8, 2019. Retrieved from www.washingtonpost.com/outlook/yes-trump-is-undigni fied-demagogues-have-to-be/2019/03/08/bd8d8d9c-4109-11e9-a0d3-1210e58a94cf_story. html?noredir

Chapter 8

Is Trump a fascist?

Paul Gottfried

What may be a reductio ad absurdum of the theme that President Trump is a fascist and that we live in a country drenched in fascist symbols and subliminal messages is a "perspective" that appeared last year in *The Washington Post*. This comment concerns a recent remake of *The Lion King*, and its American author is currently a professor at the University of Utrecht. The fact that this interpretation of *The Lion King* as a "fascistic story" is prominently featured in *The Washington Post* would suggest that the editorial board regard it as worthy of our consideration. Supposedly the new version of *The Lion King*, like the older one, is full of authoritarian elitist teachings. The reviewer, Dan Hassler-Forest, highlights "Disney's historical obsession with patriarchal monarchies," which "places the audience's point of view squarely with the autocratic lion, whose Pride Rock literally looks down upon all of society's weaker groups—like a Trump Tower of the African savanna." Further:

> Just as fascist leaders constantly pinpoint specific groups to vilify and cast out from their view of a 'balanced' society, the film's heroes are pre-occupied with keeping their kingdom free of contamination by undesir-able characters who are consigned to the shadowy ghetto-like areas 'beyond our borders'—on the wrong side of the tracks.

Hassler-Forest is particularly concerned that Hollywood has still not changed its ways. In *The Lion King*, "explicit Nazi historiography serves primarily to distract from the hero's own fascism." But this may be only the tip of the cinematic iceberg. The reviewer is almost equally upset with Disney's repris-ing of "sexist fairy tales" and at least implicitly racist children's movies, in which the voices of black performers are used to hide fascistic sentiments. Hollywood, it is charged, still hasn't done enough to "improve the way women of color, LGBT people, and the disabled are made visible to our popular culture." This has become particularly unsettling "at a moment when the far right is on the rise, when we debate whether to call the horrific shelters on our borders concentration camps, and when anti-Semitic and Islamo-phobic hate crimes continue to increase" (Hassler-Forest, 2019).

What warrants attention here is how children's entertainment furnished by mostly black performers is thought to be reeking with bigotry. Is it even conceivable that as late as ten years ago a national newspaper would denounce Disney classics for children as sexist, xenophobic, Islamophobic, and homophobic? And would a scholar in the same newspaper call for making these films more politically correct, in the face of a menacing Far Right? Supposedly we are now dealing with a xenophobic executive in the U.S. whose hatred of dark-skinned foreigners is unique in its brutal intensity. But this hardly accords with easily verifiable facts. According to Axios, "under the Obama administration, total ICE deportations were above 385,000 each year in fiscal years 2009 to 2011 and hit a high of 409,849 in fiscal 2012" (Kight & Treene, 2019).

Despite widespread criticism of his deportations, Trump's numbers are well below those reached by Obama in any year between 2009 and 2012. In 2015 and 2016, around 250,000 deportations took place. This number of deportees fell during Trump's first year in office and then reached a high point for his administration in 2019, with 282,242 deportations taking place by the end of June. One can also find statements about illegal immigration by Trump's predecessor that sound strikingly similar to his (Miller, 2019). Needless to say, these remarks emanating from a Democratic President caused little comment from an unfailingly friendly media. Travel bans on predominantly Islamic countries were issued under Obama and many of his predecessors before Donald Trump entered the White House. These refutations are certainly not meant as a defense of the current President's peevish, incoherent tweets, embarrassing interviews or inability to resist trading insults with Hollywood celebrities. But the degree of hysteria caused by his supposedly bigoted, xenophobic administration raises questions that should be objectively engaged.

Another point that merits discussion is where the invectives against Trump are coming from. Not all of those who have thundered against his presidency have been the usual suspects. Accusations of fascism have not arisen entirely from verbally loose, political opponents or from 24/7 Trump haters on CNN and MSNBC. Nor is it peculiar to freshman Congresswomen grouped around AOC, who are reveling in the public attention that obliging media are lavishing on them. More significantly perhaps, Anti-Trump attacks have also emanated from successful academics, who on the subject of Donald Trump sound even more impassioned than the President's less well-educated enemies. Like Trump's other detractors, these educated anti-Trumpers routinely reach for the F word in describing a hated chief executive. Allow me to suggest that at least some vociferous Trump-haters are simply too smart and too well educated to believe their own rhetoric. I am calling attention to their errors not because I consider those who commit them to be ignorant fools. Rather I would submit that they are no less aware than I of the misstatements that they repeatedly engage in.

It would be a mistake to describe these critics as radical leftists in the sense of being Marxists. Although their works abound in favorable references to Communist and Communist-front groups of the interwar years, their immediate interest seems to be creating a popular front against what they decry as "fascism." These writers strongly favor the building of a multicultural society under the auspices of a sympathetic public administration and an educational system attuned to their values; and they view America's chief executive as standing against everything they wish to implement. They declaim against him furiously in publications that share their general perspective and give the impression that the hour is fast approaching when it may become too late to hold back the forces of evil (Gottfried, 2019).

For example, in *The Guardian* (October 30, 2018), an eminent European historian Timothy Snyder flails away at Trump with total abandon. According to Snyder: "The governing principle of the Trump administration is total irresponsibility, a claim of innocence from a position of power, something which happens to be an old-fashioned fascist trick." Like Trump, "the Nazis claimed a monopoly of victimhood." Like the fascists, "Trump and some of his supporters mount a strategy of deterrence by narcissism: if you note our debts to fascism, we will up the pitch of the whining." And whenever the media attack him, like the fascists, Trump "seizes the occasion, as always, to present himself as the true victim. The facts hurt his feelings" (Snyder, 2018).

Even if one objects to the President's free-swinging rhetorical style, this by itself does not prove that he's a "fascist." Snyder, who is a distinguished professor of European history at Yale University, seems to let it all hang out in this editorial. But all that he manages to prove is that Trump behaves like past presidents when confronted by an almost uniformly hostile press. He has surely not been more temperamental in this respect than, say, FDR, who loudly scolded and tried to ban from press conferences abrasive Republican journalists (Beito, 2017). How does Trump compare as a media-hater to Harry Truman, who, while he was president, wrote to *The Washington Post* music critic Paul Hume threatening to punch him in the nose? Truman wrote this in response to Hume's panning of a voice recital by the president's daughter Margaret (Truman, 1950).

Snyder turns his complaint about Trump's security guards into a warning about "paramilitaries." We are reminded that "in Austria in 1938 the SA quickly took advantage of the absence of local authority to loot, beat, and humiliate Jews, thereby changing the rules of politics and preparing the way for the Nazi takeover of the country" (Snyder, 2018). One has to enter an alternative reality in order to figure out what this description has to do with Trump's security people urging a heckler to leave a rally—or if necessary escorting him to the entrance. Presidential candidates in both national parties in the U.S. receive trained security. It's also unlikely that a screaming disrupter would have been allowed to stay at a rally for Hillary Clinton or Bernie Sanders in 2016. And even if Trump behaved more indignantly in the face of hecklers than some other hypothetical candidate, it's hard to imagine how his behavior would have resembled that of Nazi thugs beating up hapless victims on the streets of Vienna in 1938.

A colleague of Snyder's at Yale, Jason Stanley, Jacob Urowsky Professor of Philosophy, devotes his booklet *How Fascism Works: The Politics of Us against Them* (Stanley, 2018) to even more desperate efforts to link Trump to the European fascist past. Stanley points to a fit between fascism and Donald Trump's connections to entrepreneurial capitalism: "In 'fascism' the state is an enemy to be replaced by the nation, which consists of self-sufficient individuals …" and "fascist ideology involves something at least superficially akin to the libertarian ideal of self-sufficiency and freedom from the state" (ibid., 43). Apparently, fascists share with other social Darwinists the ideals of "hard work, private enterprise and self-sufficiency" (ibid., 178–179). They also follow in the path of Mussolini "who denounces the world's great cities such as New York, for their teeming populations of nonwhites" (ibid., 153). Pace Stanley, Italian fascism famously glorified the state and taught "*tutto nello stato, niente fuori dello stato.*" It was German Nazism, which Stanley never bothers to distinguish from Italian fascism, which placed *das Volk* above the state. But neither movement followed libertarian teachings or even pretended to. Stanley also insists that "right-to-work laws were originally advanced in language that mirrored exactly Hitler's attacks on trade unions in *Mein Kampf*" (ibid., 172–174) This is another startling assertion for which no proof is furnished.

Nor is there evidence for this sweeping accusation: "Such antiunion policies paved the way for a presidential candidate running a white nationalist campaign with open nostalgia for the 1930s to sweep to victory across the once proud labor union states of the Midwest" (Stanley, 2018, 195–196). This last statement tries to paper over the fact that it was Trump, not his Democratic opponent, who in 2016 ran as the candidate of blue-collar America and who pulled the labor vote away from the Democrats. One might wonder how the GOP candidate achieved this if his purpose was to grind the laboring class under his heel. That said, Stanley needn't worry about unfriendly responses to his charges. The back cover of his book extols his bold, independent judgments, according to academic and literary celebrities who agree with his tirade. Princeton Dean Jan T. Gross seems especially grateful that Stanley has exposed "xenophobic populism" and "the insidious mechanisms at play that are threatening today's democracies around the globe."

Stanley becomes even more enraged when he attacks Trump's travel ban on certain Muslim countries; and he compares this act to Hitler's steps in dehumanizing hapless victims. Such attempts to depict Trump as a Nazi tyrant sin grievously against the law of proportion. Because Trump has failed to expand on certain social policies embraced by the previous administration and because he has not consistently adopted Politically Correct phrases, intellectuals feel justified in comparing him to mass murderers. This goes well beyond expressing disagreement with a specific policy or noticing that the current occupant of the White House doesn't always mind his manners.

96 Paul Gottfried

Stanley's diatribe has less to do with his illustrations drawn from the fascist and Nazi past than it does with his anxiety about the American present. His stepmother Mary is praised for helping Stanley "see the centrality of U.S. history to fascism" (ibid.). For Stanley, the U.S. has long been teetering on the brink of fascism and as one travels away from its coastal havens of diversity and LGBT rights, one encounters the face of something that for Stanley resembles interwar Europe. The victory of Donald Trump in 2016 confirmed Stanley's ingrained fears as the child of European refugees. As a student in his hometown of Syracuse, New York, Stanley tells us, he was held up to ridicule as the only Jew in his classes. Even in this Eastern urban center, non-Jews whom he encountered thought that Stanley, like other Jews, wore horns. Because of this traumatizing mockery, the author came to understand that the LGBT community needed protection against the current reign of bigotry. Thus, when a gathering of Christian philosophers recently concluded that homosexuality was a "disability" of sorts, he savagely responded by hurling unmentionable obscenities at the participants. Given the grim situation in which Stanley imagines the U.S. to be at the present time, he believes that it's necessary to fight any prejudice that betokens a fascistic mentality (ibid.).

Another form of the argumentum ad Hitlerum that expresses alarm at the fascist tendencies in Trump's America, comes from a distinguished scholar in the field of German history, Christopher R. Browning. Browning's anxious remarks appear in the conspicuously "anti-fascist" *New York Review of Books*:

> Trump has been the beneficiary of long-term trends predating his presidency in the decline of organized labor. To consolidate his dictatorship, Hitler had to abolish the independent unions in Germany in a single blow. Trump faces no such problem. In the first three postwar decades, workers and management effectively shared the increased wealth produced by the growth in productivity. Since the 1970s that social contract has collapsed, union membership and influence have declined, wage growth has stagnated, and inequality in wealth has grown sharply.

Equally important:

> Governor Scott Walker's triumph over public sector unions in Wisconsin and the recent Supreme Court decision striking down mandatory public sector union dues (Janus v. AFSCME) simply accelerate a process long underway. The increasingly uneven playing field caused by the rise in corporate influence and decline in union power, along with the legions of well-funded lobbyists, is another sign of the illiberal trend.

Somehow the weakening of labor unions in what is becoming a post-industrial America suggests that contemporary America is moving toward Nazi *Gleichschaltung*, that is, forcing all social institutions into the framework of a

Nazi dictatorship. Trump and his party are imagined to be the "beneficiary" of this development, although the economic trend that Browning mentions is unrelated to fascist coercion. Even more misleading is the equation of German *Gewerkschaften*, which were labor unions in the traditional sense, with organized blocs of public sector employees (Browning, 2018).

Professor Browning presumably knows that progressive Democratic presidents like FDR and Harry Truman never equated public sector unions with traditional associations of private sector workers (Brands, 2009, 373–393). Strikes unleashed by public sector employees in 1946 and 1947 caused a backlash from the Truman administration and were reflected in provisions of the Taft-Hartley Act. After World War II neither national party felt an urgent need to cater to the public sector, as a toiling labor class. Actions taken by former Wisconsin Governor Scott Walker to limit the pensions of public sector employees had nothing to do with what Browning characterizes as an abridgement of the "social contract." This contract, at least as it was understood up until the day before yesterday, pertained to workers and management being able to share "increased wealth produced by growth in productivity" (Browning, 2018). If any such contract existed as a concept, it pertained to dividing up increased wealth that arose from increased productivity. It is hard to see how it applied to government workers, who are consuming, not increasing, wealth. By way of relevant information, Browning's hated Mr. Walker lost in his bid for another term as governor. His Democratic opponent who won was heavily backed by the public sector.

One may speculate on the reasons why scholars who should know better twist historical facts to make Trump look like an interwar fascist or Nazi leader. In this matter I would bring up two observations that I arrived at while researching a book on the rise and permutations of antifascism since the 1920s. First of all, the identification of "fascism" as the ultimate evil is now so widespread in Western countries that calling one's adversary a fascist has become the ultimate put-down. Racist, sexist, and homophobe are also injurious to one's reputation in our increasingly PC culture but fascism seems to say it all. Fascism implies every conceivable form of politically incorrect behavior carried to the nth degree; and what makes the F word an even more devastating term of attack is that it brings up memories of Nazi genocide. Although there were other less murderous fascist movements, in most people's minds and certainly in media accounts, fascism immediately evokes the horrors committed in Nazi extermination camps.

Nor is the identification of fascism as the ultimate evil limited to the political Left in the U.S. and other Western countries. Some of the most egregious abuses of the term have come from overeager Republican propagandists. Jonah Goldberg's bestseller *Liberal Fascism* attempts to turn the tables on the Democrats by claiming that it's the other party that is linked to historic fascism. Goldberg, who is a nationally syndicated Republican columnist, focuses on the putative parallels between the rhetoric and policies of Mussolini and

Hitler and the proposals of Democratic presidential hopeful Hillary Clinton. Because Hillary Clinton favored extensive social programs that Italian fascists and German Nazis also advocated, this supposedly reveals a connection between fascism and the Democratic Party. Hillary Clinton's references to a "new village" under government auspices should be seen as a throwback to Hitler's *Volksgemeinschaft*; and the Democratic Party's endorsement of affirmative action programs for minorities and women is an updated version of Hitler's exclusion of Jews from German public life as a result of the Nuremberg Laws of 1935 (Goldberg, 2007, 243–278). Goldberg's reproduction at the end of his book of the 1920 Nazi Party Platform in translation is intended to point out that the Democratic Party of 2008, even before Barack Obama arrived on the national scene, was on its way to replicating the politics of the Third Reich (ibid., 404; Gottfried, 2016, 7–8, 98–101).

This work provides a template for more recent efforts by Republican publicists and media stars to go after the Democrats and their allies as "fascists." For example, Republican talk show host Dennis Prager has produced commentaries for his "Prager University" that assure us that "fascism is necessarily leftist." On the basis of a sketch about the life of neo-Hegelian Italian philosopher Giovanni Gentile (1875–1944), Prager can state with confidence that Gentile proves that "fascism bears a deep kinship to today's Left." After all, "Democrat progressives, in full agreement with Gentile, love and push for a centralized state, which manifests itself in stuff like recent state expansion into the private sector" (Gottfried, 2017). It would seem that Prager is saying that any thinker, regime or movement that has advocated an expansion of the state (except possibly for authorized Republican reasons) exemplifies both fascism and "today's Left." One may also search (in vain) for evidence that Prager and his guest Dinesh D'Souza have read the philosophical writings of Gentile or even his essay "*La Dottrina Politica del Fascismo*." Although anti-fascist polemicists like Tim Snyder who go after Trump as the new Hitler or Mussolini may be sullying their scholarly reputations, Republican anti-fascists usually have no scholarly reputation to compromise. They are political operatives trying to solicit votes for their party.

D'Souza has bestowed on the public an entire book, *Big Lie: Exposing the Nazi Roots of the Left*, which aims to demonstrate that the Democratic Party, which is the "Left," exudes fascist and Nazi tendencies (D'Souza, 2017). In an interview with the Breitbart website, the author explains that the Left, since the election of Obama, is driven by "the glimpse of being able to establish exactly what the fascists always wanted: a complete centralized state." He also sounds this warning:

> Remember, for example, that with the NSA today there are surveillance technologies that were completely unavailable to Mussolini in the 20s or Hitler in the 30s. So, in a sense, true fascism, full-scale fascism, is more possible today than it was in the twentieth century.
>
> (Kraychick, 2018)

Again, one has to ask the question that came up with regard to Prager and Goldberg: "Does any progress toward centralized state power represent a movement in the direction of fascism?" The consolidation of state power has been going on for a long time in many places. Do all these political developments betray the influence of a unitary fascist ideology?

Fighting fascism for electoral gain, wherever one looks for this evil, is just too tempting a political weapon to be ignored. Snyder, Stanley, Browning, Goldberg, Prager, D'Souza and other partisans are all reaching for the same weapon by attacking their political opponents as fascists. But allow me, in my second observation, to call attention to the idealism of at least some on the anti-fascist Left. Unlike Republican publicists who never leave the arena of party politics, these leftist critics seem interested in higher goals than helping their patrons win the next national election. Among the more cerebral Trump-haters, we may discern a concern about a Thermidorean Reaction, that is, a short-circuiting of a process of social change that these advocates have worked to advance. Like the reaction to a galloping French Revolution, which came to a halt in the summer of 1794 during the revolutionary eleventh month of Thermidor, when Robespierre, Saint-Juste and other Jacobin leaders were overthrown and executed, Trump's victory in 2016 and his subsequent presidential tenure were for the cultural Left, including educators, a traumatic setback.

Trump's presidency and the rise of populist leaders and parties in France, Italy, Spain, Austria, Denmark, Hungary, and to a lesser extent England and Germany, have brought the "Far Right" back into prominence. It matters little to some observers whether any or all of these populist manifestations are as far to the right as our intellectual and journalistic Left wish us to believe. What does matter is that the political change desired by the Left has been interrupted. And Trump has been the villain here. Although he has not tried to rescind gay marriage or any of the rights won by the LGBT lobby under the preceding administration, he has also not labored to promote them. Finally, he has unceremoniously revived the immigration question, after the departing Obama administration came to view illegal immigration more indulgently in its last year or so than it had done before.

What makes this setback look like fascism (quite broadly understood) is Trump's appeal to revolution as he supposedly slows down or reverses certain leftist tendencies. An apostle of perpetual revolution as well as early Bolshevik leader, Leon Trotsky developed the concept of a Thermidorean reaction and famously applied it to Stalin's takeover of the Soviet state after Lenin's death. Once revolutionary change, according to Trotsky, slows down, the reaction does not stabilize itself but continues to move in a counterrevolutionary direction. American historian Crane Brinton published a famous study in 1938, *The Anatomy of Revolution*, detailing the phases through which various revolutions have passed (Brinton, 1956). According to Brinton, every great Western revolution reaches a Thermidorean point, at which stage its zeal and energies crest.

Trump, as viewed by some of his critics, represents the operation of Thermidor. His victory and taking of office were blows against the hope of continued Cultural Revolution and against a globalist, radically anti-traditional society. This may provide the context for why otherwise serious scholars allied to the Left insist that Trump is a fascist. In Ernst Nolte's lapidary definition, "fascism is a counterrevolutionary imitation of the Left" (Nolte, 2000, 35–42). It is a movement grouped around a charismatic leader which imitates a revolutionary force but serves reactionary interests.

Thus, Trump's enemies on the Left elevate him and European populists, whom this president has praised, to the contemporary equivalents of interwar European fascists or Nazis. The role ascribed to Trump is a supposed continuation of the one played by long-dead celebrities of the interwar Right. In line with this view, Mark Bray in his *Antifascist Handbook* compares the struggle against Trump with the Popular Front of the 1930s, against fascism. Bray and other organizers of Antifa view themselves as the natural successors of those who fought Hitler, Mussolini and Franco, in alliance with European Communism. Although Bray is often viewed as a vulgarizer of better credentialed anti-Trump polemicists, he also extracts the implications of what others have left unsaid.

He addresses at length the current forms of fascism and likens them to those forms that the fascist movement took in interwar Europe (Bray, 2007, 3–39). Although both "fascisms" were devised to serve the ruling class and to keep down impoverished minorities, they nonetheless reveal noticeable differences. For example, the older fascism was primarily an interwar Central European phenomenon, while the fascism that Bray focuses on pervades the current Western world. Moreover, the older form was more explicitly militaristic and less friendly toward a global economy. Despite such variations, Bray assures us, there is enough of an overlap between the old and new fascisms to make clear the family resemblance. Also, the comparison has strategic value. The enemy whom the anti-fascists have in their crosshairs is so grim that its very existence provides "solidarity" for the protestors (ibid., 134–135).

Bray also devotes almost 20 pages of the *Antifascist Handbook* to questions concerning how much free speech or tolerance in general his movement should be willing to grant their opposition. For Bray, these questions are mostly irrelevant distractions from revolutionary activities:

> The antifascist principle of individual and collective autonomy promotes a vision of human diversity and plurality at odds with the stifling homogeneity of capitalist consumer culture. If fascists were to start organizing in such a society, antiauthoritarian antifascists would still organize to shut them down, but they would not construct massive prisons to lock them up as the American government has done to countless political prisoners over the generations.

Further: "even if you agree that shutting down fascist organizing constitutes an infringement upon the free speech of fascists, it is still patently obvious that anti-fascists advocate for more free speech in society than liberals both quantitatively and qualitatively."

It is essential for understanding such statements to recognize that, for Bray, the anti-fascists are in mortal combat with fascist institutions deriving their power from a capitalist ruling class. "Militant antifascism challenges the state monopoly on political legitimacy by making a political case for popular sovereignty from below." "Rather than buying into the liberal notion that all political 'opinions' are equal, anti-fascists unabashedly attack the legitimacy of fascism and institutions that support it" (ibid., 156).

The underlying assumption in such assertions is that we're already deep into a civil war between fascists and anti-fascists; therefore, the question of providing a "platform" for one's adversary is no longer worth considering. Bray warns against "the liberal alternative to militant anti-fascism" offered by those who "have faith in the power of rational discourse." In his view,

> given the documented shortcomings of 'liberal anti-fascism' and the failure of the allied strategy of appeasement leading up to World War II, a more convincing argument can be made that allowing fascism to achieve public respectability runs the risk of sliding into 'totalitarianism'.
>
> (ibid., 158)

Putting aside the question of who exactly the "liberals" were who tried to appease the Nazis, Bray is forthright in his determination to close down the opposition to his anti-fascist ideology. He also leaves no doubt that Trump and his European populist counterparts are the "fascists" whom he intends to close down or overthrow.

In summary, this chapter has not attempted to whitewash either Trump or his anti-fascist adversaries. What it has tried to do is show why some critics have viewed the current administration and more generally the rise of populist movements here and in Europe as a return to the equivalent of interwar fascism. Although this is clearly not my position and although the comparisons in my view are based on a flagrant misuse of historical data, genuine concern about derailing a process of social and cultural change fuels this crusade. The appeal to violence and the call to suppress dissenting opinions are the natural outcomes of the anxieties expressed by those who insist that Trump is a Nazi or fascist. After all, these militants are not engaging in routine partisan politics, like the "anti-fascist" Republicans who benefit financially from calling the other side names. The leftist anti-fascists are working to prevent what they consider the contemporary version of a Nazi takeover; therefore, for them, the hour for "rational discourse" may well be over.

References

Beito, D. (2017). FDR's War against the Press. *Reason*, May. Retrieved from https://reason.com/2017/04/05/roosevelts-war-against-the-pre/

Brands, H. W. (2009). *Traitor to His Class.* New York: Random House.

Bray, M. (2007). *The Anti-Fascist Handbook*. London: Melville House.

Brinton, C. (1956). *The Anatomy of Revolution*, rev. edn. New York: Vintage.

Browning, C. (2018). The Suffocation of Democracy. *New York Review of Books,* October 25, 2018. Retrieved from www.nybooks.com/articles/2018/10/25/suffocation-of-dem ocracy/.

D'Souza, D. (2017). *The Big Lie: Exposing the Nazi Roots of the American Left*. Washington DC: Regnery.

Goldberg, J. (2007). *Liberal Fascism: The Secret History of the American Left, from Mussolini to the Politics of Meaning.* New York: Doubleday.

Gottfried, P. (2016). *Fascism: Career of a Concept.* DeKalb, IL: Northern Illinois University Press.

Gottfried, P. (2017). Right-wing Celebrities Play Fast and Loose with History. *American Conservative*, December 27, 2017. Retrieved from www.theamericanconserva tive.com/articles/right-wing-celebrities-play-fast-and-loose-with-history/

Gottfried, P (2019). *The Strange Death of Marxism: The European Left in the New Millennium*. Columbia, MO: University of Missouri Press.

Gottfried, P. (2020). *Conservatism: The Vanishing Tradition.* Ithaca, NY: Cornell University Press.

Hassler-Forest, D. (2019). 'The Lion King' Is a Fascistic Story. No Remake Can Change That. *Washington Post*, July 12, 2019. Retrieved from www.washingtonp ost.com/outlook/2019/07/10/lion-king-is-fascistic-story-no-remake-can-change-that/

Kight, S. & Treene, A. (2019). Trump Isn't Matching Obama Deportation Numbers. *Axios*, June 21, 2019. Retrieved from www.axios.com/immigration-ice-deportation-trump-obama-a72a0a44-540d-46bc-a671-cd65cf72f4b1.html

Kraychick, R. (2018). Dinesh D'Souza: 'Bigotry' Is 'Unifying Glue' for 'Progressives and the Democratic Party.' *Breitbart*, August 3, 2018. Retrieved from www.breitbart. com/radio/2018/08/03/dinesh-dsouza-bigotry-is-unifying-glue-for-progressives-and-the-democratic-party/

Miller, M. (2019). People Roast Trump and Then Find Out It Was Obama. *Daily Caller*, July 25, 2019. Retrieved from https://dailycaller.com/2019/07/25/people-roast-trump-it-was-obama/

Nolte, E. (2000). *Der Faschismus in seiner Epoche*, 10th edn. Munich: Piper Verlag.

Snyder, T. (2018) Donald Trump Borrows from the Old Tricks of Fascism. *The Guardian*, October, 30, 2018. Retrieved from www.theguardian.com/commentisfree/2018/oct/30/trump-borrows-tricks-of-fascism-pittsburgh

Stanley, J. (2018). *How Fascism Works.* New York: Random House.

Truman, H. (1950). Letter to Paul Hume. Harry S. Truman Library. Retrieved from www.trumanlibrary.gov/education/trivia/letter-truman-defends-daughter-singing.

Part III

Social and historical factors in the rise of Trump

Chapter 9

American Exceptionalism on steroids

David Lotto

Trump's chief campaign slogan "Make America Great Again" embodies a fundamental aspect of Trump's appeal to the electorate. Trump is the symbolic leader, the delegate of the national group fantasy, who will restore the U.S. to its rightful place in the world, which is to be the most powerful, wealthy, and influential nation on the face of the Earth. It expresses the Trump enthusiasts' wish to restore a lost paradise, to return to a time when the U.S. was the greatest and always won, particularly when it came to wars. One of the major tropes of Trump's campaign and his presidency is about winning. America will become great again because it will now, under Trump's leadership, start winning again.

In her book, *Strangers in Their Own Land*, Arlie Hochschild comes to the conclusion that the people of rural Louisiana whom she interviewed and spent time with, virtually all of whom were Trump voters, are united by what she calls their "deep story" (Hochschild, 2016). The story is that these people see themselves as hard-working, morally virtuous, law-abiding, rule-following, patriotic Americans who should be, but have not been, sufficiently rewarded for their efforts and their virtues. So when they see things like people receiving Social Security disability benefits, or getting food stamps, subsidized housing, free health insurance, or worst of all, someone getting a good job through an affirmative action program or minority preference, they see red and vote Republican. Hochschild uses the metaphor of people standing patiently in line to receive what is rightfully theirs—a piece of the American Dream—which essentially means wealth. When she presented this image to the people she interviewed, of standing in line and working one's way forward to collect your piece of the American Dream with pampered minorities unfairly cutting into the line ahead of them, they enthusiastically concurred.

I think Hochschild misses the essence of the deep story here, which is that at its heart lies a sense of entitlement. Her Tea Party people are true blue, red-blooded, patriotic Americans who love their country and would sacrifice anything for it—including their lives and the lives of their children when their beloved country calls them to war. They do this because America is great. It is the exceptional nation, the most powerful and wealthiest the world has ever seen and, as loyal Americans, they deserve to share in this wealth and power. And when they don't get what they think they deserve, they react to this narcissistic injury with anger and search for someone or something to blame whom they can punish and thus avenge the blow they have suffered. Criminals, immigrants, welfare recipients, and the government that enables all this to happen are the usual suspects. They become the targets, the designated scapegoats, toward whom it is appropriate to act in violent or coercive ways.

Carolyn Marvin, Professor of Communication at the Annenberg School for Communication, published a book with David Ingle in 1999 entitled *Blood Sacrifice and the Nation: Totem Rituals and the American Flag*. They suggest that the sociologist Emile Durkheim's theory of the totem—a sign that each clan uses to distinguish itself from the others—very much applies today in the way the American flag is treated in contemporary America (Marvin & Ingle, 1999). One pledges one's allegiance to it, and one is prepared to die for it. If you want to win an election, you had best make sure you wear your American flag lapel pin. It is mandatory for an American flag to be prominently displayed at any political campaign event.

The flag is frequently associated with the military. Military rituals and displays, such as Fourth of July parades, illustrate one of its primary meanings; that it is a symbol of power, potency, and, most of all, military prowess. In these times, military strength is about the only way that the U.S. is truly exceptional compared to all the other nations in the world. America is number one in military firepower. It can destroy more in less time, in more places, and in more ways than any other nation in history.

Another perspective on the significance of the flag is to see how it functions as a fetish object. According to Freud (1927), fetish objects function to allow us not to see something important, while elevating the importance and the value of something else in its place, the fetish. The flag is the symbol and magic shield which protects Americans from harm as well as serving to hide, misdirect, and disguise the tattered state of the American Dream. It serves to aid in the denial of the unpleasant realities of life. These include the grim financial realities of stagnant or declining wages for most of the people of this country that have resulted from the deindustrialization of the last 30-plus years, and the disappointment and disillusionment accompanying the realization that one may never achieve the American Dream of increasing one's standard of living or fulfilling the expectation that one's children will be wealthier than you.

American Exceptionalism

American Exceptionalism has been around for quite a while. It is the belief that the U.S. is special; that it is exceptional or has virtues and values that make it exceptional among nations. Because of this, the U.S. has a mission to provide education and guidance to others. The term was first used by Alexis de Tocqueville in his 1835 book, *Democracy in America* (Tocqueville, [1835] 2002).

American Exceptionalism has evolved as America has grown and developed from colonial times to the present. The first expression of American Exceptionalism is most often said to be John Winthrop's sermon in 1630 on board the *Arbella* on its voyage to New England. The famous quote is:

> The lord will be our God, and delight to dwell among us, as His own people, and will command a blessing upon us in all of our ways ...We shall find that the God of Israel is among us, when ten of us shall be able to resist a thousand of our enemies; when He shall make us a praise and a glory, that men shall say of succeeding plantations, 'the Lord make it like that of New England.' For we must consider that we shall be as a City upon a hill. The eyes of all people are upon us.
>
> (Winthrop, 1630)

The main form American Exceptionalism took in the seventeenth century was the combination of missionary zeal to convert the native "savages" to Christianity in times of peace, and incredible brutality toward the native people in times of war. In Virginia, in 1622, the colonists fought the Powhatans (Pocahontas' people) which ended with the colonists inviting several hundred of them to the signing of a peace treaty and serving them poisoned tea, killing more than 250.

The early nineteenth century was the era of manifest destiny where the U.S. asserted its right to expand its contiguous territory by any and all means— buying from anyone who was selling, as in the Louisiana Purchase in 1803, or by massive ethnic cleansing of the Native American population, and military conquest, as in the Mexican-American War of 1846–1848. All of which resulted in the creation of an enormous amount of wealth; vast tracts of fertile land, and an abundance of natural resources. This wealth, along with its technological and military superiority over the native people and neighboring countries and the fact that it was protected from external enemies by two huge ocean buffers allowed the U.S. to experience uninterrupted growth in population, wealth, and military power throughout the nineteenth and twentieth centuries.

Turning to foreign policy, starting in 1823, the Monroe Doctrine claimed American hegemony over the entire Western Hemisphere, although it was rationalized by saying that the U.S. was protecting the hemisphere from the malevolent influence of European powers.

Starting with the Spanish-American War at the turn of the century, the United States began the practice of using substantial military force in areas which were not contiguous with its borders. As always, acts of war and exploitation (as in Cuba and the Philippines) were not a problem because they were expressions of benevolent wishes to bring freedom, democracy, and free enterprise to the backward peoples of the Caribbean and the Philippines.

Following the Spanish-American War the U.S. became the policeman of the hemisphere—a policy that continued into the Reagan administration in the 1980s, with the brief hiatus of Roosevelt's "good neighbor policy," where it mostly refrained from direct military interventions.

In the twentieth century, Wilson had his campaign to make the world safe for democracy. Initially, there was the idealistic rhetoric of the 14 points and the creation of the League of Nations. Following the Great War of 1914–1918, the United States became a fully-fledged world military and economic power and increased its presence and influence throughout the world, again always ascribing the noblest of motives to its actions.

Following World War II, when the country emerged as the dominant military and economic power in the world, American Exceptionalism took the form of leading the struggle for freedom and democracy in a life and death struggle against communism.

One of the consequences of these exceptional circumstances is that the U.S. has had a remarkable run of successes. The American nation has grown in territory, wealth, power, and influence in a virtually uninterrupted progression from colonial times until the present. Of particular importance is that, at least until the Vietnam War, it was possible to maintain that the U.S. had never been defeated in war. This is a claim that most other nations have not been able to make. When a grandiose group fantasy, such as American Exceptionalism, coincides with an external reality that appears to confirm it, the power of that fantasy is greatly strengthened.

Patriotism, nationalism, and American Exceptionalism are central aspects of the American identity. The mythic image of rugged individualism—that Americans are freedom-loving, gun-toting cowboys—serves to disguise and direct attention away from the communality Americans share. Americans are united by love for their country and shared identity as Americans. Americans love and adore their country with a devotion and fervor that are usually associated with religious worship. They are communicants of the secular religion of American patriotism whose primary symbol is the flag and whose current spiritual leader is the President.

I am referring not just to the Trumpists and flag-waving, right-wing patriots who are acknowledged devotees of the religion of American patriotism. Most of those who voted for Hillary Clinton would also say that they are patriots who love their country. They may not be foreign policy hawks and may have liberal or even leftist political inclinations but they share with Trump voters a deep love for their exceptional nation. They may cite different reasons for their love of America but they love it nonetheless.

Trump continues to use his slogan "America First" despite being asked by the Anti-Defamation League not to use it because of its historical associations. America First was a political movement, active in this country in the 1930s, whose chief spokesman, Charles Lindbergh, was an avowed anti-Semite and Nazi sympathizer.

As some of the many examples of the importance of the religion of patriotism, American chauvinism and the flag in Trump's message, here are some passages from Trump's inaugural speech—which was a total of 1,326 words long:

> From this moment on, it's going to be America first ... We will ... unite the civilized world against Radical Islamic Terrorism, which we will eradicate completely from the face of the earth ... America will start winning again, winning like never before ... At the bedrock of our politics will be a total allegiance to the United States of America, and through our loyalty to our country, we will discover our loyalty to each other. When you open your heart to patriotism, there is no room for prejudice ... We will be protected by God ... whether we are black or brown or white we all bleed the same red blood of patriots. We all enjoy the same glorious freedoms, and we all salute the same great American flag.

And he ends with: "Together we will make America strong again, we will make it wealthy again, we will make America safe again. And yes, together, we will make America great again. Thank you, God bless you, and God bless America" (Trump, 2017).

And now, the deconstruction of the myth of the American Dream and the valorization of America, the exceptional land of the free, home of the brave, and the pinnacle of democracy; a light to the nations, a shining city on the hill where anyone who works hard can become rich—whose greatness has become a bit tarnished lately but can be restored under the Trump regime. But then there is the reality of how America became great; wealthy colonists given title to or allowed to buy, at very low prices, vast areas of North America, who, immediately upon arrival, commenced a campaign of ethnic cleansing and genocide directed at Native Americans, which continued unabated for the next 250 years; an economic system that relied on either outright slave labor in the South or the also uncompensated labor of indentured servants in the North. Starting in the nineteenth century, the U.S. embarked on numerous offensive military operations, initially against its North American neighbors, the Canadians during the war of 1812, the Spanish in Florida, the Mexicans in Texas and later California and then expanding overseas starting with the Spanish-American War of 1898.

Economically, the class system was one in which a relatively small number of wealthy oligarchs—landowners, planters, merchants, and skilled artisans; later industrialists, capitalists, some professionals, the 1 percent (or perhaps 2 or 3 percent) of their time, continued to rule the nation (see Isenberg, 2016, for an account of the class system realities in this country from colonial times to the present). What remained constant throughout U.S. history is that wealth accumulation was always based on the exploitation of the poor majority, slaves and servants in colonial times and later underpaid workers. Currently, the economic mobility of the United States is less than that of Canada, all the Scandinavian countries, Australia, New Zealand, Germany, France, Spain, and Switzerland (Gould, 2012). American children are more likely than children from these countries to end up in the same place on the income distribution as their parents. Mobility is particularly low for Americans at the bottom of the earnings or income distribution. A quite different reality from the myth of upward mobility with its belief that anyone can become wealthy if they just work hard enough at it or if they're smart or lucky.

Economic mobility was far greater in the past, from colonial times right through until the 1970s, except for the periods of economic recession and depression, chiefly because of the vast amount of cheap land, rich in fertile fields, abundant natural minerals, coal, oil, and ample water power, all of which became available to Americans after the native inhabitants had been killed, or moved elsewhere. However, those days seem to be gone for good. Ninety-two percent of children born in the 1940s made more money than their parents. The number drops to 50 percent, net stagnation, for children born in the 1980s (Leonhardt, 2016).

But whatever grim realities faced as Americans pursue the dream of wealth, they can still feel good about themselves and their life if they feel themselves to be American.

One of the implications of viewing Trumpism, which I would describe as a right-wing political movement with populist, nativist, and authoritarian aspects, as American Exceptionalism gone wild, is that it makes it much less of a unique phenomenon or even a radical shift in American politics. There is even a presidential precedent in Andrew Jackson, similarly a populist, authoritarian, and belligerent, militarist vulgarian, whose central appeal was that he was a man of the rural people who would punish and humiliate the urban elite who had been governing the country through the first six presidencies: Washington through John Quincy Adams. Jackson actually refused to comply with the Supreme Court ruling in favor of the Cherokee nation, seizing their land and sending them off on the "Trail of Tears" to Oklahoma. Jackson was also a strong believer in American Exceptionalism, particularly in regard to the right to land owned and occupied by non-American others.

Historian Richard Hofstadter's classic (1964) article, "The Paranoid Style in American Politics," traces the history of the right-wing, nativist, super-patriotism that has always been a part of America's political reality, including the "Know Nothings," the Klan, lynchings, the waves of anti-immigrant hatred with the ever-present refrain that these newcomers were spoiling, polluting, and endangering the purity of its noble republic. Animus has been directed against the Chinese, Irish, Italians, Southern Europeans, Mexicans, and lately Muslims. In recent times, there has been the John Birch Society, the presidential campaigns of George Wallace and Pat Buchanan, and the rise of the hundreds of groups characterized by the Southern Poverty Law Center as hate groups (Southern Poverty Law Center, 2017). The vast majority of these hate groups are politically right-wing: the militias, patriot organizations, racist, anti-Semitic, and anti-government groups.

The Obama and what might have been a Clinton administration and the Trump regime all share a firm belief in American Exceptionalism and the validity of the mythical American Dream. They all wear their American flag lapel pins when they're out in public, following incidents in which they were criticized for not wearing them. Obama has proclaimed his belief in American Exceptionalism on numerous occasions. One of his strongest was in April of 2012 when he said: "It's worth noting that I first arrived on the national stage with a speech at the Democratic Convention that was entirely about American exceptionalism, and that my entire career has been a testimony to American exceptionalism" (Farley, 2015).

It's just that the Democrats and mainstream liberals have a softer, subtler, and more nuanced version than the Trump supporters. But the underlying belief system is identical; America is the sole superpower on the planet. Americans are entitled, nay obligated, to promote the spread of their special values to the rest of the world. These are foremost freedom, which includes freedom for capital to move with minimal restriction to wherever its owners wish, along with the selective protection of certain human rights for certain people at certain times. It also means that the U.S. is entitled to take whatever steps judged necessary to protect the safety of the people of the Homeland. This includes the right to violate the human rights, particularly the civil liberties of people considered as potential threats, even though they have taken no hostile actions other than to have engaged in political speech, which is supposed to be a right guaranteed under the First Amendment of the Constitution. The right of self-protection trumping all other considerations becomes the right not just to discourage but to forbid other countries, such as Iran and North Korea, from acquiring nuclear weapons. And the final shared tenet is that, because the U.S. is the world's only superpower, it is entitled to, selectively for sure, take on the role of the world's policeman. On these matters, both Democrats and Republicans as well as Trump and his followers are united.

There has been a measurable rise in hate crimes and related activities with the ascendancy of the Trump campaign and election. It seems that Trumpism has allowed much that has been latent to become manifest. According to the Southern Poverty Law Center (SPLC), there has been a significant increase in hate crimes and incidents of bias. In the first 34 days after the November election, there were 1,040 bias incidents reported around the country. In 37 percent of them, Trump, his campaign slogans, or his remarks about molesting women were mentioned. The SPLC also conducted an online survey of more than 10,000 teachers and other school employees in which 80 percent reported heightened levels of anxiety among Muslim, African American, immigrant, and LGBTQ students. More than 2,500 of the 10,000 gave accounts of students being harassed by other students using rhetoric directly related to the election.

The SPLC also regularly monitors the many (917) active organizations it classifies as hate groups. The biggest increase was that 67 new anti-Muslim groups appeared, from 34 in 2015 to 101 in 2016. There was a decrease in the number of anti-government "patriot groups" from 998 in 2015 to 623 in 2016. The peak number of these groups was 1,360, which was in 2012, the year Obama was elected for his second term (Southern Poverty Law Center, 2017).

In this chapter I have argued that the heart of Trumpism is the uninhibited expression of American chauvinism which has been very much an essential aspect of American identity throughout its history. American exceptionalism on steroids. What is most disturbing about the rise of Trumpism is the increased danger, brought on by the combination of the exaggerated sense of narcissistic entitlement and need to win in America's relations with other countries, particularly those that have nuclear weapons.

I end with the sobering observation that the *Bulletin of the Atomic Scientists* has expressed their concern about the danger by moving the hands of the doomsday clock to 2½ minutes before midnight; the closest to doomsday it has been since 1953 when it was set at 2 minutes to midnight after the Soviet Union successfully tested their hydrogen bomb, nine months after the United States first tested its thermonuclear weapon.

References

Farley, R. (2015). Obama and "American Exceptionalism." Retrieved from www.factcheck.org/2015/02/obama-and-american-exceptionalism

Freud, S. (1927). Fetishism. In *The Standard Edition of the Complete Psychological Works of Sigmund Freud*, vol. XXI. London: The Hogarth Press.

Gould, E. (2012). U.S. Lags Behind Peer Countries in Mobility. Economic Policy Institute, October 1, 2012. Retrieved from www.epi.org/publication/usa-lags-peer-countries-mobility/

Hochschild, A. (2016). *Strangers in Their Own Land*. New York: The New Press.

Hofstadter, R. (1964). The Paranoid Style in American Politics. *Harper's Magazine*, November, 77–86.

Isenberg, N. (2016). *White Trash: The 400-Year Untold History of Class in America*. New York: Viking.

Leonhardt, D. (2016). The American Dream, Quantified at Last. *New York Times*, December, 8, 2016. Retrieved from www.nytimes.com/2016/12/08/opinion/the-american-dream-quantified-at-last.html?searchResultPosition=1

Marvin, C. & Ingle, D.W. (1999). *Blood Sacrifice and the Nation*. New York: Cambridge University Press.

Southern Poverty Law Center. (2017). Active Hate Groups 2016. *Intelligence Report*, Spring 2017 2017. Retrieved from www.splcenter.org/fighting-hate/intelligence-report/2017/active-hate-groups-2016

Tocqueville, A. de ([1835] 2002). *Democracy in America*. Chicago: University of Chicago Press.
Trump, D. (2017). The Inaugural Address. The White House, January 20, 2017. Retrieved from www.whitehouse.gov/briefings-statements/the-inaugural-address/
Winthrop, J. (1630). A Model of Christian Charity. Retrieved from www.winthrop society.com/doc_charity.php

Chapter 10

What in our politics, history, economy, and culture enabled Trump's rise?

Ken Fuchsman

Politics and culture

First, we should look at our governmental structure. In the United States, someone who wins the majority of the Electoral College is elevated to the Presidency. A candidate can have a plurality in the popular vote, but not triumph in the Electoral College. This has now happened twice in the twenty-first century.

In the British government, a Prime Minister is a Member of Parliament, who has been selected as the leader of a political party or coalition that wins a majority of seats in the House of Commons. Trump would not be eligible to be the nation's political leader in Great Britain; nor would he be President in a system where the candidate with the most actual votes is victorious.

Second, no other industrial nation has as lengthy election seasons as we do. The British length is four weeks, the official French campaign is either two or three weeks, and the Germans about a month (Library of Congress, n.d.a; n. d.b; n.d.c). For these nations, the focus is more on governing than running for office. Not so in the U.S. where the first Republican Presidential debate for the 2016 election was a full 15 months before election day.

The lengthy, ritualistic contests have become a center of our national life. The talk of who is going to be running for President in the next election is frequently front and center long before any primaries are on the horizon. As political strategist David Axelrod quips, "In Washington, every day is election day" (Dionne Jr., 2016, 119).

The pursuit of a romantic partner for some may be more exciting than maintaining the actual relationship. American culture tends to be more riveted on the courtship of campaigning than the marriage of actually governing. Many follow the ups and downs of political campaigns as if it was a competitive sporting contest. This occurs in a nation where the nation's other most unifying ritual is the Super Bowl,

Third, campaigning and governing were once quite different, but not so much now. A viable presidential candidate must have a distinct persona, develop a campaign theme such as "Yes, We Can," "Make America Great

Again," "Feel the Bern," etc. The aspirant should know how to get media attention, and hold spirited rallies. To govern effectively, a president needs to have knowledge of the issues, develop detailed policy proposals, work together with Congress, implement a coherent foreign policy, provide for the common defense, be a party leader, a good public spokesperson, and take care that the laws are faithfully executed.

The competencies required for governing effectively are not those needed to win elections. As President, Trump is more frequently in campaign mode than he is devoted to his administrative duties. In the 26 months from his election in November 2016 until the end of 2018, Donald Trump held 58 domestic political rallies, averaging more than two a month. In an age of polarization and mass rallies, perpetual campaigning can have often trump governing in the way our political life is evolving.

Fourth, American political campaigns contain rituals with religious overtones. Many successful candidates running against the status quo have been adept at pointing out the nation's problems, and then making grand promises that will supposedly solve our difficulties. It is not only Donald Trump's mass events that are long on promises and short on specifics. I attended a 2016 Bernie Sanders rally and found he articulately enumerated our nation's defects and corruptions. He promised change, gave few specific proposals, and did not mention the obstacles to bringing about his revolution. In 2008, I watched a detached Barack Obama brilliantly make the large crowd enthusiastic, thus fulfilling the function of these campaign events to arouse the audience's emotions. Obama skillfully applied religiously derived rhetoric to political campaigning.

Political rallies can resemble revival meetings. Supporters get their hopes high as the candidate is there to convert the crowd. Once in office, not all the grandiose promises are fulfilled. Some people remain faithful to the nation's leader. Others become disappointed and/or disillusioned, and may either search for another promising candidate in the next election, or may just stop voting.

This cycle of hope and disenchantment has recently become a recurring phenomenon. Much is achieved by our government, yet we seem to be susceptible again and again to a cycle of electing candidates who promise more than they deliver. Donald Trump is part of this tradition of presidential candidates who make fantastic promises, and know how to rouse a crowd. He also adhered to the ritual of portraying those in power as leaving the country in a terrible state that only he could fix. Over and over in recent decades, many Americans have fallen for political salesmen who cannot fulfill the campaign promises they boldly make.

Over the last 60 years, we have gotten tired of the party holding the presidency. Since 1952, only once has a president of the same political party occupied the White House for more than two consecutive terms. Between 1896 and 1952, it was different. Our political parties went on long runs of electing presidents. Republicans won all the presidential contests between 1896 and 1928, except the eight years when Woodrow Wilson was President. Democrats were victors in every presidential election from 1932 to 1948.

Another element in our contemporary campaign melodramas is polarization. This ritual of us versus them has become central to our perpetual campaigning. Donald Trump's campaign was superb on awakening the animosity that has become central to our political theater. In our presidential elections, making great promises and denigrating one's opponents are more important than spelling out programs that can bring promises to fruition.

Fifth, the media play a central role in the phenomenon of endless campaigns. Mainstream news itself has been transformed: there is more of a tabloid sensibility, while verifying claims before publishing, broadcasting, or repeating them has too frequently gone by the wayside.

"All The News That's Fit to Print" is the slogan of *The New York Times*. One aspect of a news story should be accuracy. Of course, not all news publications adhere to verifying before publishing. Certainly the New York tabloid newspaper wars of 1898 that helped lead to the Spanish-American War focused on sensational headlines that were factually dubious.

Then half-a-century later in 1950, along came Senator Joseph McCarthy. Newspapers across the nation printed his sensational claims that card-carrying Communists were influential in the U.S. State Department. Few if any newspapers factually checked McCarthy's figures before printing them. The demagogic McCarthy never uncovered an actual State Department communist. Yet his accusations struck a deep chord in the early days of the Cold War. By not verifying before publishing, the news media played a substantial part in his rise. Nowadays there is even less reluctance to publish, broadcast or send over the internet wild unsubstantiated claims when made by newsworthy individuals.

This reflects the tabloidization of the news. Tabloid dailies feature big headlines on sensational incidents, human interest stories, scandals, and gossip about celebrities; this is called soft news. Between 1977 and 1997, such soft items in the U.S. news media increased from 15 percent to 43 percent (Cashmore, 2006, 26).

The U.S. has also become a celebrity culture, where many are hungry to be entertained. As historian Christopher Lasch wrote, there is a "cult of celebrity" promoted by the "mass media" that encourages "the common man to identify himself with the stars" and their "glamour and excitement" (Lasch, 1978, 21). For "we now live in an amusement society," writes sociologist Lauren Langham, "in which entertainment values displace all others." In our culture, the "difference between leaders and stars" has become "blurred," and not surprisingly "politics has become a moment of entertainment ... In the new era of telepolitics ... self-presentations replace platforms and agendas" (Langham, 2002, 513, 521).

Ellis Cashmore concurs: "news values have been subverted by entertainment values" (Cashmore, 2006, 32). Columnist Leslie Gelb, "Truth is judged not by evidence, but by theatrical performances ... Truth has become the acceptance of untruths" (Bernstein, 2007, 224). We now have a President who has long been a celebrity and who specializes in multiple false and misleading statements on a daily basis.

It is easy to see how our political structure, our fascination with lengthy political campaigns, the cult of personality and celebrity, the degradation of hard news, a tabloid sensibility featuring slogans over policy, and elections as entertainment have all laid the foundation that have enabled Trump to rise to the top.

No candidate in our history has been more effective at grabbing media attention than Donald Trump. During the primary season, his rallies were televised live on cable news channels, a privilege rarely granted to his opponents. Trump said the reason this was done is that he brought up their ratings. Then Chairman of CBS, Les Moonves, said Trump's candidacy "may not be good for America, but it's damn good for CBS ... The money's rolling in and this is fun ... bring it on, Donald. Keep going" (Collins, 2016).

By mid-March 2016, candidate Trump had been given $1.9 billion in free media coverage, which was three times more than the other leading Republican candidates (Tomasky, 2016). As of March, 2016, during the primaries, CNN had devoted 55.4 percent of its coverage to Trump while the rest of his Republican opponents received 44.6 percent, Fox News gave 47.6 percent of its coverage to Trump, and MSNBC 50.4 percent (Miller, 2016). These patterns did not cease once Trump was inaugurated. In a Harvard study of news coverage of the first 100 days of the new president, the investigators examined national newspapers, broadcast and cable news networks. They found that Trump was the center of 41 percent of new stories, which was three times the amount of coverage of his predecessors (Patterson, 2017).

Trump knows how to get media coverage. While many running for office hardly vary from their standard stump speech, Trump's off-the-cuff style includes bringing up something new and sensational regularly. This not only garners headlines; it keeps interest in his shenanigans ongoing. Trump was the candidate as celebrity, and now is the tabloid president.

He knows how to use the dominance of soft news to his advantage. When in doubt, he goes to the gutter, the outrageous, and the partisan. His exploitation of the sensationalist rituals of American politics has enabled him to dominate our discourse despite his false statements, lack of interest in knowing policy details, and abandonment of civility. Donald Trump is the all-time champion in the carnival of our political theater.

History and politics

The combination of the media and our preoccupation with endless campaigns partially explains the political rise of Donald Trump. For how he attracted so many ardent followers, we also need to turn to another aspect of American political history.

Of the many recurring strands within the history of the Republican Party, I will first focus on just one: the paranoid style, which has brought political suspiciousness and conspiracy theories to the mainstream (Hofstadter, 1965). In the 1930s Great Depression, intervention by the state in the economy and social welfare legislation led factions within the Republican Party to consider that Roosevelt and his fellow travelers were violating sacred principles of capitalism and were thus un-American. After World War II, a second Red Scare emerged, like the one right after World War I.

These aforementioned periods of political hysteria cannot be separated from the fact that, for many, capitalism and Americanism go together. For years, capitalism was a central element in our civic religion. The Republican Party from its beginning embraced free enterprise. Steel baron Andrew Carnegie in 1889 preached "The Gospel of Wealth" (Carnegie, [1889] 2006). In the 1920s, President Calvin Coolidge proclaimed that the "business of America is business," and that the "man who builds a factory builds a temple, the man who works there worships there" (Divine et al, 1991, 760). When this secular religious faith of capitalism falters, something cracks in the American political psyche. Many associated with the Republican Party become unsettled, angry, and search for scapegoats. To deflect the narcissistic wound of capitalism's economic failures, some seek those outside the capitalist ideology to blame. The fault cannot be in ourselves, but in some threatening force.

During the 1930s Depression, Congressional conservatives searching for a non-capitalist force to blame formed the House Un-American Activities Committee and targeted leftists of all stripes. In the 1946 Congressional campaign, many Republicans sought to identify their Democratic opponents as communists and fellow travelers. In the 1950s, Senator Joseph McCarthy made all sorts of wild and false charges about the influence of communists in our government.

From the 1930s to the end of the 1970s, despite Republican efforts to equate communism with the Democratic Party, the Democrats had Congressional majorities for all but a handful of the years between 1933 and 1980. Then came the Reagan revolution of 1980. Reagan declared that the government was not the solution but the problem, revived tax cuts favoring the wealthy by Republicans in the 1920s, and targeted so-called tax and spend liberals.

Many Republicans felt the disloyal Democratic Party had been routed, and true Americanism had been restored. Some were dismayed when after another Republican recession Democrat Bill Clinton won the 1992 election. Factions within the Republican Party think that having a Democrat in the White House is contrary to American values.

When Obama became President, it was as if the Red Scare had turned into the Black Scare. The intense fury that characterized the McCarthy era returned with a vengeance. But there was an added element, the night Obama was inaugurated, prominent Congressional Republicans met and swore to oppose anything Obama proposed, even if it had been things they had long advocated.

In the age of the internet, social media, and conservative radio, the demonized Obama was accused of being a Muslim, communist, fascist, and everything else under the sun. Birthers led by Trump even questioned if he was eligible to be President. The paranoid style was brought to a revived prominence. Part of this was due to the usual scapegoating that follows American economic crises. The Great Recession shook up many Republicans who cannot abide or understand how sacred capitalism can have major failures.

But there was another twist in this sense of betrayal. After the 2008 recession, many rebellious Republicans targeted stalwart Republicans in Congress. The 2010 elections brought to the forefront a Tea Party movement that saw the government as the enemy, and Congressional Republicans as betraying their principles of decreasing the size of the government and the federal debt.

Republicans slowly developed their own civil war. The Tea Partiers in Congress became so obstreperous that the Republican Speaker of the House resigned his position and his seat in Congress in September, 2015. These deep Republican Party divisions played themselves out in the 2015–2016 primaries. The mainstream Republican candidates fell by the wayside in a party revolt. The two candidates who received the highest vote totals were the most conservative and bold: Ted Cruz and Donald Trump. Both played upon the anger and scapegoating that drove the Tea Party.

Economics and politics

The 2008 recession left deep scars, and was preceded by years of middle-class economic decline. In 1970, the U.S. middle class had 62 percent of the nation's aggregate household income. By 2014, it was 43 percent. Between 2001 and 2013, the median wealth of middle income Americans fell by 28 percent (Pew Research Center, 2015).

Overall between 1980 and 2014, after taxes and transfers for the bottom 50 percent of working age American adults, there has been close to zero real income growth. This is despite the fact that the country's income nearly doubled in these years. In 2014 dollars, the annual income of the lower half in 1980 averaged $16,000 while the top 1 percent averaged $428,200. In 2014, those in the bottom 50 percent still averaged $16,000, but the top 1 percent $1,304,800 (Cohen, 2016).

During the Obama years through 2014 real median household income was down 2.3 percent, home ownership declined by 5.6 percent, and 3.5 percent more Americans were living in poverty (Murdock, 2016). Barack Obama was the first president since Herbert Hoover without one full calendar year of gross domestic product growth of at least 3 percent (Gillin, 2016).

Productivity had risen 96.7 percent between 1948 and 1973, while real wages almost matched that, going up 91.3 percent. Then, between 1973 and 2013, while productivity rose 73.4 percent, wages only went up 11.1 percent (Johnson, 2016). Particularly hard hit were middle-aged males with less than a college education.

In the first decade of the new millennium, in terms of job losses in manufacturing, the United States "suffered its worst performance in American history," seeing 5.7 million manufacturing positions disappear. The "decline as a share of total manufacturing jobs (33 percent) exceeded the rate of loss in the Great Depression" (Atkinson et al., 2012). The Great Recession also saw a "new high" in terms of "mean duration of unemployment" of 35 weeks compared to peaks of 20 weeks in the prior three recessions. As of 2010, among full-time workers who had been laid off and found new jobs, they were earning 21.8 percent less than in their last job. Consistent with the last three recessions, less-educated workers were more "vulnerable to layoffs" (Belsie, 2016).

Men during the Great Recession were hit harder than women, 8.5 percent of males lost their jobs, compared to 3.5 percent of females. This meant 6 million men and 2.7 million women became unemployed. Between February 2010 and June 2014, women gained 3.6 million jobs to men's 5.5 million. In other words, in 2014, men were still down half a million jobs and women were up 900,000 (Wething, 2014). If you were less educated, a male, and in manufacturing, you were more likely to have endured hardship as a consequence of the recession.

There were over 9 million jobs created between late 2007 and the 2016 election, still the economy had basically left behind less-educated white voters. *The New York Times'* Eduardo Porter reports: Whites make up 78 percent of the U.S. labor force and lost net jobs during the Great Recession. "Whites ages 25 to 54 lost some 6.5 million jobs more than they gained over the period. Hispanics in their prime, by contrast, gained some three million jobs net, Asians 1.5 million and blacks one million" (Porter, 2016).

Understandably many less-educated white men felt displaced and betrayed, and some became more conservative, nativist, resentful, sexist, and furious. Many of them feel disenfranchised. In a poll before the election, 93 percent of Trump's supporters did not feel that their concerns were being addressed in Washington (Wallace-Wells, 2016).

Following the Great Recession, a portion of the electorate became alienated, and targeted those they blamed for their troubles with a primal fury, whether it was President Obama, the Democratic Party, or establishment Congressional Republicans. In 2016, Trump tapped into this anger.

He was able to do that in large part because he too has his own narcissistic wounds. Trump characteristically displaces his faults, failures and resentments on to others. He has his own rage and paranoid tendencies. Trump's Electoral College victory is due in large part in that he held the Republican base while Hillary Clinton saw the erosion of her party's base and also because Trump could activate the discontent and anger of those who had been Democrats but felt displaced and ignored by both the Obama administration and Clinton. Trump's electoral triumph cannot be separated from the way his personal rage and sense of being a victim matched up with those of many of his ardent followers.

The 2016 election results showed that Trump's appeal to revive American greatness appealed to many who had suffered from the historically slow economic recovery. There are 3,056 counties in the United States. Donald Trump carried 2,584 and Hillary Clinton 472 of these counties. But the 15.4 percent of counties that Clinton won accounted for 64 percent of the "nation's economic activity," while the almost 85 percent of the counties that went to Trump "generated only 36 percent of America's prosperity" (Porter, 2016). Clinton lost in usually reliable Democratic states still reeling from the recession. The Keystone state went to Trump by 65,000 votes, yet 130,000 fewer African-Americans cast their ballots in 2016 than 2012 (McCormack, 2016). In Michigan, where in Detroit in 2014, 48 percent of the population earned less than $25,000, Clinton lost by 10,000 votes and got 300,000 *fewer* votes than Obama did in 2012. Wisconsin is a similar story. Hillary received 30,000 *fewer* votes than Trump, and 230,000 *fewer* than Obama did in 2012 (Chiles, 2014; Ben-Shahar, 2016). If Hillary Clinton had held serve and carried these three states, she would have been elected President.

A significant reason Donald Trump became President is that more Democrats were less impressed by Hillary Clinton than they had been by Barack Obama compared to the number of Republicans who were less enamored of Trump than McCain. In 2008, 75,128,851 voted for the Democratic presidential candidate, compared to 65,853,652 in 2016. There were 64,806,274 Republican voters in 2008, and 62,985,134 in 2016. While two million fewer voters chose the Republican Trump in 2016 than had cast their ballots for McCain in 2008, there were nine million fewer Hillary Clinton voters than Obama voters eight years earlier (Hacker, 2018).

Hillary Clinton received a lower percentage of the popular vote than any Democratic presidential candidate since 1992 (Roper Center, n.d.). In contrast, it turns out that there were more no Hillary Democrats than there were never Trump Republicans. This reflected a general Democratic Party decline. They had overwhelming majorities in Congress in 2009, but after the 2014 election there were fewer Democrats in Congress than since the beginning of the Great Depression. Hillary Clinton did nothing to stop this fall.

When all is said and done, there are multiple reasons why Trump was able to capture 46 percent of those who voted in 2016, and one major reason is that the Democratic Party under Barack Obama failed to fully meet the challenge of the Great Recession. For decades, the Democrats billed themselves as the party of prosperity.

The gaslighter currently occupying the White House gained his office by being more aware of the discontent within the electorate than were the Democrats. His lack of competence, multiple falsehoods, stoking prejudice and violence, dangerous impetuousness and tabloid sensibility did not disqualify him for higher office for many Americans. Trump and many of his supporters share something in common, a deep narcissistic wound that is manifest in resentment, anger, scapegoating and a paranoid style. These traits have recurred in the United States after a major economic downturn or unsettling international developments. They have gained renewed prominence under a Commander-in-Chief with many grievances, a demagogic sensibility, an impulse control problem, and little adherence to constitutional norms.

Acknowledgments

This chapter is based on Fuchsman (2017a; 2017b).

References

Atkinson, R. D., Stewart, L. A., Andes, S. M., & Ezell, S. J. (2012). Worse than the Great Depression: What Experts Are Missing About American Manufacturing Decline. *The Information Technology and Innovation Foundation*. March 2016. Retrieved from www2.itif.org/2012-american-manufacturing-decline.pdf

Belsie, L. (2016). Job Loss in the Great Recession. The National Bureau of Economic Research, December 5, 2016. Retrieved from www.nber.org/digest/sep11/w17040.html

Ben-Shahar, O. (2016). The Non-Voters Who Decided the Election: Trump Won Because of Lower Democratic Turnout. *Forbes*, November 17, 2016. Retrieved from www.forbes.com/sites/omribenshahar/2016/11/17/the-non-voters-who-decided-the-election-trump-won-because-of-lower-democratic-turnout/#749efc7240a1

Bernstein, C. (2007). *A Woman in Charge: The Life of Hillary Rodham Clinton*. New York: Alfred A. Knopf.

Carnegie, A. (2006). *The Gospel of Wealth Essay and Other Writings*. New York: Penguin Classics.

Cashmore, E. (2006). *Celebrity/Culture*. New York: Routledge.

Chantrill, C. (2019). What Is the Deficit? U.S. Government, January 2, 2019. Retrieved from www.usgovernmentdebt.us/federal_deficit

Chiles, R. (2014). These Are the Poorest Cities in America. *Time*, November 14, 2014. Retrieved from http://time.com/3581716/poorest-cities/

Cohen, P. (2016). A Bigger Economic Pie, but a Smaller Slice for Half of the U. S. *New York Times*, December 6, 2016. Retrieved from www.nytimes.com/2016/12/06/business/economy/a-bigger-economic-pie-but-a-smaller-slice-for-half-of-the-us.html?emc=edit_th_20161207&nl=todaysheadlines&nlid=60599755&_r=0

Collins, E. (2016). Les Moonves: Trump's Run Is 'Damn Good for CBS'. *Politico*, February 29, 2016. Retrieved from www.politico.com/blogs/on-media/2016/02/les-moonves-trump-cbs-220001

Dionne Jr., E. J. (2016). *Why the Right Went Wrong: Conservatism—From Goldwater to the Tea Party and Beyond*. New York: Simon & Schuster.

Divine, R., Breen, T. H., Frederickson, G., & Williams, R. H. (1991). *America Past and Present*, 3rd edn. New York: HarperCollins.

Fuchsman, K. (2017a). The Presidential Campaign That Astounded the World: A Psychohistory of Donald Trump and the 2016 American Election. *Journal of Psychohistory*, Vol.4, No. 4, pp. 292–309.

Fuchsman, K. (2017b). The Return of the Ghost of Thomas Dewey in 1948: Hillary Clinton and the 2016 Election. *Journal of Psychohistory*, Vol. 45, No. 1, pp. 23–40.

Gillin, J. (2016). Trump's Claims About Weak Economic Growth Under President Obama Doesn't Tell the Full Story. *Politifact*, October 31, 2016. Retrieved from www.politifact.com/truth-o-meter/statements/2016/oct/31/donald-trump/trumps-claim-about-weak-economic-growth-under-obam/

Hacker, A. (2018). Hopeful Math. *New York Review of Books*, Vol. LXV, No. 14, pp. 71–73.

Hofstadter, R. (1965). *The Paranoid Style in American Politics*. New York: Vintage.

Johnson, R. W. (2016). Trump: Some Numbers. *London Review of Books*, November 14, 2016. Retrieved from www.lrb.co.uk/2016/11/14/rw-johnson/trump-some-numbers?utm_source=LRB+online+email&utm_medium=email&utm_campaign=20161115+online&utm_content=usca_subsnonact

Langham, L. (2002) Suppose They Gave a Culture War and No One Came. *The American Behavioral Scientist*, Vol. 46, No. 4, 501–537.

Lasch, C. (1978). *The Culture of Narcissism: American Life in an Age of Diminishing Expectations*. New York: W. W. Norton & Company.

Library of Congress. (n.d.a). Campaign Finance: United Kingdom. Retrieved from www.loc.gov/law/help/campaign-finance/uk.php

Library of Congress. (n.d.b). Campaign Finance: France. Retrieved from www.loc.gov/law/help/campaign-finance/france.php

Library of Congress. (n.d.c). Campaign Finance: Germany. Retrieved from www.loc.gov/law/help/campaign-finance/germany.php

McCormack, J. (2016). The Election Came Down to 77,744 Votes in Pennsylvania, Wisconsin, and Michigan (Updated). *The Weekly Standard,* November 10, 2016. Retrieved from www.washingtonexaminer.com/weekly-standard/the-election-came-down-to-77-744-votes-in-pennsylvania-wisconsin-and-michigan-updated

Miller, M. (2016). Four Charts Show Media's Love for the Donald—Vs. All Other Candidates Combined. *International Journalism Review*, March. Retrieved from http://ijr.com/2016/03/563541-one-chart-shows-just-how-much-media-attention-trump-gets-vs-other-candidates/

Murdock, D. (2016). Obama's Pretty Words Cannot Beautify His Ugly Economy. *National Review*. May 6, 2016. Retrieved from www.nationalreview.com/article/435093/barack-obama-economy-jobs-ugly-truth

Patterson, T. E. (2017). News Coverage of Donald Trump's First 100 Days. Harvard Kennedy School, Shorenstein Center on Media, Politics and Public Policy, May 18, 2017. Retrieved from https://shorensteincenter.org/news-coverage-donald-trumps-first-100-days/

Pew Research Center. (2015). The American Middle Class Is Losing Ground. Pew Research Center, December 9, 2015. Retrieved from www.pewsocialtrends.org/2015/12/09/the-american-middle-class-is-losing-ground/

Porter, E. (2016). Where Were Trump's Votes? Where the Jobs Weren't. *New York Times,* December 13, 2016. Retrieved from www.nytimes.com/2016/12/13/business/economy/jobs-economy-voters.html

Roper Center. (n.d.). Popular Votes 1940–2016. Retrieved from https://ropercenter.cornell.edu/presidential-elections/popular-votes

Tomasky, M. (2016). Can He Be Stopped? *New York Review of Books*, April 21, 2016. Retrieved from www.nybooks.com/articles/2016/04/21/can-donald-trump-be-stopped/

United States Census Bureau. (2010). Women in the Workforce. Retrieved from www.census.gov/newsroom/pdf/women_workforce_slides.pdf

Wallace-Wells, B. (2016). How Donald Trump Could Disappear from the Political Scene. *The New Yorker*, September 30, 2016. Retrieved from www.newyorker.com/news/benjamin-wallace-wells/how-donald-trump-could-disappear-from-the-political-scene?mbid=nl_161001_Daily&CNDID=29692319&spMailingID=9614290&spUserID=MTMzMTgzMDMxNjUwS0&spJobID=1020061044&spReportId=MTAyMDA2MTA0NAS2

Wething, H. (2014). Job Growth in the Great Recession Has Not Been Equal Between Men and Women. Economic Policy Institute, August 26, 2014. Retrieved from www.epi.org/blog/job-growth-great-recession-equal-men-women/

Chapter 11

A sociologist's view of the Trump phenomenon

Charles Heckscher

The Trump phenomenon is one of a set of movements throughout the advanced industrial world aiming to disrupt politics as usual. Like the others, it is not well explained by economic or political analysis. It is not a movement of the poor (or the rich), and it is not driven by existing parties: it crosses economic lines and scrambles the political landscape, and traditional parties are struggling to adapt to it. It is better explained by the sociologist's focus on *community*. The roots of the phenomenon lie in widespread disruptions of identities, relations, and ways of life over long periods. There is good reason why so many feel that they are engaging in a "culture war."

From the sociological perspective, the Trump phenomenon is not a fluke or an isolated event: it arises from long-running and widespread forces that have spawned similar conservative or populist movements in other nations. Yet at the same time a strong counter-tendency is developing: new "progressive" institutions of civil society are also growing at a rapid pace—different from traditional associations, more open and fluid, often making use of new media of communications, often stressing social justice and inclusion.

These two kinds of movement represent contrary reactions to the social strains of the past 50 years. This has been a period of enormous opening up and expanded cultural exchange: the dismantling of the Iron Curtain, the globalization of commerce, the rapid spread of the internet and social media, the change in attitudes toward other races, genders, and sexual preferences. These developments have been extremely disruptive to established traditions. Many feel that their expectations of life have been tossed out. They have no confidence in what their careers might be, whether their community will be stable, or even how they should act toward their spouses and workmates. Some have responded by charging ahead: embracing the changes, seeking wider inclusion. Others have responded by pulling back to established values and ways of life, and erecting walls to protect against those outside their traditions. For the former, things are moving too slowly; for the latter, which form the committed core of the Trump support, things are moving too fast and threaten to destroy order and meaning.

This chapter will explore these orientations, and also the possibilities for bridging the divide and reconstructing a healthy civil society.

Conservatives and populists

At one level, Donald Trump is just a normal conservative: many of his supporters just feel that change should proceed with caution, and that more responsibility should be exercised by localities and individuals than by the federal government. If this was all, he would not be a "phenomenon": he would represent only another moment in the long oscillation of the past two centuries between the liberal impulse to hasten social change and the conservative impulse to slow it down. Both have given rise to philosophically deep and elaborated views of society—including, for instance, Burke and Tocqueville on the conservative side, Rousseau and Mill on the liberal. In periods of relative social calm, they can work together in a productive interaction, with conservatives restraining liberal haste and ideological oversimplifications, and liberals nudging conservatives—often through governmental action—out of entrenched patterns of injustice and stagnation.

Where Trump is distinctive, and different from his Republican predecessors such as the Bushes and even Ronald Reagan, is that he *also* activates a populist impulse that has been on the rise after half a century of dormancy. This is a disruptive passion that drives the most intense believers in Trumpism as a movement.

Populism in its essence is a reaction against cultural and political elites. It has appeared in various guises in the past two centuries. Currently it is mostly allied with conservatism, but it is in essence neither conservative nor liberal. It is conservative in seeking to defend an existing culture against forces of change; but it also has a radical aspect because it strikes back against dominant forces. It is often hostile and angry. While the conservative instinct is to advance slowly and carefully, the populist instinct is to tear down. Populists rally to Trump because he seeks to *destroy* the institutions that represent the new economy and the technocratic elites undermining their way of life. Populism is also anti-intellectual and anti-science, because the intellectuals are the core of the elites whose progressive tendencies threaten existing ways of life.

Populism primarily represents those who feel left out—those who have been solidly self-confident members of society in the past but are now out of the mainstream of cultural and economic change; who have done well but feel that they are losing their place (Mutz, 2018). Its focus is on preserving a valued way of life against an onslaught of outside forces. A 2016 book on the Tea Party is entitled *Strangers in Their Own Land* (Hochschild, 2016); the same phrase is used by a historian to describe the 1890s populists, adding a description that could apply equally to both movements:

> people bewildered by the complexities of the world around them … Populists saw themselves as cruelly hoodwinked for years, until the third party had opened their eyes. A greedy plutocracy controlled the government and

economy ..., and the money kings remained secure in their high places through their success in duping the citizenry.

(Turner, 1980, 369)

The social historian Richard Hofstadter (1964, 23) traces a series of similar movements that have seen the elites as engaged in a vast conspiracy to undermine their way of life—going back to anti-Masonic movements of the 1820s, anti-Catholics of the 1830s, and more recently in the McCarthy movement of the 1950s. He describes populists as

[feeling] dispossessed: America has been largely taken away from them and their kind, though they are determined to try to repossess it and to prevent the final destructive act of subversion. The old American virtues have already been eaten away by cosmopolitans and intellectuals.

(Bell, [1963] 2017, 1–38)

This is an almost perfect description of the feelings of Trump's populist base today.

Many people supported Obama in 2008, and Bernie Sanders in 2016, out of the same deep and diffuse desire for change. But Obama turned out to be a system-repairer rather than a system-destroyer, which was a deep disappointment, even to many of his supporters. The fact that Trump is (despite his wealth) so manifestly not a member in good standing of the elite—that the elite so constantly and vocally express their horror and rejection of what he stands for is—in the eyes of populists—proof that he is on the right track. He promises to dismantle the system—and he is delivering on that promise more than anyone expected.

Populism is not a movement of the *poor* because the truly down-and-out generally do not seek to preserve their way of life. It is a movement of those who have loved their lives and feel that slipping away. It maps more accurately onto the urban-rural split, because rural areas have always felt strongly loyal to their communities, while cities have always been the drivers of change. Today it also maps onto educational level. Trump "sorted" the electorate more powerfully by education than by income—primarily because many working-class voters with high school educations shifted in a populist direction.

Many classic conservatives have lamented that Trump is not really of their number. He has abandoned a number of the core tenets of "regular" conservatives, such as free trade. They want to reverse a good deal of the recent rapid spread of liberal legislation, but they wish Trump wasn't such a crudely destructive force. But so far they have found it on balance better to stick with him than to abandon him, which is crucial to his success.

Europe has also experienced a fierce populist wave (Lewis et al., 2018). The triggering issue has typically been immigration. But that fails to explain much: populism has gained strength since about 2012 as the actual incidence of immigration has sharply declined. It has become clearer that, as in the U.S., the underlying impulse is much more profound: it is about retreating and putting up walls against outside forces in general; not just against immigrants but also against global businesses, international governance mechanisms like the EU, and extensions of multiculturalism. Everywhere the desire to retreat to narrower, more homogeneous, and simpler communities has gained strength.

Characteristic features of populist movements throughout the advanced industrial nations include:

- a focus on strengthening community borders, both real and symbolic;
- a reassertion of traditional loyalties based on shared histories and cultures;
- a turn away from globalism and multiculturalism, both of which threaten the unity of these traditional commitments;
- opposition to bureaucratic state systems staffed by social elites, and to the social welfare and regulation policies that have been central to the growing reach of state programs;
- attacks on expertise and knowledge elites as out of touch;
- the emergence of new parties or the substantial transformation of existing parties.

Why now? The collapse of confidence in the postwar framework

Though there is no clear breakpoint, the trajectory that leads to Trump can usefully be traced to the convulsions of the 1960s.

For three decades after World War II, there was throughout the industrial world an extraordinary efflorescence of economic and cultural growth. The French call it *les trente glorieuses,* the glorious thirty (years). All through Europe as well as North America, and even in the defeated nations of Germany and Japan, there was a similar wave of prosperity and optimism.

All these nations had a common framework for success: economies built on corporate capitalism, with labor unions acting as an effective voice for workers, and activist governments providing social welfare programs and shaping the economy according to Keynesian economic theories. These essential similarities extended across the many varieties of the industrial democracies and across the political spectrum. They also helped to support a growing set of international institutions like the World Court and the European Union.

It was a period in which people had high confidence in large organizations and their leaders, and in experts with special knowledge to manage the big systems around them. A well-known study of the small dairy town of "Springdale" in the early 1950s sounds almost impossibly quaint today:

A sociologist's view of Trump   129

> Springdalers have a decided respect for the great institutions that characterize American society. The efficiency, organizational ability and far-flung activities of giant government and business enterprise inspire them with awe. The military might of the nation and the productive capacity of industry lend a Springdaler a sense of pride and security, and the continuous development and successful application of science assure him that he is a participant in the most forward-looking and progressive country in the world.
>
> (Vidich & Bensman [1957] 1968, 79)

I will use the term "postwar framework" for this dominant paradigm of the industrial democracies from the 1940s to the 1980s, with emphases on large organizations as managers of the system—especially corporate capitalism and the welfare state. In much of Europe it was called "social democracy," though many nations like the U.K., the U.S., and Spain, not usually considered social-democratic, shared its core features.[1]

Conservatives throughout this period were supportive of the broad outlines of this postwar framework. Richard Nixon famously declared (following the conservative economist Milton Friedman) that, "We are all Keynesians now" (Friedman, 1965). Nixon sought to extend the welfare state through a comprehensive healthcare proposal and an activist economic policy; and he intervened strongly in the economy with a freeze on wages and prices to counter inflation. He also helped to build institutions of global cooperation, most notably with his opening to China. The postwar order seemed untouchable.

But the 1960s were a turning point. Throughout the advanced economies 1968 was a year of huge popular uprisings against the established institutions and elites. In the U.S., which has the most complete polling record in that period, there is evidence, over a period of a few years, of a truly extraordinary collapse of popular trust in the anchoring institutions of the postwar framework: large corporations, unions, and government. In the early 1960s, over 80 percent of Americans felt that this constellation could be trusted to govern the country; within less than a decade, that had been cut in half, and it has never recovered. For example, Figure 11.1 is based on data from the Harris Poll of May 21, 2012 (The Harris Poll, 2012). The left axis is an index set to 100 for the 1960s. So Figure 11.1 indicates that the mean for the 1970s was about half that for the 1960s. The best evidence, though not directly comparable, suggests a further significant drop after 2010.

One can quibble about particular methods and wording of survey items, but the essential pattern repeats itself in many polls and other types of data.

This is a social catastrophe. Complex societies require high levels of trust: they work only when the large majority of citizens basically agree both on the goodwill of the population as a whole and on the legitimacy of the institutions that govern them (Heckscher, 2015, Chapter 1). When that is eroded,

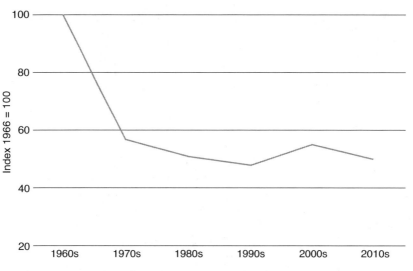

Figure 11.1 Confidence in leaders of institutions: average per decade.

The Harris Poll. (5/21/2012). Confidence in Congress Stays at Lowest Point in Almost Fifty Years. Retrieved from https://www.prnewswire.com/news-releases/confidence-in-congress-stays-at-lowest-point-in-almost-fifty-years-152253655.html

people withdraw into safer, more homogeneous islands of trust where they feel some level of control. So it is not surprising that political polarization has also increased since the 1970s, and has reached unprecedented levels in the past decade—once again, not just in the U.S. but across the advanced industrial world (Campbell, 2016).

Though there had always been a conservative critique of the welfare state, it remained marginal until the 1960s. The wider loss of faith in the postwar regime, and particularly in government, began initially among young liberals: they were the first to express their disenchantment with "the system." The movements of the late 1960s across Europe and the U.S. began as complex stews of issues, including class conflict and cultural issues of race and gender, energized by artistic and musical upheavals; but they all came to focus on government as the main obstacle to change. In the U.S., Johnson and McNamara became symbols of an old order; in France it was de Gaulle, baffled by the events and leaving the country during the May riots. In both cases the movements centered in the young and educated, who replaced the faith in the liberal welfare state with a rise of expressivist values (Dalton, 2005).

Confidence in institutions stabilized at the new, lower level during the 1980s and 1990s. Then, starting around 2000, there was another decline—this time led by the older and less-educated, especially in rural areas.[2] This second

A sociologist's view of Trump 131

decline catalyzed a populist reaction, beginning with the rise of the Tea Party. The Trump "phenomenon" emerges from this toxic spiral of mistrust.

Why?

The decline in confidence is not closely correlated with economic or political crises. The latest steep drop—since about 2010—has happened during a long period of steady growth in production and jobs. Some have suggested that the problem is the rise in inequality since the mid-1970s; but the first sharp drop in trust occurred earlier, at a point of historically high economic equity. A similar decline in confidence, moreover, is seen across Europe from the 1960s to the 1980s, though inequality has generally remained lower than in the U.S. (Pharr, Putnam, & Dalton, 2000; Korpi & Palme, 2003; Dalton, 2005) While scholars in each nation tend to blame their own particular circumstances—bad leadership at some point, a particular symbolic break—these come nowhere near explaining the scope and length of the phenomenon.[3]

No explanation that focuses on particular nations or particular events will hold. The underlying trend that makes sense of the decline in trust in the past half-century is that the world for ordinary people has grown more complex and insecure, causing a widespread feeling of anxiety across most sectors of society. The Springdalers quoted above would certainly not be speaking now with the same pride in their great institutions: in equivalent studies of recent years, residents of small towns and rural areas speak primarily with anger and often with despair about the decline of their way of life, the spiral of poverty, increasing drug use, and the arrogance of the elites (Hochschild, 2016; Vance, 2016). Twenge's extensive studies have documented a sharp rise in anxiety, and sense of loss of control, since the 1950s (Twenge, 2000; Twenge, Zhang, & Im, 2004). This is felt especially keenly among middle-aged white males: Princeton researchers were shocked to find a sharp increase in mortality among that group between 1999 and 2013—mainly from alcohol poisoning and suicide (Case & Deaton, 2015).

The rural Springdalers of the 1950s were just beginning to become aware of the larger world of powerful institutions, but still felt they could remain separate and self-determining. In the intervening decades that faith has broken down. Before World War II the vast majority of people stayed within narrow social circles for their lifetimes, rarely if ever venturing beyond their towns and hearing the news of foreign lands only as a distant echo. Today they have in their faces every day, on TV and social media, a world of strangeness and horror: fearful battles, terrorists slaughtering innocents, enormous cities in foreign lands humming with activity, terrifying natural disasters, wrenching images of poverty. During this same period, other bases of security have been whittled away. Large corporations that used to provide stable employment and benefits for a large segment of the population have abandoned those commitments.

As government was the focal point of the system in the 1950s, it became the focal point of disillusionment with the system in the subsequent period.

The reach of government, and its expenditures, have grown enormously without creating a corresponding sense of confidence. It clearly feels to most people that the future is out of control, and that government is not helping. The systems that undergirded a feeling of optimism and energy in the 1950s have lost their magic.

Perceptive scholars began focusing on this quite early. In 1975, the Trilateral Commission issued a report entitled *The Crisis of Democracy: Report on the Governability of Democracies* (Crozier, Huntington, & Watanuki, 1975), arguing that the multiplication of stakeholder demands was creating too much complexity for current institutions to handle. That same year the German sociologist Jürgen Habermas published *Legitimation Crisis,* arguing that the political system had become unable to produce meaning; "alienation" became a widespread meme (Habermas, 1975; later echoed by Pharr & Putnam, 2000).

What we are experiencing, then, is not a peculiar throw of the electoral dice, but the deep ills of advanced industrial democracy. The legitimacy of the postwar order that once integrated virtually all the advanced industrial economies is now severely weakened.

The pace of effects on political parties and events has varied: in the U.K., the Thatcher turn happened simultaneously with the Reagan turn in America; in northern Europe, where social-democratic parties were far more dominant, the decline was later and slower. By now, however, even Sweden and Denmark, the purest examples of the postwar liberal order, face strong populist reactions, and the long-standing party systems are fragmenting. Trust in parliaments is nearly as low as Americans' confidence in Congress.

What Trump's populist supporters like is not particular policies—indeed, his policies are not at all clear, since he changes tack and contradicts himself frequently. What they like is that he represents something *different* from the corrupt and failing system of the past. Some of them also liked Bernie Sanders for the same reason. As a young lawyer—a lifelong Democrat who swung to Trump in 2016—said to me, "It suddenly hit me: why would I support anyone who has had anything to do with the last thirty years?"

Populism remains a minority movement, rarely reaching as much as a third of the population in any of the industrial democracies, including the U.S.[4] It has had a disproportionately powerful impact because of this wider loss of faith in the postwar framework. The defenders of the existing order are not nearly as dedicated as its opponents: all the old parties are riven with doubts and criticisms, deeply worried about everything from climate change to genetic engineering to racial justice, uncertain and often divided on how to proceed. They tend to share with the populists a skepticism about government's capacity to deal with the complexities.

The progressive phenomenon

Populism cannot be understood, however, without attention to counter-vailing progressive movements. Populism is a reaction to anxiety that seeks to overthrow the leadership of the postwar elites, to close down the incursion of outside forces, and to return to successful models from the past. On the other side is a movement, primarily driven by the educated elites themselves, to broaden and reach out—to transform society by upending social hierarchies and aggressively pursuing equality of status among all social groups. I will refer to this as "progressivism," since that is a widely understood term today, and helps to keep it distinct from the "liberal" postwar consensus already described.[5]

Unlike postwar liberalism, progressivism is critical, or only weakly supportive, of the welfare state and unions. Its focus is on cultural inclusion—especially of identity groups of race, gender, and religion—in sharp contrast to the populist focus on cultural protection. Trump's "wall" is a perfect symbol for this difference. Progressivism builds on what sociologists have called the "expressive revolution" starting in the 1950s, with values including demands for participation, self-fulfillment, embrace of gender and racial diversity, environmental consciousness, and a shift in child-rearing focus from hard work to imagination.[6] It has increasingly colored the so-called identity movements. These started as demands for equal rights, but have gradually shifted toward demands for recognition and inclusion. It is no longer seen as enough for blacks, women, and others, merely to have the same rights as white men; the expectation is that white men will move out of the evaluative center, and that norms will be set in part by the new groups.

Progressivism continues to be driven, as it has since the 1960s, by the young and the educated. Yet those toward the left of the political spectrum, feeling gloomy about Trump, tend to underestimate the impact of these progressive and expressive values on the population more widely. The data show massive transformations since the 1960s in cultural norms around race, gender, family, religion, and other pillars of communal values. Few periods in human history have approached it for speed and scope of cultural shift. To pick a few indicative facts:

- Between 1958 and 1999, the percentage who said they could vote for "a generally well-qualified man for president who happened to be Black" went from 38 percent to 95 percent. In the South, it went from 13 percent to the same 95 percent. Over the same period, the percentage who said they could vote for a woman went from 57 percentage to 92 percentage.[7]
- In 1967, 95 percentage of law school students were male; in 2011, the gender balance was nearly equal (American Bar Association and Others, 2007).

- Since 1950 the percentage of African-Americans who have completed high school has more than tripled (20 percent to more than 60 percent) and the percentage completing college has increased ninefold (from 2 percent to 18 percent) (National Center for Education Statistics, 1993, Table 4).
- Families grew smaller and more intimate: those who believed the "ideal number of children" was three or more dropped, within a few years in the late 1960s, from 70 percent to 43 percent (Newport, Moore, & Saad, 1999). A transformation of childrearing practices was catalyzed by Dr. Spock and thousands of his successors, encouraging creativity and freedom rather than obedience to authority.
- There was a large decline in church attendance—probably by around one-half, though people tend not to admit this to pollsters.[8] Churches have certainly been feeling beleaguered. The six largest Protestant denominations together lost as much as a third of their membership between 1965 and 1990 (Marty, 1970). Moreover, as Tanya Luhrmann has noted, the character of the remaining religious faith has changed greatly, shifting towards expressivist values: "When God is your therapist," as she puts it (Luhrmann, 2012; 2013). Traditional "fire and brimstone" fundamentalism has retreated to small corners of the society.

In my own surveys in recent years, I have found an unexpectedly solid consensus in favor of a strong notion of multiculturalism. I tested support for two conceptions of diversity. The "melting pot" view, which has a long tradition in the U.S., welcomes new cultural groups only if they assimilate to the dominant American norms. In contrast, the newer and more demanding multicultural conception suggests that other cultures should be recognized and valued for themselves, and that the dominant norms should *change* to be more inclusive. My "multicultural" questions included: "People from other places and cultures help us to grow, we should learn from them," and "People should be encouraged to celebrate their cultural, ethnic, religious, and linguistic differences." I thought these were rather aggressively progressive statements and expected relatively low support for them; but in fact about three-fourths of the population was positive, with Republicans nearly as high as Democrats.[9] These and similar items were far more consensual than more classically conservative or liberal items; items like "Government should ensure that everyone is provided for" or "Government welfare programs undermine personal responsibility."

The basic multicultural sensibility, in other words, is now widely accepted as normatively valid. What's more, the trend of change has continued right through periods of apparent conservative ascendance. The movement for gay marriage took off during George Bush's (conservative) presidency: support doubled (from 31 percent to 62 percent) between 2004 and 2017, leading to a wave of legislative and judicial successes. And even in the first years of the Trump administration, the #MeToo movement brought about important changes in gender norms. Through all the sound and fury, a new consensus is developing: around two-thirds of the country as of 2018 sees sexual harassment as a very serious problem—including half of Republicans—which is twice the level of ten years earlier (Agiesta & Sparks, 2018).[10]

Progressives lament the distance still to be traveled and the gaps remaining, but the magnitude of these changes has been extraordinary. Among Republicans, though the level of support is typically lower than average, the direction of movement is similar and the slope is sometimes steeper. On gay marriage, for example, Republican support increased from 15 percent to 41 percent from 2004 to 2017.

Movements like gay marriage and #MeToo have proceeded so rapidly because this ground has been prepared. There is absolutely no indication of reversal since Trump's election, in my own polls or others, using many different kinds of indicators. Though overt racists and intransigent evangelicals appear to have more political influence than before, there is no evidence that their numbers in the society at large have grown beyond small minorities.

Though progressives have often been leery of politics, they have been growing more active. They are now a major force in the Democratic Party in the U.S., which after all was in power before Trump, and in the 2018 midterm elections they generated enthusiasm and increases in turnout to counter the energy of the populists.

Polarization

Polarization from 2000 to the Trump era has coalesced around the cultural divide between progressivism and populism—between expressivist values, with an emphasis on inclusion and multiculturalism, and more traditional religious and nationalist faiths. This gap reflects the demographic variables of education, age, population density, and economic sector (populists are generally less educated, older, from rural areas or small towns, and from manufacturing or extractive industries). They also map onto the broad progressive movement starting in the 1960s, and the populist reaction starting around 2000.

These are quite different from the orientations of conservatism and liberalism that defined politics in the earlier postwar era. Working classes and the less educated have moved toward populism; educated elites have moved toward progressivism. Political parties across the West have painfully re-sorted themselves to accommodate these energized viewpoints. In the U.S., the Republicans have moved toward Trumpian populism, while the Democrats have increasingly embraced progressive multiculturalism.

Yet when one looks more deeply into the beliefs of the population at large, the picture is much blurrier. Researchers are confronted by a paradox: polarization has evidently increased since the 1970s, but the views of *individuals* remain inconsistent. In fact, for all the fervor of the marches and rallies shown in the news, most people do not hold uniformly Red or Blue views on issues.

136 Charles Heckscher

According to a 2018 study, less than a third of the country has adopted one of the consistent ideological poles. The rest are mixed, and often ambivalent, confused, and discouraged. They constitute an "exhausted majority," containing

> distinct groups of people with varying degrees of political understanding and activism. But they share a sense of fatigue with our polarized national conversation, a willingness to be flexible in their political viewpoints, and a lack of voice in the national conversation.
>
> (Hawkins et al., 2018, 11)

This exhausted majority is pulled in several directions. Though the postwar framework is no longer consensual and has few ardent supporters, most still feel some attraction to the welfare state and corporate capitalism, with their promise of both growth and security. But *at the same time*, they often agree with populist criticisms of political leaders and elites; and *at the same time* they agree with progressive values of self-expression and diversity.

Earlier I cited the surprisingly strong evidence that multicultural views characteristic of progressivism had become near-consensual. Trump certainly does not represent that view, yet he has succeeded because he *does* represent unusually well another equally consensual feeling: the mistrust of the leaders of our major institutions, especially the government. In 1964, less than 30 percent of Americans felt that government was run by a few big interests; in 2016, it was over *90 percent*.[11] It is one of the most bipartisan results to be found in the survey world: *everyone* feels that government has lost touch with the people. Virtually *no one*, left or right, now feels that "the system" is working.

Trump draws heavily on that feeling. He is the true political outsider, the anti-system. He generates an intense visceral support from the roughly 30 percent of the population, those who strongly reject the postwar regime and its elites. But he also receives a more partial and conflicted support from the very large segment whose faith in those institutions is weak, though they may oppose many other aspects of his persona.

Aside from a small set of ideological purists on each side, the best description of most of us is that we are confused. We agree overwhelmingly that progressives have a point: we should welcome diversity—and also that populists have a point: we need to get rid of the current leadership elites. This leaves most people struggling to reconcile inconsistencies. The few who take just one of the poles disproportionately drive politics by their certainty.

Bridging the divide

In addition to the two broad agreements I have cited—support for multiculturalism and hostility to governing elites—there is one more: a general wish that the polarization would end. Over three-quarters are bothered by "politics being too divisive and there being a lack of respect for people who disagree with each other" and believe that "it is important to try to understand people we don't agree with."[12]

The foregoing analysis suggests that the problem has deep roots, growing for more than half a century, and branches spreading throughout the Western democracies. It does not point to a particular culprit that can easily be tackled. Rather, it points to a breakdown in the relation of people to government, which can be repaired—if at all—only through a long, sustained, and multipronged effort.

Society will not heal without improved relations across civil society. We need to manage high diversity while simultaneously maintaining the trust necessary to deal with complex issues. As we have seen over the last few decades, this cannot be accomplished through electoral battles. Pursuit of merely *political* solutions—trying to win majorities and offices in the voting process—does nothing to address the gaps. If the Democrats win, the Republican activists will only get angrier, and vice versa. The underlying dynamics sketched above will only continue to worsen.

Despite appearances, the problem is not primarily disagreement about particular issues. There are of course many differences, but even on the most politically polarized issues, there is much mixing and overlap in the public at large. On guns, for example, large majorities of Republicans as well as Democrats agree on the need for background checks at gun shows and private sales; and smaller majorities of Republicans join the overwhelming majority of Democrats on banning high-capacity magazines (Pew Research Center, 2018). Those policies would make a significant difference, but we can't get there because we don't trust each other. When it gets turned into *politics*, people have to pick a side—and they pick the side they trust more. The gun owners feel Democrats don't understand them or know anything about guns—so they take the NRA's word over the Democrats' experts. Democrats on the whole know very little about guns—fewer than 20 percent own one; they hate the NRA, though, so they know what to oppose.

Climate change is similar. Only 12 percent maintain that there's no problem: almost two-thirds believe some action should be taken on it, and another quarter say they don't know enough.[13] There is very wide support across the spectrum for encouragement of renewable energy, and majority support among Republicans as well as Democrats for greenhouse gas regulation and fuel-efficiency standards for cars (Mayer, Adair, & Pfaff, 2013). But again, we can't get there because of the gulf in relations: Republicans, especially rural voters, feel that proposals coming from Democrats necessarily fail to understand their concerns and so can't be trusted, and everyone fears that government involvement would be misdirected.

An age of high diversity and interdependence creates new challenges for trust. We can't rely, as we have for most of human history, on assumptions of shared traditions and culture. We have to build trust deliberately through some form of public conversation—by *talking through* differences and building relationships.

But is this practical?

Many are trying. The Bridge Alliance lists, as of mid-2019, 27 member organizations with a specific mission of bridging the political divide, most national in scope (The Bridge Alliance, 2019). For example, Better Angels conducts workshops—spreading quite rapidly across the country—in which equal numbers of "Reds" and "Blues" exchange views with each other and probe for deeper understanding of how they view the world. Living Room Conversations, the Village Square, and the National Institute for Civil Discourse, and many others have demonstrated activity and effectiveness. As far as I can tell, this spread of deliberate bridging is virtually unprecedented: it was virtually unheard of through most of human history, and the practice has accelerated only in the past decade.

On the other hand, these efforts are also, for now, very fragile and uncertain. While they often succeed in building some sense of connection among participants within the dialogue, they don't have effective strategies for building from there. They have certainly not made much of a dent on the overall political climate. And they are all very incomplete, each making use of only pieces of the available knowledge about how to build bridging conversations.

There is now a very large academic literature on public dialogue, ranging from deep philosophical works to experimental social psychology and historical cases. There is also a set of practices and techniques that have largely been invented in the past 50 years.[14] Techniques of process management, scenario-building, active listening, peer feedback, perspective-taking, reframing, and many others have been developed only since the 1960s, and have spread widely through corporations and other organizations. Some have penetrated civil society through best-selling self-help books and "Anonymous" groups. There is already a record of many community dialogues that have used these techniques.

Distilling from that enormous array, three key types of discussion must be combined to build a sense of trust and open exchange across wide differences in views. For each of these, a large set of techniques and tools is already available to facilitate discussion:

- *Understanding*: placing oneself in others' shoes, expressing one's views in a way that they can identify with—without denying the differences. It includes both emotion and rationality. Such dialogues explore where people are "coming from": their valued traditions and experiences. They do not seek *agreement*: one can continue to disagree with others yet increase one's understanding of their perspective.
- *Visioning*: building a shared image of a desirable future—where we're "going to"—in which all participants can see themselves. Whereas understanding preserves differences, visioning is unifying: ideally,

everyone should be committed to common purposes, while maintaining distinct identities.

- *Collaborating*: working together to solve problems, moving toward a shared purpose. This is where talk turns to action: it often helps move a conversation beyond platitudes. It does not need to be long-term or grandiose. The Anglican term "walking together" is appropriate: participants can take a step or two in the same direction, without committing to a long journey.

My suggestion is that over time, a network of civil society organizations with membership across the political spectrum could be developed to improve citizen capacity in these three areas. Groups like Better Angels and others have already established the foundations. They have started with a focus on improved understanding; in time they could engage in collaborative search for agreements on public policy at local and even national levels. Broad-based citizen groups could develop legislative proposals with general support; they might displace special interests, single-interest groups, and professionalized associations that push their narrow views onto an overwhelmed legislature. In the long run, this could connect civil society and government in a new way: not just through parties and votes, but through continuous exchanges that would engage citizens much more widely than at present.

This suggestion has some affinity with notions of "deliberative democracy".[15] But unlike many of those, it is not a very optimistic view for the short to medium run. We know that broad-based community deliberation *can* sometimes work—there has already been enough success for that; but we also know that it is difficult and time-consuming and often fails.[16] It seems unlikely that it can spread quickly to a larger scale.

A story (surely apocryphal) tells of Voltaire in his old age seeking to plant an *allée* of oak trees in front of his house. Informed they would take a century to achieve the height he wanted, he replied: "Then we'd better start immediately!"

The coming decades are likely to continue to be full of strife and anger. But through continued efforts to talk across the divide and to build understandings, civil society groups incorporating wide diversities of views could in time become a regular part of the political process. For all the difficulties, this seems the only path to repairing civil society and restoring its support for government.

Notes

1 Many political scientists call it "the liberal order"; but in the present polarized environment that term has been distorted and freighted with ideological stereotypes.
2 The decline since 2000 is clearly evident in these U.S. data; I have not seen good data for Europe. The association with this decline with age and lower education is somewhat indirect: I have not seen evidence testing these correlations at individual

levels, but there is evidence simultaneously of sharp decline in confidence and of disenchantment among the older and less-educated (e.g., Foster & Frieden, 2017), who have become the core of populist movements.

3 For a good overview, see Hobsbawm (1996).

4 For Europe, see (Gramlich, & Simmons, 2018). For the U.S: Support for the Tea Party was 27 percent at its height (Zeleny & Thee-brenan, 2011). Strong support for Trump is 31 percent in late 2018 (NBC News Exit Poll Desk, 2018; Quinnipiac University, 2018).

5 This progressivism is, however, quite different from that of the early twentieth century.

6 The "expressive revolution" at this time was sketched at a theoretical level by Parsons (1974; 2007, p. 453), and empirically by Inglehart (2008) and others.

7 (Newport et al., 1999; Gallup, 2016) The race question in 1958 said "Negro" rather than "Black."

8 Newport et al. (1999) report a drop from 50 percent weekly church attendance to 40 percent in the 1970s. The evidence that the drop is much greater—to perhaps 20 percent today—is developed by Hadaway et al. (1993; 1998).

9 There was some difference in *strength* of support, with 70 percent of Democrats strongly supportive versus 50–60 percent of Republicans.

10 I also conducted a repeat survey in 2018 which showed little change on the multiculturalism items.

11 Through 2012 these surveys were administered by the American National Elections Survey. The 2016 iteration asked the same question but was administered by a different group (Kull, 2016). The last ANES data point was in 2012—over 75 percent.

12 Data from my own national surveys in 2014 and 2018.

13 NBC News survey, September 14–18, 2017.

14 Google ngram of references to "public dialogue" in books takes off from near-zero in the late 1950s, see http://bit.ly/2E5tPM9

15 See, for instance, Elster (1998) and Mansbridge et al. (2012)

16 This statement is pieced together from many partial assessments and experiences. See, e.g., Helling and Thomas (2002); Heckscher et al. (2003).

References

Agiesta, J. & Sparks, G. (2018). CNN Poll: Two-Thirds Call Sexual Harassment a Serious Problem in the US Today. *CNN*, October 11, 2018. Retrieved from www.cnn.com/2018/10/11/politics/sexual-harassment-poll/index.html

American Bar Association, and Others. (2007). First Year and Total JD Enrollment by Gender 1947–2005. For the Past 20: 1971–2005. Retrieved from www.americanbar.org

Bell, D. ([1963] 2017). *The Radical Right*, 3rd edn. New York: Routledge.

The Bridge Alliance. (2019). Our Members: Bridging Ideological Divides. Retrieved from www.bridgealliance.us/our_members_bridging_ideological_divides

Campbell, J. E. (2016). *Polarized: Making Sense of a Divided America*. Princeton, NJ: Princeton University Press.

Case, A. & Deaton, A. (2015). Rising Morbidity and Mortality in Midlife among White Non-Hispanic Americans in the 21st Century. *Proceedings of the National Academy of Sciences of the U.S.A.*, Vol. 112, No. 49, pp. 15078–15083.

Crozier, M., Huntington, S. P., & Watanuki, J. (1975). *The Crisis of Democracy: Report on the Governability of Democracies to the Trilateral Commission*. New York: New York University Press.

Dalton, R. J. (2005). The Social Transformation of Trust in Government. *International Review of Sociology: Revue Internationale de Sociologie,* Vol. 15, No. 1, p. 133.

Elster, J. (1998). *Deliberative Democracy.* Cambridge: Cambridge University Press.

Foster, C. & Frieden, J. (2017). Crisis of Trust: Socio-Economic Determinants of Europeans' Confidence in Government. *European Union Politics,* Vol. 18, No. 4, pp. 511–535.

Friedman, M. (1965). We Are All Keynesians Now. *Time,* December 31, 1965.

Gallup. (2016). Dataset: "Gallup 'Black President' Question." Retrieved from www.justfacts.com/reference/gallup_black_president_question.xls

Gramlich, J. & Simmons, K. (2018). Western European Populism and the Political Landscape: 5 Takeaways. Pew Research Center. Retrieved from www.pewresearch.org/fact-tank/2018/07/12/5-key-takeaways-about-populism-and-the-political-landscape-in-western-europe/

Habermas, J. (1975). *Legitimation Crisis.* Boston: Beacon Press.

Hadaway, C. K., Marler, P. L., & Chaves, M. (1993). What the Polls Don't Show: A Closer Look at US Church Attendance. *American Sociological Review,* Vol. 58, No. 6, pp. 741–752.

Hadaway, C. K., Marler, P. L., & Chaves, M. (1998). Overreporting Church Attendance in America: Evidence That Demands the Same Verdict. *American Sociological Review,* Vol. 63, No. 1, pp. 122–130.

Hawkins, S., Yudkin, D., Juan-Torres, M., & Dixon, T. (2018). Hidden Tribes: A Study of America's Polarized Landscape. More in Common. Retrieved from https://doi.org/10.31234/osf.io/xz25v

Heckscher, C. (2015). *Trust in a Complex World: Enriching Community.* Oxford: Oxford University Press.

Heckscher, C., Maccoby, M., Ramirez, R., & Tixier, P.-E. (2003). *Agents of Change: Crossing the Post-Industrial Divide.* Oxford: Oxford University Press.

Helling, A. & Thomas, C. (2002). Community Dialogue. In N. Roberts (Ed.), *The Transformative Power of Dialogue,* Research in Public Policy Analysis and Management 12. Bingham: Emerald Group Publishing Limited, pp. 135–155.

Hobsbawm, E. (1996). *The Age of Extremes: A History of the World, 1914–1991.* New York: Vintage.

Hochschild, A. R. (2016). *Strangers in Their Own Land: Anger and Mourning on the American Right.* New York: The New Press.

Hofstadter, R. (1964). The Paranoid Style in American Politics. *Harper's Magazine,* November, pp. 77–86.

Inglehart, R. F. (2008). Changing Values among Western Publics from 1970 to 2006. *WestEuropean Politics,* Vol. 31, No. 1–2, pp. 130–146.

Korpi, W. & Palme , J. (2003). New Politics and Class Politics in the Context of Austerity and Globalization: Welfare State Regress in 18 Countries, 1975–95. *The American Political Science Review,* Vol. 97, No. 3, pp. 425–446.

Kull , S. (2016). Voter Anger with Government and the 2016 Election. Program for Public Consultation, School of Public Policy, College Park, MD: University of Maryland.

Lewis, P., Clarke, S., Barr, C., Kommenda, N., & Holder, J. (2018). Revealed: One in Four Europeans Vote Populist. *The Guardian,* November 20, 2018. Retrieved from www.theguardian.com/world/ng-interactive/2018/nov/20/revealed-one-in-four-europeans-vote-populist

Luhrmann, T. M. (2012). *When God Talks Back: Understanding the American Evangelical Relationship with God.* New York: Alfred A. Knopf.

Luhrmann, T. M. (2013). When God Is Your Therapist. *New York Times*, April 13, 2013. Retrieved from www.nytimes.com/2013/04/14/opinion/sunday/luhrmann-when-god-is-your-therapist.html

Mansbridge, J., Bohman, J., Chambers, S., Christiano, T., Fung, A., Parkinson, J., et al. (2012). A Systemic Approach to Deliberative Democracy. In J. Mansbridge & J. Parkinson (Eds.), *Deliberative Systems: Deliberative Democracy at the Large Scale.* Cambridge: Cambridge University Press, pp. 1–26.

Marty, M. E. (1970). *Righteous Empire: The Protestant Experience in America.* New York: Doubleday.

Mayer, F., Adair, S., & Pfaff, A. (2013). Americans Think the Climate Is Changing and Support Some Actions: Policy Brief. Duke Nicholas Institute for Environmental Policy Solutions. Retrieved from http://people.uwec.edu/jamelsem/papers/CC_Literature_Web_Share/Public_Opinion/CC_US_Survey_Results_Summary_Duke_2013.pdf

Mutz, D. C. (2018). Status Threat, Not Economic Hardship, Explains the 2016 Presidential Vote. *Proceedings of the National Academy of Sciences*, Vol. 115, No. 19, pp. E4330–E4339.

National Center for Education Statistics. (1993). *120 Years of American Education: A Statistical Portrait.* Washington, DC: DIANE Publishing.

NBC News Exit Poll Desk. (2018). NBC News Exit Poll: Nearly Half of U.S. Voters Strongly Disapprove of Trump. *NBC News*, November 6, 2018. Retrieved from www.nbcnews.com/card/nbc-news-exit-poll-nearly-half-u-s-voters-strongly-n932431

Newport, F., Moore, D., & Saad, L. (1999). Long-Term Gallup Poll Trends: A Portrait of American Public Opinion Through the Century. Gallup Inc., December 20, 1999. Retrieved from www.gallup.com/poll/3400/LongTerm-Gallup-Poll-Trends-Portrait-American-Public-Opinion.aspx

Parsons, T. (1974). Religion in Postindustrial America: The Problem of Secularization. *Social Research*, Vol. 41, No. 2, pp. 193–225.

Parsons, T. (2007). *American Society: A Theory of the Societal Community.* Edited by G. Sciortino. Boulder, CO: Paradigm Publishers.

Pew Research Center. (2018). Gun Policy Remains Divisive, But Several Proposals Still Draw Bipartisan Support. Retrieved from www.people-press.org/2018/10/18/gun-policy-remains-divisive-but-several-proposals-still-draw-bipartisan-support/

Pharr, S. J. and Putnam, R. D. (2000). *Disaffected Democracies: What's Troubling the Trilateral Countries?* Princeton, NJ: Princeton University Press.

Pharr, S. J., Putnam, R. D., & Dalton. R. J. (2000). A Quarter-Century of Declining Confidence. *Journal of Democracy*, Vol. 11, No. 2, pp. 5–25.

Quinnipiac University. (2018). Quinnipiac University Poll Release Detail. QU Poll, November 11, 2018. Retrieved from https://poll.qu.edu/national/release-detail?ReleaseID=2587

The Harris Poll. (2012). Confidence in Congress Stays at Lowest Point in Almost Fifty Years. Retrieved from www.prnewswire.com/news-releases/confidence-in-congress-stays-at-lowest-point-in-almost-fifty-years-152253655.html

Turner, J. (1980). Understanding the Populists. *The Journal of American History*, Vol. 67, No. 2, pp. 354–373.

Twenge, J. M. (2000). The Age of Anxiety? The Birth Cohort Change in Anxiety and Neuroticism, 1952–1993. *Journal of Personality and Social Psychology*, Vol. 79, No. 6, pp. 1007–1021.

Twenge, J. M., LiqingZ., & Im, C. (2004). It's Beyond My Control: A Cross-Temporal Meta-Analysis of Increasing Externality in Locus of Control, 1960–2002. *Personality and Social Psychology Review: An Official Journal of the Society for Personality and Social Psychology, Inc*, Vol. 8, No. 3, pp. 308–319.

Vance, J. D. (2016). *Hillbilly Elegy: A Memoir of a Family and Culture in Crisis*. New York: HarperCollins.

Vidich, A. J. & Bensman, J. ([1957] 1968). *Small Town in Mass Society: Class, Power and Religion in a Rural Community*. Urbana, IL: University of Illinois Press.

Zeleny, J. & Thee-Brenan, M. (2011). New Poll Finds a Deep Distrust of Government. *New York Times*, October 25, 2011. Retrieved from www.nytimes.com/2011/10/26/us/politics/poll-finds-anxiety-on-the-economy-fuels-volatility-in-the-2012-race.html?_r=1&hpw

Part IV

Presidential personality and performance

Chapter 12

How Trump's personality influences his policies

Michael Maccoby

The chapters in this book have offered different perspectives on Donald Trump's personality and practices. They have described his personal history and how trends in American history and culture contributed to his rise. In this chapter I apply that knowledge to explore how Trump's personality and history have influenced his policies.

Every individual has a unique personality, but psychoanalytic study shows that personalities are in part made up of motivational systems, typical combinations of human drives, shaped as children adapt to their families and culture. Trump's personality is in some ways similar to some other national and business leaders but in some ways unique.

A full description of personality includes temperamental traits, type of intelligence, philosophy of life including purpose and values, and ethical and moral reasoning. Let's consider how these elements are integrated in Trump's personality and how they are reflected in his policies.

The marketing narcissistic orientation

In Chapter 1, I termed Trump's motivational system as marketing narcissistic. Since this view of Trump's personality is different from the common views that just describe Trump as a narcissist, it is worth elaborating Trump's marketing traits to show their relation to his policies. Erich Fromm first described the marketing orientation, and he could have been describing Donald Trump. A marketing person's self-worth and identity depend on how he is evaluated by significant others.

> His prestige, status, success, the fact that he is known to others as being a certain person are a substitute for a genuine feeling of identity. This situation makes him utterly dependent on the way others look at him and forces him to keep up the role in which he had once been successful.
>
> (Fromm, 1947, 73)

148 Michael Maccoby

Fromm wrote that others are experienced by the marketing person as commodities, like himself. "The difference in people is reduced to a merely quantitative difference of being more or less successful, attractive, hence valuable" (ibid., 72).

Fromm wrote that only when the marketing individual is successful, does he feel valuable, if not, he feels worthless.

> The insecurity which results from this orientation can hardly be over-estimated. If one feels one's self-worth is not constituted primarily by the human qualities one possesses, but one's success on a competitive market with ever-changing conditions, one's self esteem is bound to be shaky and is in constant need of confirmation by others.
>
> (ibid., 72)

Fromm wrote that the marketing orientation also determines a way of thinking,

> of grasping things quickly so as to be able to manipulate them success-fully ... For manipulative purposes, all that is necessary to know is the surface feature of things, the superficial. The truth, to be uncovered by penetrating to the essence of a phenomena, becomes an obsolete concept.
>
> (ibid., 75)

Depending on the marketing person's degree of productiveness, he may also have positive qualities, including adaptability, radar-like sensitivity to people and their needs. The marketing orientation can be a strength for a politician whose success depends on satisfying the voters. Trump has this sensitivity and productive qualities of activeness with passion, perseverance, risk-taking and resiliency, but also the negatives of superficial knowledge and need for con-tinual affirmation. He can be charming and seductive with those he values, but cold and dismissive and even cruel to those he considers to be without value. A major element in Trump's success has been his ability to adapt to a knowledge-information culture, a media world where information is con-stantly being created to serve interests and truth is lost in the process.

Trump's narcissism is an attempt to overcome his marketing vulnerability. To avoid the feeling of intrinsic worthlessness, of being a commodity, he creates a grandiose self-image and attacks anyone who threatens it. He told Anthony Scaramucci, "I'm a total act" (Rucker & Leonning, 2020, 192). This grandiose act served him well on the TV show *The Apprentice* and as Elizabeth Lunbeck suggests in Chapter 3, it appeals to his base. Rather than showing his needy marketing vulnerability, it presents an image of invulnerability. He finds ways to connect with people who affirm this image, and he demands this from those who work for him. We can remember the scene where members of his cabinet, sitting around a table, lavishly praised him, all except General Jim Mattis, who didn't last very long as Secretary of Defense.

Trump has some of the negative narcissistic traits. To protect his fragile grandiose self-image, he is oversensitive to criticism. He exaggerates and lies to look good. He is overcompetitive and distrustful to the point of paranoia.

Our personalities are integrated by our philosophies of life, our sense of purpose and supporting values. Trump's purpose is to be a winner and to make every organization he heads into winners. He values whatever supports this purpose. His ethical commandment is: do not get caught; his moral decisions favor whatever serves himself and his family.

How does Trump's marketing narcissistic personality compare with other national leaders? The closest is Boris Johnson, the British Prime Minister, also known for his opportunistic political flexibility and his lies and exaggerations. Bill Clinton has some of these qualities, but he is more productive, with a philosophy that combines personal success with the public good.

Trump's marketing narcissistic personality is very different from that of productive narcissists whose strong convictions did not waver, even in the face of adversity and unpopularity, leaders like Winston Churchill and Charles de Gaulle. They, like productive narcissistic business leaders such as Steve Jobs and Jeff Bezos, don't need constant praise to bolster their self-images. They need collaborative followers to help them to implement their visions.

Trump's personality and policies

Trump's policies are influenced by both his personality and experiences as an entrepreneur who has run his own company since 1973. Trump was able to do things his own way without the constraints of a board of directors. But he had to struggle against government oversight and regulations and as President has enjoyed repealing regulations that limit business practices. His narcissism has propelled him to design grandiose visions of buildings and businesses. Some have succeeded and some have failed. He is used to talking big risks with other people's money and carrying heavy loads of debt. He has come to believe in his ability to seduce and persuade people and to pull off favorable deals.

It's hard to know whether his policies reflect his real beliefs or whether they are tailored to satisfy one of the constituencies he needs to stay in power. For example, provoking fear of immigrants plays to that part of his base that either believes immigrants from Latin America and the Middle East are destroying traditional white American culture and those who resent losing jobs to undocumented immigrants. As an employer, Trump well knows how the construction unions suffered from competition from immigrants willing to do work for lower pay, because he hired many undocumented immigrants and hid them from investigators. As reported by the *New York Times*:

> [O]ver decades in business, entertainment and now politics, Mr. Trump has approached America's racial, ethnic and religious divisions opportunistically,

not as the nation's wounds to be healed but as openings to achieve his goals, whether they be ratings, fame, money, or power, without regard for adverse consequences.

(Baker, Grynbaum, Haberman, & Buettner, 2019)

Trump can deal differently with his different constituencies. He can go against the Republican free traders and resist the hawks, because he knows that traditional Republicans will vote for him because of his appointments, especially judges, deregulations, and other policies favorable to business. He believes a strong military is a deterrent, but he doesn't want to be a war president and he believes his base also wants to bring American troops back from the Middle East. He is an American Firster who wants to win in business and politics and avoid war.

These views that conflict with those of the Republican elite appeal to his base, the group he most needs for both psychological and political reasons. Psychologically, this is the group that jams his rallies and expresses the love and adulation he needs. Politically, this group includes people who voted for Obama and could be lured back to vote Democratic. Many of them are influenced by Fox News commentators and rabid right radio commentators like Rush Limbaugh who criticize any liberal move or impulse, like supporting the dreamers or strengthening background checks on gun buyers. They egged him on to close the government when he didn't get funding for the wall on the Mexican border he promised his base.

Republicans have been trying to get rid of Obamacare (the Affordable Care Act) since it was passed by a Democratic Congress in 2009. Yet Trump took office promising to defend established healthcare programs such as Medicare and Medicaid and left the impression among some that he wanted to be a healthcare President. But Trump soon joined the fight to repeal Obamacare without a plan to replace it. After that failed, his administration has undermined it by repealing the individual mandate to buy insurance, and underfunding funds for enrollment outreach, and counseling, and they have scaled back minimum coverage standards. The result has been that 7 million Americans have lost coverage.[1]

Trump and the officials he appointed have used the regulatory process not to enhance the efficiency of industries or to protect the American public but to increase the power of business and right-wing activist groups. They have gutted environmental and consumer protection, workplace safety, and anti-discrimination policies. Their actions favor Republican donors particularly in the fossil fuel industries. Trump's actions continue a trend of increasing the power of the President and lessening that of Congress.

One of the defining characteristics of Trump's presidency is a readiness to abandon treaties or agreements that were major accomplishments of Obama's presidency. These have included the hard-won long-term agreement to prevent Iran's development of a nuclear weapon and the Trans-

How Trump's personality influences policies   151

Pacific Partnership Agreement (TPP), both of which were negotiated by Obama. In these abrupt actions, we see two motives, going it alone without dependence on allies and proving that he can make better deals than Obama, without considering the impact of his actions on America's security and reputation for honoring its commitments. So far, it would be difficult to make the case that he has improved national security, and many believe he has increased the risks of conflict.

Trump has long believed that he has mastered "the art of the deal." He has the grandiose belief that by force of his personality and by applying threats and incentives he can force heads of state to make concessions favorable to America. Since the 1980s, Trump has complained that other countries are making a mockery of the U.S. with their trade policies, and he has viewed tariffs as tools for pressuring countries to make concessions.

There is justification for Trump's challenge to China's predatory economic practices, but by refusing to sign the TPP, he lost the chance for allies who could help pressure China. The United States has turned a competitor into an enemy it must face alone.

China has answered Trump's tariffs with tariffs on American products, in particular, agricultural products from parts of the country that have supported Trump. Farmers have suffered and questioned their support for Trump. Seeming oblivious to the farmers' feelings, Trump has said, "My farmers love me." His need for adulation is so strong he invents it.[2]

Trump seems to like dealing with powerful people like Xi Jinping, Kim Jong un, Mohammad bin Salman, and Vladimir Putin. These leaders are killers, but Trump undoubtedly remembers that his father told him that people are either killers or losers. However, dealing with heads of state is different from making business deals. Heads of state may have great power only as long as their people believe they are defending their interests and improving their lives. In allowing concessions, business leaders may lose money, but national leaders could lose their power.

Trump's need for praise and affirmation translates into a demand that subordinates flatter him and express total loyalty. Trump has fired advisors not mainly for incompetence but for what he considered lack of loyalty. The list includes John F. Kelly, Chief of Staff; Jeff Sessions, Attorney General; Steve Bannon, chief strategist; H.R. McMaster, National Security Advisor; Rex Tillerson, Secretary of State; and others. Mattis resigned rather than follow a leader he didn't respect.

Trump ran against the government bureaucracy and so-called deep state. His administration has been hostile to public servants, freezing pay, cutting budgets, making it easier to fire officials. Competent people are leaving government and there has been a failure to fill many leadership positions. Except for employees in the Department of Defense and Homeland Security, employee morale has fallen.

On the positive side, the administration has supported projects to improve management, increase accountability, improve the IT systems, and make effective use of data.[3]

It is too early to judge the extent to which the Trump Administration has contributed to improving federal management. If progress on the problems addressed by the President's Management Agenda is sustained, it might have a transformative effect. Or, his disruption and distrust of the federal government as an institution could have long-term corrosive effects that overwhelm the efforts at reform.

In summary, the play-out of Trump's personality in his policies has worsened the anxiety and distrust that poisons our society. His disdain of allies leaves America more isolated. His attack on Obama's progressive policies widens the political divide. His international deal-making causes uncertainty. Trump does not offer a vision for bringing the country together to move toward a better future. For that we need the kind of leader described in Chapter 13.

Notes

1 We thank John Rotter, president of the National Coalition on Health Care for providing these facts.
2 Communication from Dan Morgan, who has been interviewing Mid-West farmers.
3 We thank Professor Steve Redburn of George Washington University for providing these facts.

References

Baker, P., Grynbaum, M. M., Haberman, M. A., & Buettner, R. (2019). Trump Employs an Old Tactic: Using Race for Gain. *New York Times*, July 21, 2019, Section A, p. 1.

Fromm, E. (1947). *Man for Himself: An Inquiry into the Psychology of Ethics*. New York: Rinehart.

Rucker, P. & Leonning, C. (2020). *A Very Stable Genius*. New York: Penguin.

Chapter 13

The president we need

Michael Maccoby

In his speech to the Athenian people in the midst of a devastating plague, Pericles, according to Thucydides, listed four competencies that he believed equipped him to lead Athens. These were:

1 Knowledge of the right policies.
2 The ability to explain them and convince people they are right.
3 Patriotism, meaning putting the interests of the nation above the leader's and his family's own narrow interest.
4 Honesty.

Pericles said that:

> [A leader] possessing that knowledge of the right policies without that faculty of exposition might as well have no idea at all on the matter. If he had both these gifts, but no love for his country, he would be but a cold advocate for her interests; while were his patriotism not proof against bribery, everything would go for a price.

I interpret the crucial ability to explain policies as not just crafting a good explanation of them, but doing so in a way that engages the values and interests of the voters. Candidates become leaders only when they gain followers.

Reflect on the Trump presidency so far. Compare what you've seen and heard to the above four qualities. I've done so, and I give Trump low to middling marks on right policies and the ability to convince people they are right and failing grades on honesty and putting the nation's interest before his own. That is what got him impeached. He expounds wrong policies like fossil fuels over renewable energy, depriving millions of health insurance, and belittling the COVID-19 threat. It's too early to score his military and trade policies. His economic policies produced a thriving economy before the Pandemic, but his tax bill increased the wealth gap, and some economists predict that these policies will prove to be negative in the future. I believe, only a minority of Americans would disagree with my report card.

154   Michael Maccoby

Before discussing the qualities we need from a president in the current context, I'll briefly describe what we can learn from the way Lincoln and Roosevelt expressed them.

They both took office at a time of challenge and political division even greater than what we are facing today. Both had knowledge of the right policies for their time, if we believe the right policies moved the country forward according to humanistic values. Both used their ability to communicate, to explain the reasons for their policies in a way that first connected with the voters who elected them, then with a wider constituency.

Both Lincoln and Roosevelt were patriots who did not take bribes and who put their country before self-interest. Lincoln's honesty was so well known that he was called "Honest Abe." FDR scores less well on honesty because he tried to hide the facts that he was a cripple and that he was very sick when he ran for his fourth term. But unlike Trump, he sought and valued the truth relevant to political issues. Lincoln and Roosevelt fought courageously for the common good against special interests that fought progressive change. Although Trump talks about loving this country and proclaims he is putting America first, he supports regressive special interests and his own interests, and he attacks democratic institutions, such as a free press.

The right policies

Pericles didn't define what he meant by the right policies. I suggest that for America it has to do with responding to existential and national challenges, consistent with the humanistic values and rights enshrined in the Declaration of Independence and the Constitution. The Declaration states that we are born equal with rights for life, liberty, and the pursuit of happiness. The Constitution adds that the purpose of the Constitution is to create a more perfect union, to establish justice, provide for the common defense, and promote the general welfare. In Lincoln's time, the main challenges and right policies not only had to do with slavery and the threat to the union by the Confederacy, but also government initiatives to improve the economy.

Lincoln expounded his policies about slavery and union in his carefully prepared Cooper Union speech on February 27, 1860. He said that while the Constitution protected slavery in the original 13 states, the founding fathers had clearly indicated that slavery should not be allowed to spread into new territories. Lincoln went to war to preserve the Union, but in his speeches and debates with Stephen A. Douglas, he had condemned slavery as unjust. By the end of his presidency, he had signed the Emancipation Proclamation that freed most slaves and initiated the 13th Amendment to the Constitution that made slavery illegal. He also signed the Homestead Act that gave settlers federal land, a policy that led to the development of farms and towns. This Act, together with his support for railroads and public universities, brought prosperity to post-Civil War America. His ability to communicate and explain his policies was developed by his history of speeches, debates and experience as a trial lawyer.

When Roosevelt became president, his main challenge was national depression, both economic and psychological. In the first 100 days of his presidency, Roosevelt's response to the Great Depression was to institute policies to get people back to work, protect their savings, and provide relief for the sick and elderly. He increased his support with programs like Social Security that provided benefits for everyone, not just the disadvantaged. Throughout his presidency, Roosevelt effectively expounded his policies in his "fireside chats" over the radio.

Leadership philosophy

These competencies to develop the right policies and clearly expound and explain them were strengthened by the humanistic philosophy and productive personality of these leaders. People are more likely to trust leaders when they know and approve of the philosophy that directs their policies and priorities. Lincoln expressed his philosophy, his purpose and values, in many speeches and interactions with people. A humanistic philosophy is built on the belief that every human being has the potential to develop their productive and loving potential, but this depends on the support of society as well as their own responsibility to live a productive life. The measure of national progress is not just material, but also the well-being of the people. Today, it also includes protection of the environment.

Lincoln said he was for "the man and the dollar, but in case of conflict the man before the dollar." He believed that everyone should enjoy "the fruits of their labor," and that slavery was "a social, moral, and political wrong." He also believed in fighting for what was right, but not wars for conquest as he saw the Mexican War he voted against during his term in Congress.

Lincoln and Roosevelt also understood that good values are sometimes in conflict. They were *principled pragmatists*, able to adjust their policy so that it furthered their main purpose. When General John C. Frémont proclaimed the liberation of slaves in Missouri at the start of the Civil War, Lincoln fired him and reversed the proclamation. He was criticized by the abolitionists, but he reasoned that he lacked a Constitutional right to end slavery and by freeing the slaves, he would lose the slave-holding border states that remained in the Union. Then the South would be more likely to win the war and spread slavery to the West. In August 1862, he wrote Horace Greeley that his goal was to preserve the Union and what he did about slavery had to fit into that goal. A month later, he argued that the South was using slaves to strengthen its armies, and he issued the Emancipation Proclamation as both a practical and moral decision. The Proclamation only freed slaves in Confederate states. It took the 13th Amendment to make slavery illegal in all states.

At the start of his presidency, Roosevelt expressed the humanistic values that drove his policies. He said, "In these days of difficulty, we Americans everywhere must and shall choose the path of social justice, the path of faith, the path of hope, and the path of love toward our fellow man." He ran as a fiscal conservative but quickly realized that the Federal Government needed to restart the economy. In his second term, he said, "The test of our progress is not whether we add to the abundance of those who have much; it is whether we provide enough for those who have too little."

The challenges we face

In Lincoln's time, the challenges were national, as they were for Roosevelt before World War II. Now a president faces challenges on the global as well as the national level. No country by itself can deal with the major threats to human life on planet Earth. The president needs to develop international collaboration to avoid wars, protect the environment and care for survivors of wars and disasters. Although global trade has enriched countries, it has also caused some people to lose their jobs. Global trade agreements need to take account of their social and political impact, and the national government should aid people who have lost their jobs because of these agreements.

On the national level, the challenge for the United States is the humanization of capitalism in a time of historic changes in the economy and society. The dominant mode of production in America and other advanced economies has changed from manufacturing to service, led by the producers of information and knowledge. Even much manufacturing has been automated, with the result that remaining factory jobs require knowledge to run the automated systems. More advanced knowledge work requires both technical and social skills. People with the skills and personality traits that fit the knowledge mode of production have become much richer than those lacking these qualities.

At the same time that work is changing, the empowerment of women and minorities has been transforming the traditional culture. Trump exploits the nostalgia and resentment of white traditionalists for whom the changing social values and loss of status rankled even more than their worries about jobs. He promised this constituency a return to an idealized past. He addressed some neglected problems such as trade with China and military policy. But his election resulted in further enriching and empowering the monied interests and increasing ideological conflict. America has boasted about being a land of equal opportunity, but if that were true in the past, it is no longer true in the knowledge economy. Unless people have guaranteed healthcare and schools that develop both adaptive skills and social character, they have little chance of prospering in the new economy or narrowing the income gap.

The socioeconomic challenges America faces today are in some ways similar to those Teddy Roosevelt faced at the start of the twentieth century when new technology and innovation in production led to the growth and power of corporations. When the country moved from a farming and craft-based economy to a dominantly industrial economy, as at the present time, there were winners and losers. Farmers and craftsmen became workers and bureaucrats. Unions were formed to protect workers. Teddy Roosevelt's Square Deal defended customers and small businesses against the powerful monopolies and trusts. When FDR initiated the New Deal, he was attacked by the large corporations that had been humbled by TR but had increased their power during the 1920s. Running for re-election, FDR said that these moneyed interests "consider the Government of the United States as a mere appendage to their own affairs." He went on to say:

> Never before in all our history have these forces been so united against one candidate as they stand today. They are unanimous in their hate for me and I welcome their hatred.
> I should like to have it said of my first Administration that in it the forces of selfishness and lust for power met their match. I should like to have it said of my second Administration that in it these forces met their master.

Roosevelt was re-elected by over 60 percent of the voters and won 523 of 531 electoral votes.

When Donald Trump ran for president, his policies appealed to many Americans, especially the white families who felt they were the victims of social and economic change. He claimed he would make America great again and get unemployed workers jobs by keeping out unskilled and poor immigrants, partly by building a wall on the border with Mexico, and by getting better deals with our trading partners. He promised to end Obamacare and replace it with a much better healthcare system, and that he would save money and American lives by bringing our troops home from the Middle East. In fact, he has somewhat improved the North American trading treaty but it is highly questionable whether some of his other policies would improve the country. They do not deal with the real challenges caused by the effects of changing technology, the nature of work, and threats to the environment. His policies on immigration, climate change, healthcare, and education are divisive and not humanistic.

In his first inaugural address, Roosevelt told an anxious country that fear paralyzes us and "we have nothing to fear but fear itself." His optimism turned fear into hope and activated the country. Trump told voters they should fear that terrorists, immigrants, and trading partners who were threatening their lives and stealing their jobs. Now, the country is suffering from an increase in anxiety and uncertainty, augmented by a pandemic.

The personality of leaders

The philosophy that directs the policies of leaders is rooted in their personality. Even though they came from very different backgrounds—FDR was rich and Lincoln was poor—they shared key personality traits. They were both visionaries who embraced new social and economic complexities. They did not try to maintain the status quo or promise a return to an idealized past. Both presidents were conscientious and had experienced suffering and setbacks that made them more sensitive to the sufferings of others. Lincoln suffered from the tragic deaths of his mother and sister when he was young and his sons when he was president. Roosevelt struggled to recover enough from his crippling polio to gain the strength to run for office. Both fought for their ideas against attacks from both the Right and the Left, but they did not denigrate their opponents. Both had a sense of humor, the emotional equivalent of intellectual realism and a weapon they used to disarm and poke fun at their attackers.

Contrast these traits with those of Trump. In Chapter 1, I wrote that in his book, *Think Like a Billionaire*, Trump avers that the description in my book, *Narcissistic Leaders*, of productive narcissists like Steve Jobs and Jeff Bezos fit him, that like them, he works to realize his visions. Productive narcissists are typically ambitious and competitive. They have weak superegos, so their moral sense and visions are shaped by their philosophies and ego ideals. Lincoln and FDR were productive narcissists with humanistic philosophies. Lincoln's ego ideal was George Washington, FDR's was his cousin, TR. According to Steve Bannon, Trump's is Douglas MacArthur, a grandiose general who was an impressive viceroy in Japan after World War II, but who went on to lead American troops in Korea and almost got us into a war with China. President Harry S. Truman fired him as insubordinate. Trump is a visionary, but his visions are not humanistic. They are aesthetic visions of beautiful buildings, a beautiful wall, and an idealized past. Leaders like Trump with a strong aesthetic drive tend to distort reality to make it sound and look good to them. Business leaders like Steve Jobs with a strong aesthetic drive and a tendency to distort reality don't do as much damage as do political leaders with this tendency. The worst was Adolf Hitler with his destructive vision of a racially pure thousand-year Reich.

It is essential for leaders with a narcissistic personality to recruit advisers they trust and who will help to keep their egos in check. Unlike Lincoln and Roosevelt, Trump has been unable to build a first-rate team at a time when increased complexity and speed of change call for a leadership team with complementary expertise as well as shared values. Trump listens, if at all, only to powerful people—generals, leaders of state, billionaires, some politicians—whom he believes respect him. Lacking a sense of humor, Trump lashes out at anyone who criticizes him. He fires aides who don't agree with him.

Like Lincoln and Roosevelt, Trump is a street-smart politician who has been able to tune into the aspirations and emotions of some voters. But while Lincoln and Roosevelt measured their success in terms of realizing their humanistic visions, success for Trump, the marketing narcissist, is gaining applause and admiration for his winning deals. So far, these deals have not proved beneficial for most Americans.

Neither Lincoln nor Roosevelt was perfect. No leader is. Lincoln was slow to take leadership in the Civil War and left General George B. McClellan in charge of the armies too long. Roosevelt tried to pack the Supreme Court and exercise dictatorial powers. Both learned from their mistakes.

In summary, these two presidents had the right policies, the ability to express them and engage followers, put their country above self-interest, and, especially Lincoln, were honest. They had a humanistic philosophy and some of the personality traits we needed in a president then and that, in a different historical context, we need now. But would the electorate recognize these qualities in a candidate? Some people recognized them in Lincoln and Roosevelt, but a number of experts did not. Edward Everett, a former President of Harvard wrote his view of Lincoln in his diary during the presidential campaign. "He is evidently a person of very inferior cast of character, wholly unequal to the crisis." Congressman Charles Francis Adams wrote, "His speeches have fallen like a wet blanket here. They put a flight to all notions of greatness." Lincoln was elected president with only 39.8 percent of the popular vote. The fact that there were four candidates contributed to his victory, but those who voted for him agreed with the policies he had so well expressed. (Trump has an approval rating around 40 percent but it's over 55 percent in 17 states.)

When Roosevelt ran for president, Walter Lippmann, the distinguished columnist, described him as "an amiable boy scout" and H. L. Mencken, another influential columnist, wrote that he was "somewhat shallow and futile."

In his study of Pericles, Donald Kagan wrote, "The paradox inherent in democracy is that it must create and depend on citizens who are free, autonomous, and self-reliant. Yet its success—its survival even—requires extraordinary leadership" (Kagan, 1991, 9). Kagan could have added that this leadership depends on voters who recognize the qualities of competence and character needed in a leader. Americans have not always elected the leaders most needed. Sometimes they have elected leaders with the wrong policies like Herbert Hoover who tightened the money supply during the Depression or the wrong policies and philosophy like Donald Trump whose main purpose is to be an admired winner and who has a humorless authoritarian personality. And sometimes they have elected a president with the right policies and philosophy but who lacked the ability to explain them effectively and gain followers, like John Quincy Adams who sought justice for blacks and Native Americans, but lost the election to Andrew Jackson, a racist.

But sometimes, particularly in less challenging times, they have elected patriotic and honest presidents with the right policies who have more balanced personalities, such as James Madison, Harry S. Truman, and Dwight D. Eisenhower. These presidents were more cautious than Lincoln and FDR, more problem-solvers than visionaries. In times of great change, like the present time, some people are attracted to visionaries who give them hope for a more just and prosperous future, but the philosophy and competencies of the president we need are important than her or his personality.

Although we can't be sure a president will be able to express these qualities before he or she takes office, we can ask each candidate the following six questions as an aid to deciding who is most likely to have these qualities:

- What are the main challenges facing Americans?
- What policies are needed to deal with them?
- How will you convince people these are the right policies?
- What is your philosophy and how does it direct your policies and practice of leadership?
- How do you deal with attacks on you and/or your policies?
- What is your vision for America?

The president we need will answer these questions in ways that make sense to us and also give us hope for creating a better future.

Reference

Kagan, D. (1991). *Pericles of Athens and the Birth of Democracy.* New York: The Free Press.

Chapter 14

Conclusion

Ken Fuchsman

In February 1964, Beatlemania seemed to take over American public life. The four young British musicians caused a craze across the land in their television and concert appearances. They had an unprecedented eleven hits on the Billboard Top 40 in the first five months of the year (Whitburn, 2004, 51–52). Their 1964 summer film, *A Hard Day's Night*, was a smash hit, but the same year *Mary Poppins* had seven times the gross as did the Beatles' film (IMDb, 2019). As extremely popular and as much a sensation as the Fab Four remained, Beatlemania itself had passed its peak in half a year.

Trumpmania, on the other hand, was still going strong after five years from the time he declared his presidential candidacy in June, 2015. Many news cycles have Donald Trump as the featured star. During the 2016 Republican primary season, other Republican candidates were at a disadvantage as the coverage the broadcast media gave Trump dwarfed what the other candidates received.

The connection between television, newspapers, social media, and Trump contributed to his rise and continued during his presidency. The marketing narcissist, as Michael Maccoby calls Donald Trump, has exploited the frequent hunger in some media for the sensational, the outrageous, and the controversial.

Trump's insatiable appetite for public attention leads him to want to be front and center all the time. A former top adviser told *New York Times* reporters that after two or three days, Trump "could not handle watching the news without seeing himself on it." The journalists concluded that the President is on a "perpetual quest" to have himself be on television (Haberman, Thrush, & Baker, 2017). His drive for media attention is facilitated by the instrument of Twitter, where, as of April 2019, he had almost 60 million followers (Bort, 2019). With a media climate where stars come and go, in the television age no one else in American public life has been able to have such a long-term daily hold on the public's attention as has Donald Trump.

Understanding Trump's influence on the American consciousness is a complex topic; it needs input from various disciplines. Psychoanalysts, historians, and a sociologist in this book have addressed the topic of explaining

Trump's personality and what in our life and culture has enabled his rise. What is striking in reviewing these various chapters is how much they complement each other, how much one runs into another. I will try to show these interconnections in this Conclusion.

A celebrity culture has infiltrated the political arena to the extent that marketing narcissists can be elected President of the United States. As Trump is more engaged with his being on public display than in the nitty-gritty details of administering the executive departments, he has accelerated a trend where an American President can be more involved with promoting themselves than in governing.

Maccoby's quite original notion of marketing narcissism brings together Erich Fromm's description of a marketing personality with the psychology of the narcissist. Maccoby collaborated for years with Fromm and has written about narcissism in a number of influential books. The marketing personality tries to find effective ways of getting himself or herself in the public eye. This orientation indicates that the person does not self-validate, but is dependent on others' acclaim. This fits in with a narcissist's grandiose need to be the center of attention and to devalue others who are perceived as competitors. In contrast, a productive narcissist, such as Steve Jobs, is concerned with getting attention through the innovative products he seeks to perfect.

Any aspiring presidential candidate battling for the nomination needs to be skillful at getting his or her campaign extensive media coverage. No one has been better at that in recent decades than Donald J. Trump. His trait of being a superb marketing narcissist helps us understand the phenomenon of Trumpmania.

Harvard historian Elizabeth Lunbeck's Chapter 3 on the allure of Trump's narcissism complements Maccoby's insights. She finds that it is Trump's narcissistic charisma and charm that enable him to appear as a heroic figure to Trumpites, At the 2016 Republican Convention, Trump presented himself in grandiose terms by saying that he was the only one who could make America great again. Trump has managed to convince the "disenfranchised and aggrieved" that he understands their problems. By enthusiastically backing Trump, they get to participate in his greatness. Lunbeck cites Trump's assessment that he appeals to people's fantasies. He uses his own self-definition of being a genius to induce others to fantasize about being part of something greater than themselves. This marketing strategy has been extraordinarily successful.

Of course, marketers are seeking ways to sell their products and/or themselves. They may not always be accurate. and may even deceive the public. Billionaire Michael Bloomberg said that Trump is a con man pulling a fast one. To appeal to an audience, people must find the marketing campaign speaks to them. And this leads us to the concept of gaslighting. Psychoanalyst Robin Stern's (2007) *The Gaslight Effect* explained this phenomenon. In Chapter 6, she says that gaslighting is a phenomenon between two individuals, the first one seeks to have the other disbelieve their own perceptions, doubt their integrity and sanity, and another person who buys into what the gaslighter is trying to do.

The term comes from the 1938 play, *Gaslight*, by Patrick Hamilton and is best-known from the 1944 film with Charles Boyer, Ingrid Bergman, and Joseph Cotton. Stern first noticed this phenomenon in her clients, friends, and herself. To her, gaslighting takes two to tango. When applied to Donald Trump, it would focus on why his deceptions would appeal to so many American voters. During the 2016 presidential election, events occurred that led Stern to conclude that gaslighting was becoming as much a socio-political as a personal phenomenon.

Psychoanalyst Judith Logue more fully applies the concept of gaslighting to Donald Trump. She does so in a variety of ways. One of the recurring phenomena of Trump's 2016 campaign rallies was his guaranteeing that Mexico will pay for the wall between the two countries to stop illegal immigration. Trump would ask the crowd, "Who is gonna to pay for the wall?," and they would respond in unison "Mexico." And then he might repeat his question a few more times, and get the same enthusiastic response (CNBC, March 3, 2016). This is an example of gaslighting in a different sense. Trump was misleading his audience and they happily joined in. Not surprisingly, Mexico is not paying for any wall. If one is built, it will be paid for the American taxpayer.

Trump during the 2016 campaign made other bold promises, such as he would eliminate the national debt in eight years, and as President he said that he could make a deal to get North Korea to dismantle their nuclear weapons. As Logue points out, in President Trump's first two years the debt has increased by two trillion dollars and is going up and not down. North Korea, after talks with Trump, has resumed testing ballistic missiles and has done nothing to disarm. Still Trump's political base has mostly bought into his gaslighting through the first three years of his Presidency.

A gaslighter seeks to destabilize the psyche of the other party, to disturb the internal equilibrium of his or her target. In Chapter 4, historian and psychoanalyst Paul Elovitz says that Donald Trump is the Great Disrupter. To Elovitz, the need for both adoration and combativeness has characterized Donald Trump since childhood. These two qualities mean that wherever Trump is prominent, disorder, confusion, and destabilization are always present. Since his "childhood he has persisted in saying erroneous things despite repeatedly being told of his error." In both domestic and foreign affairs, Elovitz writes, as President, Trump's "greatest successes are as a disrupter of the status quo."

His exceptional skill in branding, stereotyping, and demeaning others is the major source of his appeal to his base. At his rallies he may say the most dreadful things, urge the crowd to chant lock her up or send her back, or incite anger and talk about doing violent things to dissenters. This demagoguery has worked well for Trump.

What makes for a successful demagogue? In Chapter 7, Michael Signer says there are four tests to being a demagogue: (1) be a man of the masses; (2) arouse passion; (3) use it for political benefit; and (4) break the established rules of governance. Demagogues relish being vulgarians and renegades. Many of Trump's followers, Signer thinks, no longer believe that leaders who are decent and dignified can solve their problems. These Trump adherents relish how inflammatory he is.

As Trump's appeal in part is to disrupt the status quo, be vulgar, and violate political norms, that he is happy to do so pleases many in his base. Not all of his followers are disturbed by some of his characteristics that might make him seem incompetent and unqualified to be Commander-in-Chief. I address some of these issues in Chapter 5.

Trump makes false and misleading statements at an astounding rate, often he reverses his viewpoints not long after finishing the first claim, remains willfully ignorant of the information he needs to govern intelligently, and specializes in demeaning others, often for what he also does himself.

He is also preoccupied with his public image. Trump reportedly watches television between 4 and 8 hours a day (Haberman, Thrush, & Baker, 2017). It is unclear whether Donald Trump averages spending more time a day actually performing his constitutionally mandated duties or watching cable news. When he sees things he does not like, he takes to Twitter to stereotype and denigrate others, whether they are Democrats or Republicans. Much of this can be categorized as the actions of a narcissistic gaslighter.

Whether we view Donald Trump as a marketing narcissist, a gaslighter, an incompetent disrupter, or a thin-skinned demagogue, it is clear it is not only his personality that explains the condition we are in. The issue is not only Trump, but us. How can we explain how the U.S. went in 2008 from electing Barack Obama, a candidate who promised hope and reconciliation to in 2016 electing Trump, a political divider who incites nativism and violence? To understand the Trump phenomenon entails looking at the economic, cultural, psychological, and historical factors that have enabled him to be elevated to the Presidency.

As with Trump's personality and character, our contributors address this problem from different angles that often have common features. In Chapter 2, psychoanalyst Otto Kernberg says that "there are culturally fostered negative dispositions that under ordinary circumstances don't have much weight." In times of crisis, "personal identity is threatened by social disorganization and a second skin is established by being part of a regressed social group." Part of this psychological regression entails identifying with a powerful leader and against an outgroup. There can then be an intensification of nationalism and a "freedom from moral principles." We have seen this phenomenon, Kernberg says, in Yugoslavia, Rwanda, Nazi Germany, and the Russian Revolution.

Conclusion 165

If it is in conditions of social disorganization that a society becomes susceptible to regressive leaders, how would this apply to Donald Trump? With Trump, it is important to distinguish "between the characteristics of his public behavior, that may fit nicely the symptoms of 'political narcissism' and a clinical diagnosis as a person that could only be assessed by seeing him personally." Kernberg connects social conditions to individual and group psychology.

So does Maccoby. To him, we live in an age of anxiety that is characterized by "weapons of mass destruction" that

> are primed to kill millions of people, that climate change and viruses threaten human life, that terrorists can suddenly turn a pleasant outing in places ... into a bloodbath, that children at school, concert goers. and worshippers in a church or synagogue can suddenly be murdered by a fanatic

Added to these threats is the pace of social change in a "rapid transition from a bureaucratic-industrial culture to a culture based on information and knowledge."

There are a variety of responses to these anxieties. One characteristic of recent times is that a "regressive transference" leads many to join "tribalistic political groups that are vulnerable to demagogues, narcissistic leaders who project power and certainty." This can then "feed the group's narcissism, blame others for their problems, and promise magical solutions to the causes of their anxiety." A product of these psychological mass regressions is "the election of Donald Trump, a narcissistic leader who has increased the fragmentation of society and our existential anxiety." Again, psychological regression in an age of terror and anxiety has resulted in a narcissistic, divisive leader.

In Chapter 11, sociologist Charles Heckscher begins with the "extremely disruptive" social strains of the last half-century. These include the collapse of the Soviet Union, commerce's globalization, the internet, social media, and changing attitudes about race, gender, and sexual preferences. Among the varied responses to these stressors are two brands of "populism," one on the conservative side has led to Donald Trump, and another is more progressive.

Populism represents those who feel left out, dispossessed, and oppose cultural and political elites. The angry and hostile populists want to tear down the world of the privileged. These "populists rally to Trump because he seeks to *destroy* the institutions that represent the new economy and the technocratic elites undermining their way of life." Trump's demagogic populism seeks to destroy as much or more than build. He plays upon the decline of confidence in institutions that accelerated around 2000, which was accompanied by a widespread feeling of anxiety. The sense of the legitimacy of advanced industrial democracy is being severely weakened. Trump supporters like that "he represents something *different* from the corrupt and failing system of the past."

The other brand of populism is the progressive, with a focus on cultural inclusion. It emphasizes "expressive revolution" which includes "demands for participation, self-fulfillment, embrace of gender and racial diversity, environmental consciousness, and a shift in child-rearing focus from hard work to imagination."

Since about 2000, there has been political polarization, often centering around these two opposed versions of populism, both of which represent a minority, while the "exhausted majority" is pulled in different directions. Neither the populist minorities nor the exhausted majority feels the system is working. Trump takes advantage of this disenchantment.

As do Kernberg, Maccoby, and Heckscher, I stress the social/political climate in explaining Trump's rise. Capitalism has long been a central element in the American civic religion. It is based on a faith in material prosperity and individual opportunity. When major failures in the economy happen, something cracks in the American political psyche, and often a paranoid style develops. Scapegoats are targeted as being to blame for our social and economic ills. The periods following economic difficulties are accompanied by political polarization. This has happened after the 1893 depression, the 1930s Great Depression, and the 2008 Great Recession. On the politically conservative side, in the 1890s, radical populists such as William Jennings Bryan were portrayed as dangerous radicals. In the 1930s, New Dealers were often labeled as un-American, After the outbreak of World War II, many conservatives supported an America First movement. Following the 2008 economic downturn, the Tea Party campaigned against a demonized national government, and nativism once again reared its head. Donald Trump campaigned on America First and targeted "un-Americans," such as Mexican rapists and Muslim terrorists.

Another factor in Donald Trump's rise grows out of the rituals of Presidential campaigns. Since the end of World War II, when a sitting President is not up for re-election, aspiring candidates present themselves in an almost religious manner. They blame the sins of the political status quo for a dangerous decline, and sell themselves as agents of political salvation. Since the 1968 election, mass political rallies are held that often resemble religious meetings. Candidates rouse the crowd with slogans such as getting the country moving again, and making America great again. Renewal and redemption are alluded to either directly or indirectly. Not surprisingly, the candidates promise more than they can deliver. Down the political road, some disillusionment inevitably follows. In another election cycle, the disenchanted among the electorate seek another candidate as hero, who again cannot deliver on all their promises, and round and round we go in a political circle game. The competitiveness of campaigns almost begs candidates to create an image of themselves as superior to others. Campaigns encourage those skilled in self-marketing and projecting grandiose self-images.

In Chapter 9, psychoanalyst David Lotto emphasizes what can be called an American group narcissism: American Exceptionalism. This notion has its origins in 1630 in the Massachusetts Bay Colony, when Governor John Winthrop proclaimed that America is a city on a hill, a model for the rest of the world. It was Alexis de Tocqueville who in 1835 called this American exceptionalism. This sense of American superiority is a perennial in our politics. Lotto finds it in Woodrow Wilson's desire to have America lead the way to make the world safe for democracy, or when Ronald Reagan would regularly cite Winthrop's phrase that America is that blessed city on a hill. Trump has given a nativist, often racist, twist to America being exceptional. Trump plays on the fear of many that the precious American way of life is being threatened by immigrants, Muslims, and other targets of the day. This fear of outliers is nothing new in American history. In the Trump era, American exceptionalism is both strong and under siege.

Some claim that the political movements that have enhanced Trump's rise are fascistic, and that this label might even be applied to Trump. In Chapter 8, Paul Gottfried examines this claim. He finds that highly respected academics, no matter their political orientation, loosely throw around the word fascist, sometimes applying it to Trump. There is an overinflated rhetoric, and a confusion of contemporary conservative populism with the fascist governments in Europe after World War I. Trump's response to illegal immigrants supposedly shows how the current president is fascistic. Gottfried points out that in many years Obama annually deported more immigrants than Trump has done his first two years in office. To claim that Trump is a fascist turns out to be a form of name calling, sometimes by noted scholars. Not surprisingly, the problem of excessive rhetoric and claims is not restricted to any particular political persuasion.

To conclude, Donald J. Trump is a larger-than-life figure, a master of controversy, a brilliant self-promoter, self-centered to the extreme, with an amazing ability to market himself, and possessing a special gift to turn most any issue to himself. Through skillful branding, he knows how to elevate himself and denigrate others. This celebrity President somehow has staying power and has not become a fad whose fame fades away overnight.

In an age of excess, he is among the elite of those who are consistently excessive. In many a period of American history, such a person would not be nominated by a major political party. It took a special set of circumstances to make him a viable candidate. As our contributors say, it is a time of social disorganization, intense anxiety, distrust, and psychological regression. The economic suffering and disaffiliation accompanying the Great Recession made many people into conservative populists wanting to disrupt the status quo. They became receptive to a demagogic gaslighter who could con others into believing what he says and stay with him through thick and thin.

With Trump in the White House, the nation has been thrust into a continuous soap opera. The perils of Pauline have become the daily melodramas of discontented Donald. A President who is less concerned about the details of governing is adept at getting headlines about himself. An exceptional marketing narcissist has found a moment in history when he would not be laughed off the stage. Rather, he takes bow after bow as many in the audience give him a standing ovation while others cannot stop booing. Barack Obama's claim that we are unified as one America has turned into an age of partisan polarization, of divide and conquer, of stereotypes and slurs, of inciting fury and violence. If across the land conditions alter and there becomes less of a mass psychological need for social regression, will that mean that Trump's personality will appeal to a smaller base, and that Trumpmania will no longer characterize America's social discourse? Or will it take the kind of leader Maccoby proposes in Chapter 13, a leader who like Abraham Lincoln and Franklin Delano Roosevelt inspired a more progressive age in America?

References

Bort, R. (2019). Trump's Twitter Problem? He Has Less Followers than Obama. *Rolling Stone*, April 24, 2019. Retrieved from www.rollingstone.com/politics/politics-news/trump-twitter-followers-obama-826471/

CNBC. (2016). Trump: I Guarantee Mexico Will Pay for the Wall. CNBC, March 3, 2016. Retrieved from www.cnbc.com/video/2016/03/03/trump-i-guarantee-mexico-will-pay-for-the-wall.html

Haberman, M., Thrush, G., & Baker, P. (2017). Inside Trump's Hour-by-Hour Battle for Self-Preservation. *New York Times*, December 9, 2017. Retrieved from www.nytimes.com/2017/12/09/us/politics/donald-trump-president.html.

IMDb. (2019). Feature Film, Released between 1964-01-01 and 1964-12-31. Retrieved from www.imdb.com/search/title/?title_type=feature&year=1964&sort=boxoffice_gross_us,desc

Stern, R. (2007). *The Gaslight Effect: How to Spot and Survive the Hidden Manipulation Others Use to Control Your Life*. New York: Harmony.

Whitburn, J. (2004). *The Billboard Book of Top 40 Hits*, 8th edn. New York: Billboard Books.

Index

Note: italic page numbers indicate figures; numbers containing n refer to chapter endnotes.

9/11 attacks (2001) 79
1984 (Orwell) 76

Acosta, Jim 79
Adams, Charles Francis 159
Adams, John Quincy 110, 159
affect systems 33
Affordable Care Act 19, 38, 51, 150, 157
African Americans 11–12, 31, 52, 111–112; and education 134; voters 121
aggression 26, 27, 29, 30, 32, 33, 39, *see also* anger; rage
alpha personalities 46
Alzheimer's disease 46
"America First" 108, 109, 150, 154, 166
American Civil War 154, 155, 159
American Dream 105–106, 109, 111
American Exceptionalism 6, 105–112, 167; and American flag 106; as group fantasy 105, 108; and hate groups/crimes 110–112; history/evolution of 106–108; and manifest destiny 107; and Obama/Hillary Clinton 108, 111; and patriotism/American Dream 105–106, 111; and Trump 108–109, 110, 111, 112; and U.S. as world's policeman 108, 111; and wealth accumulation 105–106, 107, 109–110
American flag 88, 90, 106, 108, 109, 111
American identity 6, 108, 112
anger 2, 38–39, 67, 120, 126, *see also* aggression; rage
anti-establishment stance of Trump 5, 22n1, 51, 75, 84, 89, 126, 136

anti-government groups 111, 112
anti-Semitism 2, 15, 27, 30, 52, 79, 92, 94, 96, 111
anti-social personality/behavior 26, 27, 29
Antifa 100–101
anxiety 15, 25, 31, 67, 81, 131, 133, 157, 167; treating 21–22, *see also* Trump anxiety disorder
anxiety, age of 1, 11–12, 19, 165; Trump's exploitation of 2, 12, 15
Apple 14, 18
Apprentice, The (TV show) 52, 66, 148
approval rating of Trump 43
approval, Trump's need for *see* praise/admiration, Trump's need for
Aristophanes 90
Aristotle 90
Art of the Deal, The (Trump/Schwartz) 37, 55n15, 82
attention span of Trump 48, 49, 62–63
attention-seeking behavior 4, 44, 47, 48, 50, 52, 54n3, 58, 161, 162
Attorney General 44, 84, 151
Austria 32, 94, 99
authoritarianism 53, 110, 159
Axelrod, David 114

backtracking 44, 49, 58
Baker, P. 149–150
bankruptcies 39, 54–55n10, 61
Bannon, Steve 50, 62, 151, 158
Barr, William 78, 84
Barron, John 45
Beatlemania 161

170 Index

Begley, Sharon 80
Bell, D. 127
Bensman, J. 129
Bergman, Ingrid 72–73, 75, 163
Beria, Lavrentiy 30
Berlusconi, Silvio 53, 83
Bernstein, C. 117
Better Angels 138, 139
Bezos, Jeff 149, 158
Bin Salman Al Saud, Mohammad
    18, 151
Bion, Wilfred 28
birther controversy 52, 55n20, 119
Blair, Gwenda 45, 50, 55n14, 60
blame 12, 15, 22, 65; and gaslighting 72
Bloomberg, Michael 61, 162
Bolsonaro, Jair 79
border wall 18, 47, 48, 54n9, 76, 133,
    157, 163
Bornstein, Harold 80
Boyer, Charles 72–73, 75, 163
Bozos, Jeff 16
Brackett, Marc 73
Brandeis, Louis 74
Bray, Mark 100–101
Breitbart 98
Bridge Alliance 138
Brinton, Crane 99
Britain (UK) 78, 114, 129, 132
Brokaw, Tom 80
Browning, Christopher R. 96–97, 99
Bryan, William Jennings 166
Bryce, James 74
Buchanan, Pat 110
Buettner, R. 149–150
bullying 48, 73
Burke, Edmund 126
Burns, Alexander 59
Bush, George H.W. 43, 126
Bush, George W. 43, 126
Bush, Jeb 43
business career of Trump 18, 47, 50, 51,
    54–55nn10,21, 149; bankruptcies in
    39, 54–55n10, 61; lying in 59, 60–61

California 109
Campbell, W. Keith 35
Canada 78, 110
capitalism 19, 27, 54n1, 95, 100, 118,
    156, 166; corporate 128, 129, 136
Caribbean 22
Carnegie, Andrew 118

Cashmore, Ellis 116
CBS 117
Cedar Rapids, Ohio 63
celebrity culture 55n20, 77–78,
    116–117, 162
centralization 98–99
change, social/economic/technological 1,
    27, 125, 131, 156, 157, 165; and
    populism 126, 127; and progressive
    movements 133–135
charisma 36, 37, 72, 162
Chávez, Hugo 79, 89, 91
child-rearing 133, 134, 166
childhood of Trump 44–45, 55n14,
    82–83, 163; at military academy 44,
    47, 49, 50; ill-health/emotional
    unavailability of mother 4, 47, 48, 83;
    and walls 46–48
China 28, 43, 49, 53, 62, 129, 151, 156
Chris Wallace 67
Christian Right 96
Christianity 107, 133, 134, 139, 140n8
Churchill, Winston 149
CIA (Central Intelligence Agency) 62, 75
civil society 125, 137, 138, 139
class system 109–110, see also middle
    class; white working class
Cleon 90, 91
climate change 11, 137, 157
Clinton, Bill 14, 17, 43, 64, 83, 149
Clinton, Hillary 45, 54n4, 61–62, 64, 75,
    83; accused of fascism 98; and
    American Exceptionalism 108, 111;
    "crooked"/"Lock her up" 2, 3, 30, 58,
    63, 67, 163; loss of support for
    120–121
CNN 79, 89, 93, 117
cognitive functioning 28, 80, 85
Cohn, Roy 50, 52
Cold War 112, 116, 165
Collins, E. 117
colonialism 31, 107, 109, 110
Comey, James 45, 54n4, 62, 79, 84
Committee for a Responsible Federal
    Budget 61
communism/communists 15, 30, 94, 100,
    108; and McCarthyism 89, 116, 118
community 125, 128
competency/fitness of Trump 1, 2, 4, 7, 58,
    58–67, 121, 164; and business career
    60–61; and demeaning opponents see
    demeaning of opponents; and financial

backing 64; and gaslighting 75; and ignorance of policies 58, 62, 63; and impulsiveness 58, 65–66; and indecision on policies 61–62; and lack of political experience 1, 4, 34, 62; and lies *see* lies of Trump; and paranoia 6–67; and proposal of illegal actions 62; and sexual misconduct 2, 39, 59, 60, 63, 64; and slander 65; and temperament/character 63–66; and U.S. national debt 61–62
competitiveness 3, 25, 50
concentration camps 32, 92
Congress 46, 48–49, 77, 79, 121, 132; and non-partisanship 84, 85
Conservative Political Action Conference (CPAC) 88, 89, 91
conservatives/conservatism 7, 22n1, 84, 88, 118, 166, 167; critical of Trump 127; and disenfranchisement 79, 120; and media 119; philosophical 126; Trump as 51, 53; and welfare state 129, 130
consumer protection 79, 150
Conway, Kellyanne 78
Cook, Tim 18
Coolidge, Calvin 118
Corker, Bob 54n2, 58
corporations 129, 131, 138, 157
Cotton, Joseph 75, 84–85, 163
Coughlin, Charles 89
counterpunching 48–49, 51, 65
COVID-19 153
CPAC (Conservative Political Action Conference) 88, 89, 91
Cruz, Ted 2, 63, 64, 65, 67, 119
cults 13

Dale, Daniel 59
D'Antonio, Michael 45, 48, 50
Davidson, Amy 59
Davis, W.P 51
Dayton, Ohio 51
de Gaulle, Charles 130, 149
death drive 33
debt, personal 12
debt, U.S. national 55n10, 61–62, 76, 119, 163; and tax cuts 62
deep state 75–76, 151
demagogue, Trump as 5, 7, 12, 88–91, 163–164, 167; compared with historical examples 90–91; and four

tests of demagogues 89, 164; and indignity/vulgarity *see* vulgarity of Trump
dementia 80
DeMirgian, K. 58
democracy 6, 95, 107, 108; deliberative 139; and postwar framework 128, 129, 132
Democrats 43, 46, 48–49, 52, 54n2, 66–67, 95, 116; accused of anti-Americanism 118; accused of fascism 97–99, 101; and American Exceptionalism 111; decline of 120–121; and progressive movements 135
denigration of rivals 4, 6, 59, 62, 64, 65, 79; *see also under* Clinton, Hillary
Denmark 53, 99, 132
"Deplorables, Les" 88
deportations 93, 167
depression 12, 25
Dershowitz, Alan 78
Detroit, Michigan 121
diagnosis, overview of 81–82
Diagnostic and Statistical Manual of Mental Disorderssee DSM
Diamond, J. 63, 65
Dicks, Henry 32
dignity 12, 13, 88, 89
disabled people 92
Disney movies 92–93
disruption 43–53, 125, 126, 163, 164; and backtracking 44, 49; and competitiveness 50; as counterproductive in office 51; and good/bad splitting 45–46; of interpersonal relationships 4; and misunderstanding boundaries 44; and need for admiration 45, 47, 50, 51; and personalizing of issues 43–44; of political system 2, 4, 6, 43; and presidential/personal power 44; and psychic defense 45, 50; and racism 52; in Trump administration 4, 34, 43, 46, 48; and Trump as counterpuncher 48–49, 51; in Trump's childhood 44–45; and Trump's hollow personality 50–51; Trump's need for 43, 44; and tweets 48–49, 51, 53, 54n8; and vulnerability of Trump 53; and walls 46–48
distrust of political class 2, 75–76, 79, 129–132, *130*, 136, 166; and bridging strategies 137–139, *see also* anti-establishment stance of Trump

172 Index

diversity 96, 100, 133, 134, 136, 137, 166
Dodes, Lance 82
Douglas, Stephen A. 154
draft avoidance 49, 55n18
draining the swamp 34
drugs 12, 21, 24, 25, 131
DSM (*Diagnostic and Statistical Manual of Mental Disorders*) 34, 35, 36, 76, 81, 82
D'Souza, Dinesh 98, 99
Durkheim, Emile 106

economic mobility 109–110
economy 6, 14, 17, 118, 120, 153, 154, 157, 165, 166; knowledge 12, 20, 156; and postwar framework 128, 129, *see also* Great Depression; Great Recession (2008)
Edina, Esther 17
education 12, 19, 127, 134, 156; of Trump 44
ego 14, 15, 46, 85, 158
Eisenhower, Dwight D. 160
El Paso, Texas 11, 51
election campaigns 77, 114–115, 166; and accusations of fascism 99; and length of season 114, *see also* presidential election campaign, 2016
Electoral College 4, 59, 120; and popular vote 77, 114
electoral cycle 6, 77, 114, 166
elites 5, 12, 15, 31, 51, 84, 108–109; and demagogues 89, 90; and populism 126–127, 165; and progressivism 135, 136
Elovitz, Paul 44, 50, 83
empathy 25, 35, 50
employment 2, 11, 12, 20, 52, 84, 105, 120, 131, 153, 157; and automation 156
entertainment qualities of Trump 2, 77–78
enthymemes 90
environmental protection 19, 54n1, 79, 157
envy 3, 24, 25, 35, 79
Erdogan, Recep Tayyip 79
erotic personality type 13, 14
ethical values 19, 22, 25, 26, 27, 83–84, 147, 149
Europe 31, 78, 99, 100, 101, 130, 131; populism in 127–128, 167

Everett, Edward 159
exaggeration/hyperbole 17, 37, 149

Facebook 73
fake news 43, 65, 66, 76, 78, 79
families 133, 134
Far Right 92, 93, 99, *see also* fascism
Farley, R. 111
fascism 5, 92–101; and academics' attacks on Trump 93–97, 167; and Antifa 100–101; and attacks on Democrats 97–99; and Disney movies 92–93; and entrepreneurial capitalism 95; and Thermidorean reaction 99–100; and Trump's rallies 94–95; and U.S. history 96; and weakening of labor unions 96–97, *see also* Nazis
FBI (Federal Bureau of Investigation) 67, 76
FDR *see* Roosevelt, Franklin Delano
fear *see* anxiety, age of
Ferenczi, Sandor 14
fetish objects 106
fight–flight 33
Fisher, M. 66
Flake, Jeff 54n2
Florida 61, 89, 109
Flynn, Michael 49
Forbes, Malcolm 65
foreign policy 4, 62, 77, 107, 108, 112, 115
Fox News 52, 61, 65, 66, 67, 117, 150
France 5, 31, 99, 110, 114, 130
Frances, Allen 35, 76, 77
Franco, Francisco 100
freedom 38, 95, 107, 108, 109, 111
French Revolution 5, 99
Freud, Sigmund 13, 15, 85; on fetish objects 106; and libido/death drive 33; mass formation theory 28; and Modern Conflict Theory 82; on narcissistic leaders 36
Friedman, Milton 129
friends of Trump, lack of 18, 50
Fromm, Erich 13, 147–148, 162

Gaddafi, Muammar 64
Gajanan, M. 66
Gartner, John 29
Gaslight Effect, The (Stern) 71, 72, 73, 75, 162

Gaslight (play/movie) 72–73, 75, 84–85, 163

gaslighting 4–5, 7, 71–85, 162–163, 164, 167; and blame 72; as co-creation 71; cultural factors in 76, 77–78; defined 71, 75–76; effect on gaslightee of 72, 73; growth in use of term 73–74; and media 5, 77; and populism 74, 78–79; and psychohistorical perspective 74–79, 85; and societal sickness 76, 77, 79; as socio-political phenomenon 74–75, 85; strategies to prevent 83–84; and Trump 5, 74, 75, 76, 77–80, 84–85, 121

gay marriage 134, 135

Gelb, Leslie 116–117

gender 133, 165, 166

genocide 13, 27, 97, 109

Gentile, Giovanni 98

Germany 31, 55n18, 99, 110, 114, 128, *see also* Nazis

Gerson, Michael 88

Gewerkschafen 96–97

Giuliani, Rudy 78

globalization 11, 125, 156, 165

Goebbels, Joseph 30

Goering, Hermann 30

Goldberg, Jonah 97–98, 99

Goldman Sachs 64

Goldwater Rule 81, 82

golf, Trump's cheating at 17–18

governmental structure of U.S. 54n1, 77, 114–117; and campaigning/governing 114–115; and changes of ruling parties 115–116; and elections as entertainment 114, 117; and Electoral College *see* Electoral College; and length of campaign season 6, 114, 117; and media/celebrity culture 115, 116–117

grandiosity 7, 12, 13, 24, 25, 26, 27, 29, 53, 55nn19,21, 67, 83, 149; as aspect of Trump's appeal 34, 39, 148; in Trump's childhood 50

Great Depression 118, 120, 155, 159, 166

Great Recession (2008) 6, 119, 120, 121, 166, 167

Greece, ancient 90, 91

greed 24, 76

Greenland 53

Gross, Jan T. 95

groups *see* regressed social groups

Grove, Andy 18

Grynbaum, M.M. 149–150

Guardian, The 94

guilt/shame 14, 25, 32

gun control 61, 137

Haberman, Maggie 59, 149–150

Habermas, Jürgen 132

Hamilton, Alexander 91

Hamilton, Patrick 75, 163

Hassler-Forest, Dan 92

hate groups/crimes 111–112

hatred *see* aggression; anger

Hawkins, S. 136

health of Trump 79–80

healthcare 17, 20, 22n3, 129, 156; and COVID-19 pandemic 153; *see also* Affordable Care Act

Hispanics *see* Latinos/Hispanics

Hitler, Adolf 3, 14, 15, 24, 30, 32, 53, 89, 95, 96, 97–98, 100, 158

Hochschild, Arlie 105, 126

Hofstadter, Richard 110, 127

Hollywood 92–93

Holt, Lester 66–67, 80

Homestead Act 154

homophobia 96, 97

Hoover, Herbert 119, 159

Hoover, J. Edgar 76

House Un-American Activities Committee *see* McCarthy, Joseph

human rights 111

Hume, Paul 94

Hurt, Harry 49

Hussein, Saddam 24

hyperbole/exaggeration 17, 37, 149

hypocrisy of Trump 47, 65

id 50, 85

identity 27, 147, 164; American 6, 108, 112; shared 13, 55, 108, 133

identity movements 133

ideology 3, 27, 28–29; and media 28; and slogans 30

ignorance of Trump 4, 58, 62, 63

immaturity of Trump 63, 82

immigration 2, 3, 5, 15, 18, 28, 38, 43, 55n11, 79, 106, 149, 157; and deportations 93, 167; in Europe 31, 127–128; and large group regression 31–32; Mexican *see* Mexican immigrants; and Obama 93, 99

impeachment 52, 62, 91

174 Index

impulsiveness of Trump 46, 58, 63, 66, 67, 81, 122; and id functioning 85
inaugural address of Trump 75, 109
inclusion 7, 125, 135
incomes 19, 110, 119, 156
individualism 108
inequality 7, 11, 15, 19, 131, 153
infantilism 3, 25
Ingle, David 106
innovation 16–17, 20, 157, 162
institutions, erosion of trust in 6, 78, 126, 129–132
international system 4, 43, 128, 129, 156
intimacy 25, 26, 38
Ionesco, Eugène 32
Iran 84, 111, 150
Iraq 59, 60, 64, 66
Isis 32, 59, 84
Islamophobia 15, 47, 52, 84, 92, 95, 109, 111–112, 166
Israel 84
Italy 53, 83, 99, *see also* Mussolini, Benito
Ives, Joni 18

Jackson, Andrew 110, 159
Japan 33, 52, 128
Jews 2, 15, 27, 52, 79, 96
Jobs, Steve 14, 16, 17, 18, 149, 158, 162
Johnson, Boris 149
Johnson, Lyndon B. 130
Justice Department 44, 62

Kagan, Donald 159
Katrina, Hurricane 51
Kavanaugh, Judge Brett 60
Kaylan, Melik 78, 79
Kelly, John 49, 151
Kennedy, John F. 63, 65, 76
Keynesian economics 128, 129
Kight, S. 93
Kim Jong-un 18, 76, 78, 151
King, Martin Luther Jr. 76
Klein, Melanie 24
knowledge economy 11, 12, 20, 156
Knowledge is Power Program (KIPP) 20
Kohut, Heinz 37, 39
Kranish, M. 66
Kraychick, R. 98

labor unions 95, 96–97, 128, 133, 149, 157
Langham, Lauren 116
language of Trump, deterioration in 80
large group regression *see* regressed social groups
Las Vegas 63
Lasch, Christopher 116
Latin America 21–22, 149
Latinos/Hispanics 11–12, 52, 120, *see also* Mexican immigrants
leadership 11, 17, 54n5, 153–160; candidates, six questions for 160; and charisma 36, 37; and communication skills 154–155, 159; effective, qualities of 19–20, 153–155; and engagement with political process 22; and humanistic philosophy 2, 7, 155, 156, 158; and personality 158–160; and pragmatism 155; trust/distrust in *see* distrust of political class
Letterman, David 80
Levine, Ted 47
Lewis, Charles 76
LGBT people 92, 96, 99, 111–112
liberalism/liberals 7, 84, 118, 130, 132, 133, 135; and American Exceptionalism 108, 111; and fascism 96, 101; philosophical 126; Trump as 17
libido 33
Libya 64
lies of Trump 2, 4, 7, 15, 17, 55nn20,21, 59–61, 117, 121, 164; in business career 60–61; as gaslighting 76, 84, 85; patterns of 60; and Presidential debate 66–67
Limbaugh, Rush 150
Lincoln, Abraham 14, 17, 18, 154–155, 156, 168; personality of 158, 159, 160
Lindbergh, Charles 108
Lingiardi, Vittorio 81
Lion King, The (movie) 92
Lippmann, Walter 159
litigiousness 31, 66
Long, Huey 5, 89, 90–91
"losers" 38, 45, 52
Louisiana 105
Louisiana Purchase (1803) 107
love 22, 91
Luhrmann, Tanya 134

MacArthur, Douglas 158
McCain, John 45, 50, 121

McCarthy, Joseph 75, 83, 89, 116, 118, 127
Maccoby, Michael 16, 36, 45, 46, 54n5, 55n19, 161–162
McConnell, Mitch 49
McGahn, Don 62
Machado, Alicia 59, 63, 64
McIver, M. 45
McMaster, H.R. 49, 151
McNamara, Robert 130
McWilliams, Nancy 81
Madison, James 160
Maher, Bill 74
Make America Great Again 6, 36, 38, 43, 58–59, 61, 105, 109, 114–115, 157, 162; as gaslighting 75
malignant narcissism 3, 13, 26–28, 34; and anti-social personality 29; danger of diagnosing Trump with 29, 30; and Hitler/Stalin 24, 30; and paranoia 26, 27
Manhattan Javitz Center 60
manifest destiny 107
Mao Zedong 30
Maples, Marla 34, 64
Marcus, Ruth 63
marketing 33, 167
marketing narcissistic leadership 1, 2–3, 7, 11–22, 147–149, 159, 161, 164, 168; and aesthetics 17–18; and celebrity culture 162; and commodification of people 18; and exploitation of anxiety 11–12, 15; and innovation 16–17; and lying/exaggeration 17; and narcissistic personality disorder, compared 15; and narcissistic traits 12–15; and paradigm of winners/losers 3; and paranoia 13, 18; and partnership 18; productive 16–17, 18; and Trump's father 16
marketing personality 13–14, 21, 162
marriages of Trump 50, 51, 64, 83
Marvin, Carolyn 106
mass formation theory 28
mass shootings 11, 61, 165
Mattis, James 49, 63, 65, 148, 151
media 2, 30, 34, 36–37; accusations of fascism in 92–93, 94, 97; and fake news 43, 65, 66, 76, 78, 79; and gaslighting 5, 77; and ideological formation 28; and political campaigns 115, 116; and racism 92, 93; tabloid

65, 83, 116, 117, 121; Trump's attacks on 43, 45, 47, 51, 76, 79, 89, 94, 154; Trump's exploitation of 6, 77–78, 117, 148, 161; and Trump's lies 4, 65
Mencken, H.L. 90, 159
mentalization 85
#MeToo movement 134–135
Mexican immigrants 2, 31–32, 84, 88, 92; labeled as rapists 2, 79, 166; and wall 18, 47, 48, 54n9, 76, 133, 157, 163
Mexico 78, 107
Michigan 121
middle class 79, 119
Middle East 17, 149, 150, 157
Milgram experiments 32
militarism 6, 100, 110
military 18, 49, 53, 150, 153, 156, 157; and American Exceptionalism 106, 107–108, 109; soldiers' pay, Trumps lie about 60
Mill, John Stuart 126
Modern Conflict Theory 82–83
Monroe Doctrine 107
Moonves, Les 117
Moscovici, Serge 28
MSNBC 34, 93, 117
Mueller, Robert 53, 66, 67, 84, 85, 88, 91
multiculturalism 5, 94, 128, 134, 135, 136, 140n10
Muslims 15, 27, 47, 52, 84, 92
Mussolini, Benito 53, 89, 95, 97–98, 100

Napoleon 18
narcissism 1, 12–15, 106; allure/fantasy of 3; characteristics of 3, 12–13; continuum 13; and foreign policy 112; Freud/Fromm on 13–14, 15; group 13, 15; and leadership see leadership; malignant see malignant narcissism; marketing see marketing narcissistic leadership; and millennials 35; and paranoia 13, 33; productive 16, 17, 36, 149, 158, 162; range of qualities associated with 35–36; visionary 13, 14, 15, 16
narcissistic appeal of Trump 34–39; and anger 38–39; and autonomy/freedom 38; and bankruptcies 39; and charisma 36, 37; and hyperbole 37; and identification with supporters 37; and intimacy 38; as overlooked phenomenon 34, 35; and range of qualities associated with

176 Index

narcissism 35–36; and rule-breaking/
secret-sharing 39; and self-transcendence 38
narcissistic leadership 1, 3, 14–15, 24–33,
54n5, 158; and aggression/rage 26, 27,
29, 30, 32, 33; and dangers of
analysing living politicians 29–30; and
large group regression *see* regressed
social groups; and malignant
narcissism 24, 26–28; and narcissistic
personality disorder 24–26; and need
for affirmation/adulation 45; and
paranoia 29, 30, 33; and parents 14;
and sadism 26, 32; and splitting 45–46
narcissistic personality disorder (NPD)
12, 13, 15; characteristics of 24–26;
DSM criteria for 35, 36; inapplicable
to Trump 1, 3, 15, 35; and malignant
narcissism 24
Narcissistic Personality Inventory 36
narcissistic wounds 118, 120, 121–122
National Enquirer 65
National Rifle Association (NRA)
61, 137
nationalism 6, 28, 108, 135
Native Americans 107, 109, 110, 159
nativism 79, 110, 120, 164, 166, 167
Nazis 15, 27, 28, 30, 32, 94, 95, 96–98,
100, 101, 164; and "America First"
108
NBC News 61, 80
Nelson, Louis 63
neo-Nazis 2
neurolinguistics 80
New Deal 14, 157, 166
New York City 45, 46–47, 55n10, 60,
72, 95
New York Military Academy (NYMA)
44, 47, 49, 50
New York Times 59, 60, 77–78, 116, 120,
149–150, 161
New Yorker, The 59
Nixon, Richard 14, 51, 52, 83, 129
Nolte, Ernst 100
North Korea 43, 54n1, 59, 76, 111, 163
NPD *see* narcissistic personality disorder
NRA (National Rifle Association)
61, 137
nuclear weapons 11, 19, 43, 54n1, 59, 76,
82, 111, 112, 150, 163, 165
NYMA (New York Military Academy)
44, 47, 49, 50

Obama, Barack 5, 14, 17, 38, 43, 62, 66,
98, 121, 127, 150, 164, 168; and
American Exceptionalism 111, 112;
and birther controversy 52, 55n20,
119; and immigration 93, 99, 167; and
incomes/employment 119, 120; policies
reversed by Trump 150–151, 152;
political rallies of 115; and Republican
rage 118–119
Obamacare (Affordable Care Act) 19, 38,
51, 150, 157
obsessive personality type 13, 14
Oklahoma 110
Oliver, John 5, 74
Ortega y Gasset, José 19
Orwell, George 76
Oswald, Lee Harvey 65

pandemics 153
Panksepp, Jaak 33
paranoia 65–67, 121, 149; and American
culture 31, 166; and malignant
narcissism 26, 27; and marketing
narcissistic leadership 13, 18; and
narcissistic leadership 29, 30, 33; and
narcissistic personality 13, 33; and
narcissistic personality disorder 12; and
Republicans 118–119
Parkland, Florida 61
pathological grandiose self 24, 25
patriotism 6, 15, 105, 108, 109, 110
PDM (*Psychodynamic Diagnostic
Manual*) 81
Pelosi, Nancy 46
Pericles of Athens 7, 153, 154, 159
personality types 13–14
Pew Research Center 12, 78, 119, 137
Philippines 107
Philipson, Ilene 20
phraseology of Trump 3, 30, 80
Poland 31
polarization, political 7, 58, 115, 116,
130, 135–137, 166, 168; inconsistencies
in 135–136; strategy to resolve
136–139
policies of Trump 7, 147–152, 153–154,
156, 157; and deal-making 151, 152,
159; and demand for loyalty 151; and
marketing orientation 147–149; and
personality 149–152, 158, 159; reversals/
indecision in 4, 58, 61; and undoing of
Obama's policies 150–151, 152

policy proposals, reversals/indecision in 4, 58, 61
political experience of Trump 1, 4, 34, 62
political rallies 115, 166
political rallies of Trump 38–39, 45, 52, 62, 76, 117, 150, 163; post-election 115; protesters at 63, 94–95
Politico 63
Politifact 59
populism 6–7, 51, 95, 99, 100, 101, 110, 126–128, 165–166; and anger/disenfranchisement 126–127, 131, 132, 165; as anti-intellectual and anti-science 126, 127, 128; characteristics of 128; European 127–128, 167; and gaslighting 74, 78–79; progressive 133, 165, 166; and progressivism, polarization between 135
Porter, Eduardo 120
Post-Trumpmatic Stress Disorder 31
postwar framework 128–132, 136; collapse of 129–132, *130*; and economic/cultural growth 128–129; second decline in 130–131
poverty 119, 131
power 72, 106, 107, 108; presidential/personal 44
Prager, Dennis 98, 99
praise/admiration, Trump's need for 4, 13, 15, 16, 24, 34, 55n19, 82, 148, 151, 162; as disruption 45, 47, 50, 51
presidential election campaign, 2016 58–59, 66; castigation of opponents during 2, 3, 4, 30, 58, 62, 63, 64, 67, 163; and gaslighting 5, 163; and Trump's health 80; Trump's ignorance during 58, 63; Trump's lies/broken promises during 59, 115; and Trump's polarization strategy 116; Trump's rallies *see* political rallies of Trump
presidential TV debate 63; moderators in 66–67
productivity 96, 97, 119, 131
progressive humanistic leadership 2, 7, 155, 156, 158
progressive movements 133–135; and liberalism, compared 133; and multiculturalism/diversity 134–135; and populism, polarization between 135; and Republicans 135; and social/cultural change 133–134

projection/projective identification 45, 64–65
psychiatric analysis, dangers of with living politicians 29–30, 35; and Goldwater Rule 81, 82
psychic defense 45, 50, 79
psychoanalytic diagnosis, overview of 81–82
Psychodynamic Diagnostic Manual (PDM) 81
psychohistorical perspective 74–79, 85
psychopathy 29, 30, 76, 82, 83–84
public dialogue 138–139
public sector 96, 97
Putin, Vladimir 18, 53, 58, 78, 79, 151

race 133, 165, 166
racism 11–12, 31, 52, 66, 67, 79, 84, 97, 135, 159; and American Exceptionalism 110–111, 167; and Disney movies 92–93; and narcissism 13, 15
rage 33, 46, 53, 120, *see also* aggression; anger
Ramirez, Rafael 17
Rappeport, A. 44
Reagan, Ronald 14, 17, 18, 43, 46, 108, 118, 126, 132
regressed social groups 27–28, 29, 31–32, 164–165; Trump's followers as 2, 30, 165
Reilly, Rob 17–18
religion 133, 134, 135; secular/civic 6, 77, 108, 109, 115, 118, 166
Republicans 1, 4, 7, 43, 46, 53, 58, 116, 150; attacks on Democrats by 97–99, 101; divisions amongst 119; and paranoia 118–119; and progressive movements 134–135, *see also* supporters of Trump
revolution 99–100, *see also* French Revolution
Rhinoceros (Ionesco) 32
Roosevelt, Franklin Delano (FDR) 7, 15, 18, 78, 94, 97, 108; leadership qualities of 154, 155, 156, 157, 168; and New Deal 14, 157; personality of 158, 159
Roosevelt, Teddy (TR) 157, 158
Rose, Charlie 80
Rousseau, Jean-Jacques 126
Rubio, Marco 88
Rucker, P. 8

178 Index

rural areas 105, 110, 127, 130, 131, 135, 151
Russia 28, 49, 79, 84, 164, *see also* Putin, Vladimir; Soviet Union
Russian Revolution 27, 164
Rwanda 27, 28, 32, 164

sadism 13, 26, 32
Sanders, Bernie 115, 127, 132
scapegoating 2, 118, 119, 121
Scaramucci, Anthony 148
Schiff, Adam 88
school shootings 61
Schwartz, Anthony 43, 55n15, 82
Second World War 33, 75, 108, *see also* Nazis
self, sense of 24, 36, 72
self-defeatism 49
self-esteem 3, 7, 11, 13, 20, 147, 148; of Trump's supporters 39
self-interest 7, 53, 154, 159
self-reflection 28, 72
sexism 67, 79, 84, 92, 93, 97, 120
sexual misconduct 2, 39, 59, 60, 63, 64, 134–135
sexual promiscuity 24, 25
Siemaszko, C. 80
Singapore 19
slander 65
slavery 109, 154, 155
slogans 6, 30
smartphones 21
Snyder, Timothy 94, 95, 98, 99
social contract 96, 97
social democracy 129
social media 12, 21, 73, 119, 131, 161, 165, *see also* Facebook; Twitter
social regression *see* regressed social groups
societal sickness 76, 77, 79
sociological perspective 1, 2, 6–7, 8, 125–139, 161–162, 165; and bridging strategies 136–139; and civil society 125, 137, 138, 139; and community 125, 128; and inclusion 7, 125, 135; and polarization 135–136; on populism 126–128; and postwar framework *see* postwar framework; and progressive movements *see* progressive movements
sociopathy 76, 77, 82, 83–84
Southern Poverty Law Center (SPLC) 110–112

Soviet Union 99, 112, 165
Spain 99, 110, 129
Spanish-American War (1898) 107, 108, 109, 116
Special Counsel *see* Mueller, Robert
splitting 45–46
Spock, Dr. 134
"squad, the" 52, 79, 93
Stalin, Joseph 3, 24, 30, 32, 99
Stanley, Jason 95, 96, 99
Steele, Robert David 75–76
stereotyping 2, 52, 79, 163, 164, 168
Stern, Howard 44
stock market 44
Stockholm syndrome 32
strongman rule 78–79
superego 14, 15, 158
supporters of Trump 15, 22n1, 34, 35, 36–38, 54n6, 164; and American Dream 105; and distrust of political system 132; and education 127; ex-Democrat voters 120–121, 150; and Republican Party historical context 117–119; signs of decline of 49, 51; and Trumpmania 161–162, 168; and unemployment 120, *see also* narcissistic appeal of Trump
Supreme Court 54n1, 110, 159
surveillance 98
Sweden 19, 132
Syria 49, 59, 84

Talleyrand 18
tax reform 53, 54n1, 60, 62, 118, 153
Tea Party 38, 105, 119, 126, 131, 166
television career of Trump 52, 53, 55n10, 117, 148
terrorism 11, 47, 51, 79, 89, 109, 157, 165, 166
Texas 109
Thatcher, Margaret 132
therapy: and gaslighting 5
Thermidorean reaction 5, 99–100
Think Like a Billionaire (Trump) 16, 46, 158
Thompson, Derek 77–78
Tillerson, Rex 62, 151
Tocqueville, Alexis de 106, 126, 167
totem, theory of 106
trade 4, 18, 19, 79, 153, 156, 157; tariffs 76, 151; Trump's disruption of 43, 76
trade unions *see* labor unions

Index 179

Trans-Pacific Partnership Agreement (TPP) 150–151
travel bans 93, 95
Treene, A. 93
Trilateral Commission report (1975) 132
Trotsky, Leon 99
Truman, Harry 94, 97, 158, 160
Trump administration 151–152; disruption in 4, 34, 43, 46, 48; downsizing of 79; failure of 54n1; morale in 151
Trump anxiety disorder 30–31
Trump, Donald Jr. 38
Trump, Fred (father) 4, 16, 46, 50, 55nn16,17, 60, 82
Trump, Ivanka 44
Trump, Mary Anne (mother) 4, 47, 48, 83
Trumpmania 161–162, 168
Trump's grandfather 44–45, 55n18
trust, facilitating 137–139, 155, *see also* distrust of political class
Turkey 79
Turner, J. 126–127
Turner, Ted 16
Turquet, Pierre 28
Twenge, Jean M. 12, 20, 131
Twitter 2, 4, 18, 35, 38, 48–49, 53, 54n8, 58, 59, 63, 93, 164; extent of Trump's followers on 51, 78, 161; responses to Trump on 88
Tyson, Mike 52

United States (U.S.): electoral cycle in 6, 77, 114, 166; governmental structure of *see* governmental structure of U.S.; as open culture 31–32; as paranoid culture 31; psychoanalytic description of 76, 77
U.S. Constitution 4, 58, 62, 111, 154

Venezuela 79, 89
Veterans of Foreign Wars National Convention 76
Vidich, A.J. 129
Vietnam War 45, 49, 108

violence 63, 88, 89, 121, 163, 168
viruses 11, 153
Vitali, A. 80
Volkan, Vamik 27, 28
Voltaire 139
volunteering 21–22
vulgarity of Trump 5, 88, 89–91; and context of political vulgarism 90–91, 110; and "Les Deplorables" 88

Walker, Scott 96, 97
Wallace, George 5, 89, 110
walls 46–48, 54n9
war mentality of Trump 48, 50–51, 66, 79
Washington, George 158
Washington Post, The 59–60, 76, 88, 92, 94
wealth accumulation 105–106, 107, 109–110; and middle class 119
weapons of mass destruction *see* nuclear weapons
welfare state 105, 106, 128, 129, 130, 133, 136, 155
White House *see* Trump administration
white working class 11, 15, 31, 95, 120
Williams, Joan C. 11
Wilson, Woodrow 108, 116, 167
Winfrey, Oprah 80
winning, Trump's obsession with 17, 50, 105, 149, 159
Winthrop, John 107, 167
Wisconsin 96, 97, 121
women 72, 73, 74, 79, 92, 133, 156, *see also* sexual misconduct
Wright, Frank Lloyd 14

xenophobia 93, 95
Xi Jinping 18, 151

young people 11, 12
Yugoslavia 27, 32, 164

Zero Dark Thirty (movie) 73
Zingales, Luigi 83

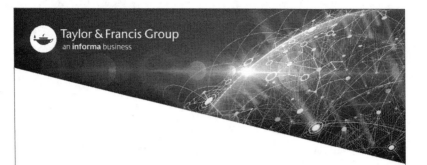